THE
GREATEST
MONEY BOOK
EVER WRITTEN

BY
BRUCE
GOULD

ISBN 0-918706-42-4

TABLE OF CONTENTS

OBSERVATIONS

The price graphs used in this book are used with the permission of CRB chart service, 75 Montgomery Street, Jersey City, New Jersey, 07302. If you are interested in learning how to make money, I recommend their graphs and charts as being one of your most valuable tools.

This book is part truth and part fiction. Certain names have been changed to protect identifiable persons and other names have been created to illustrate a principle to be applied to an actual money making situation. The price illustrations used are all true and all reflect actual history. When you examine any price, you are examining historical truth.

It is not easy to start with nothing and emerge with a large fortune. It is not easy, but it can be done. Just the fact that success is possible blesses those who search for hope on the horizon. This is a book about making money, very large sums of money, and making it in extremely short periods of time. I must warn you, however, that other readers who came before you have written me that once opened, these pages cannot be put down until the end of the book is reached. May you find this story as captivating as you find it enlightening. And may you emerge at the end, a changed person forever.

Happy Reading!

DEDICATION

This book is dedicated to
two of the world's most wonderful people.

Tiffany Anne Gould,
our daughter born October 2nd, 1984,
and her very beautiful mother,
Christine Anne Gould.

May God take good care of them forever.

Bruce Grant Gould
June 26, 1985
My Forty-Third Birthday

PART ONE:

THE BEGINNING

TAKE A BALL...

ROLL IT DOWN A HILL.

Chapter One

T AKE A BALL. ROLL IT ACROSS A TABLE. YOUR HAND has given momentum to the ball, the amount of momentum determines how far the ball will roll before stopping. This is the simplest form of momentum.

Take a ball. Roll it down a hill. Your hand begins the momentum, but an additional force, gravity, will supply additional momentum. The ball will roll faster and faster, gaining speed until a counterforce acts against it. The same flick of your wrist that rolled the ball a few feet across a table has started it down the hill, yet momentum has sent the ball rolling at 5, 10, 25 miles per hour: other forces can act on momentum.

Chapter Two

ROCKY AND KAREN BECKET ENTERED THE DECADE of the 1980's as champions. They had achieved a level of success, security and personal comfort that is the aspiration of most people on this earth, yet they could accept this success as their due for years of hard work. It was no more than their expectation. They had achieved, but their values were such that they saw no limit to what they could still achieve in the future.

They were told that there were indeed limits.

Rocky and Karen did not believe this.

The Beckets own a modest nursery and flower shop in Modesto, California. It is a thriving business in a competitive field; Rocky and Karen devoted the early years of their marriage to fourteen and sixteen hour days to make it so. Their customers were friends, and very loyal; their mail-order business in Bonsai tree seedlings is growing, with three employees working solely on this enterprise. Rocky works ten hours a day in the nursery. Karen still works five or six hours a day as the cashier, and cares for their two toddlers, Michael and Tanya, who can often be found amidst the bromeliads and ferns, chasing each other and breaking pots.

I said they were champions, and I do think they are heroes. By study and hard work, Rocky and Karen have achieved a life of great personal comfort and enjoyment. They have thrived financially, and as employers, provide livings for three others. They are part of the great Middle Class that has made their country strong, and they look forward to a life of personal achievement and growth, of giving and love. They are upwardly mobile; wealth is not their sole goal, but they think it is a goal well worth the achieving, and they want to go for it. Their question is: how?

The nursery is a living; a good living, but Modesto would someday be saturated with Asparagus fern. There was no question in Rocky and Karen's mind that they would have to venture out of the area of their expertise in order to find a degree of wealth.

It was by sharing the values of their parents that Rocky and Karen *have* become champions. It was the ethic of hard work and determination that had made a success of the nursery. Their personal happiness was a measure of their instruction in the giving of love and the enjoyment of day to day living, middle-class lessons given by middle-class parents, attributes that Rocky and Karen would pass to Michael and Tanya. So it was to those values that Rocky and Karen turned to when they decided to pursue wealth.

They found them wanting. The sound and prudent approaches that their parents took when entering the decade of the 1950's would have seemed to be eternal and safe, but Rocky and Karen discovered them to be patched and wounded. Not only would the approaches to investment and wealth accumulation that helped build the middle-class not work, but they could even be disastrous to a couple like Rocky and Karen, who only want to get ahead.

GETTING AHEAD

T O GET AHEAD AND STAY AHEAD. ROCKY AND Karen had reached a point in their lives where that seemed an attainable goal. They had money to invest; not a great sum, but enough to work with. They wanted to invest that money in the typical fields that did so well for their parents: that is their financial background, and they value the stable, controlled quality of such investments. They believed that wealth stood behind such investments. They want to pay for the children's education, set aside a fund for their retirement, perhaps retire early and sail to Maui (after first learning how to sail). Not extravagant desires, nothing beyond that of their parents. They are already secure. They are hard workers with some capital to invest, and they wouldn't be adverse to accumulating a little wealth, if it could still be done.

They approached the question of investment and wealth accumulation with the care, work, and study that had made the nursery a success. They would seek the best advice, the best surest investments, agree on an investment strategy, and go for it. They expected it would be exciting; the nursery had been exciting in the early going. They had barely survived those early days, but they had battled and thrived. Rocky and Karen knew that their parents had invested all their lives, and were still on their feet, with major victories behind them. Rocky and Karen expected and planned to do equally as well.

The first thing they learned was that they were not to be trusted with their own money. Everyone wanted to manage it for them.

They had gone into San Francisco to talk to stockbrokers. They were given tours, given pep-talks, given sober, sound advice: "Investment is not a world for you to get into alone. If you are going to buy and sell stocks and bonds, you had better have experienced professional help taking control of your portfolio. It's a jungle out there."

Rocky and Karen listened to this piece of advice unhappily, but they were in the presence of experts, and would have to seriously consider this advice. It seemed odd to them that two people who could turn a small business into a success story by study and hard work could not be trusted with their own money.

The second major piece of information passed on to Rocky and Karen was that they had only two basic decisions to make with respect to their money. They were the same choices that their parents had had to work with. They could either turn their money over to banks, savings and loans, or money market funds, to earn regular rates of interest, or they could subject themselves to the rigorous study and uncertainty of stocks, bonds, real estate and other similar entities. "You can certainly build up a library in investment books and devote yourself to their study, if you insist on investing on your own, but it's tough work researching thousands of investment opportunities. That's why we recommend that we manage your money. We have the resources; we have the researchers; we have the computers."

The investigation was getting drearier and drearier. Rocky and Karen didn't have the **time** to become economics students. They could visualize what lay ahead of them if they went it alone, and they didn't have the hours or the energy for that path.

Finally, Rocky and Karen learned the cornerstone of traditional investment, the concept of **diversification**. Oh, how they discussed diversification! "Get in there and diversify." "If you have a little of this and a little of that, you won't get hurt when the Crash comes again." "Put 10% in bonds, 30% in the stock market, 30% in real estate, 10% in insurance, and 20% in cash for future opportunities: that's what I tell all my clients." "Diversification is the **answer**. Believe me. Financial success is **diversification!**"

Rocky and Karen learned that the well-diversified portfolio shines like the Nativity Star. Diversification, they were told, was the hallmark of conservatism, of responsible money management, of Success, from time immemorial to the end of time. Wise men took their knickered sons and petticoated daughters by the shoulders and pointed them to the Well-Diversified Portfolio with a gentle shove; it was the way of the world, and wherever those sons and daughters go to seek money wisdom, the avatars of mammon burnished the leather of the portfolio and said, "Seek no more: thou hast found it."

Found what? Found wealth? No, found diversification. It worked for their parents; it would work forever.

It was a very glum Rocky and Karen who came home to Modesto to consider all the wisdom they had acquired from the stockbrokers and bankers.

A plant nursery can be a very quiet place, full of small puttering chores that occupy the hands while the mind ponders. They had a lot to think about.

Did they really want to entrust their money to a manager? They were independent people; they believed in finding their own way. Who, they asked themselves, cares more about our money? Us, or a stockbroker?

But the option, the research of a thousand opportunities seemed burdensome. We have a business to run. **Our** balance sheets are confusing enough; what are we going to make of IBM's balance sheet?

And diversification. Diversification sounds like you pay for bad investments with your good investments. Diversification basically means that everybody will get a little bit of our wealth to work with. Maybe it is acceptable once you have accumulated your wealth, just as a means of preserving the wealth, but it doesn't seem like a program for gaining that wealth.

They thought more about these great pieces of traditional advice. A money manager must handle money, invest it all in only **two fields** of investment, and dilute it by spreading it out over **many** opportunities, good or bad. It is what everyone does. But everyone is not rich.

But it was tradition, and respect for tradition was high on Rocky and Karen's list of values. They resigned themselves to researching the fields of investment further, to see what could be salvaged from these traditional ventures.

A PORTFOLIO OF TRADITIONAL INVESTMENT

Where Americans Put Their Savings

	Percentage of Total Savings
Savings accounts, time deposits	28.8%
Corporate stock	22.3%
Life insurance, pension reserves	21.6%
Demand deposits, currency	6.4%
Other U.S. government securities	5.1%
Money-market funds	3.9%
Corporate bonds, open-market paper	2.3%
State, local securities	1.9%
U.S. savings bonds	1.4%
Other investments	6.2%
Real Estate	— —
Their Own Businesses	— —

U.S. NEWS & WORLD REPORT

It seemed like quite a menu, these entities that worked for Rocky and Karen's parents. For many years these investments provided steady growth, security, reliability. For many years they worked, but they won't work for you today.

These are the traditional investments for the traditional investor with traditional expectations. Most of these investment areas

did make our fathers and our grandfathers wealthy, if they became wealthy at all. If you are under the age of fifty, it is likely that these areas of investment contributed to your education, or your first car, or the endless shoes you wore out, or the 287 pizzas you ate during your teen-age years. They were solid investments in their time; they helped build the middle-class. But that was a different time. This list won't help you today, and it won't help your son or daughter tomorrow.

Each of these fields of investment were new and vital and exciting at one time, and investment in these fields created many a fortune. But we are entering a new age. Our parents faced a new age; our grandparents faced a new age. These fields of investment opened at each age, offered each generation a chance to cut the pie, to accumulate their share of the growing wealth of the nation and the world, and then closed tight.

Your grandfather could not give advice to your father about IBM stock, that was a world he had never known. And so, on his own, your father would buy those shares of IBM in his youth and hold throughout his lifetime. He bought it and held onto it, and it returned munificent rewards. And now your father gives you the very best and only financial advice he knows, "Buy IBM, child. Buy IBM and hold onto the stock. It will make you rich." But he is wrong. He is not at fault; IBM was a brilliant investment on his part, but IBM cannot do for you what it did for him. He is wrong; he may be disastrously wrong.

The litany of the collapses of traditional investment are familiar. Look again at the two major fields the stockbrokers said were available to the Beckets: interest-bearing investments and speculation in stocks or real estate. Then take a close look at this table.

The Relentless March of Prices

Item	Eight Years Ago	Three Years Ago	Today's Price	Change
Time and *Newsweek* magazines	$0.50	$1.25	$1.50	+ 20%
Barron's	0.50	0.75	1.25	+ 67
Wall Street Journal	0.20	0.30	0.40	+ 33
New York Times	0.15	0.25	0.30	+ 20
TV Guide	0.15	0.35	0.50	+ 43
McDonald's milkshake	0.40	0.69	0.80	+ 16
McDonald's quarter-pounder w/cheese	0.79	1.35	1.69	+ 25
Baskin-Robbins ice-cream cone (one scoop)	0.30	0.60	0.85	+ 42
Slice of pizza	0.35	0.65	0.85	+ 31
Good Humor toasted-almond bar	0.25	0.50	0.75	+ 50
Chock Full O'Nuts melted cheese sandwich	0.50	0.88	1.10	+ 25
Chock Full O'Nuts doughnut	0.10	0.25	0.35	+ 40
Sandwich for Battery Park picnic (Turkey on rye w/Russian dressing)	2.10	3.00	3.60	+ 20
Coca-Cola (from street vendor)	0.20	0.50	0.60	+ 20
Dietetic pear dessert	0.25	0.40	0.50	+ 25
Martini (silver bullet)	1.25	2.25	2.75	+ 22
Bone-dry Beefeater martini at Plaza Hotel	1.75	3.75	4.50	+ 20
Stein of beer at singles bar	0.50	1.25	1.50	+ 20
Taxi (2-mile, or 40-block, ride)	1.75	2.20	2.70	+ 23
New York subway and bus fares	0.30	0.50	0.75	+ 50
Shoeshine (with tip)	0.50	1.00	1.40	+ 40
Razor haircut (plus tax)	4.00	6.00	8.00	+ 33
Woman's hair care (wash and set)	6.00	8.75	11.00	+ 26
New heels (Drago shoe repair)	2.00	4.50	6.00	+ 33
Suit cleaned and pressed	2.37	3.25	5.00	+ 54
Podiatrist	9.00	18.00	20.00	+ 11
Bounced check (courtesy of a friend)	3.00	5.00	6.00	+ 20
First-class postage stamp	0.08	0.15	0.20	+ 33
First-run movie	3.00	4.50	5.00	+ 11
Theater ticket (Broadway musical)	9.00	20.00	32.50	+ 63
Obscene greeting card	0.60	1.00	1.25	+ 25
Brooks Bros. standard "gentleman's" necktie	7.50	14.00	16.50	+ 18

Spearmint gum	0.10	0.30	0.35	+ 17
Paperback book (avg. of 200)	1.25	2.65	3.30	+ 25
Dog license	6.10	8.10	8.50	+ 5
Panhandler's request	0.10	0.25	1.00	+300
American Express fee	15.00	25.00	35.00	+ 40
Daily parking fee (pier at foot of Wall Street)	3.25	5.75	9.65	+ 68
Wall Street Tennis Club	12.00	20.00	24.00	+ 20
Sunday church donation*	1X	2X	2½-3X	+ 37

The writer's modesty—or guilt—prevents his disclosing how much he contributes each week.

BARRON'S MAGAZINE

Not many years ago, a passbook savings account at 3% interest would put you ahead of the game, way ahead. But today all savings accounts merely fight against the loss of value due to inflation. When you have money in savings accounts—and in this I include money market funds, bonds, savings bonds, and credit union deposits—you are merely putting your fingers in a dike. You are holding on bravely, but your fingers are cold, and for all your efforts the flood of inflation is seeping by you, with the potential for crashing over your head. The further irony is that savings accounts also pump flood waters back into that ocean you are trying to hold back. For that reason, no fixed-dollar interest return can ever gain much against inflation. Never. A savings account is a hope for a kinder, more benign future, and I don't know where the basis for such a hope can be found.

What about stocks? Won't they make us wealthy like they did our parents? Perhaps. Perhaps you can pick a few winning stocks, hold onto them for years, and cash in, hoping that their return has not been eroded by inflation. Perhaps you can churn through the stock market, buying and selling, buying and selling, scalping a small profit here, a small profit there, in constant and frenzied activity. Perhaps one of these approaches will work for you. However, in recent years thousands, even hundreds of thousands, of people have tried these approaches, but they haven't yet taken much money out of the stock market, and in battling the market, they often lose sight of the purpose of their investments, which is to accumulate real wealth.

Ultimately, the Stock Market is a never ending horse race. The horses run in a pack, and one noses ahead for a moment, while another trails a length for a furlong. All the while, lap after lap, investors place bets on who will be ahead for a little while. But the race never ends. There is no respite for the horses or the bettors; the only winners are the people selling the pari-mutuel tickets. So much speed, so much activity, yet no one asks why the race is never over?

Would you like an afternoon of fruitless activity? Search your city for someone under forty who has accumulated wealth by investing in the stock market. I would like to meet such a person before my time is out: it is a search like Diogene's lifetime quest for an honest man.

Savings accounts are devastated by inflation, and are not a road to either wealth or security. Corporate stock is a possibility, but a long ways from offering sure returns, even on winning tickets. Life insurance? Life insurance pays off big only one time—and by then you are dead. Although the question of whether you can take it with you is still discussed, the consensus is that you cannot. This is not a book about how to make a widow rich or a widower secure. It is a book about how **you** can accumulate some wealth during your lifetime. The only way that I can think of that life insurance can make you wealthy would be for you to get your neighbor high on one illegal substance or another, have him sign up for a large policy, name you as the sole beneficiary, take him to the top of the World Trade Center and convince him that he can fly like a grackle. However, the Beckets are far too imbued with middle class values to consider this scheme, and, after some deep reflection, most of us wouldn't dare it, either. But if there is a different way to acquire wealth through life insurance, I don't know about it.

Bonds are an integral part of the shiniest well-diversified portfolio, like a vest on a three piece suit. Bonds are, of course, another form of savings account, with a few built-in disadvantages. Savings accounts are guaranteed safe to a certain amount by the United States Government, whereas bonds carry no such guarantee. However, bonds do seem to be guaranteed to decline in price whenever interest rates rise, which is quite often, if that is the guarantee you are looking for.

Why do bonds fall in value with a rise in interest rates? They seem such a secure, conservative investment. But bonds are simply the loaning of money from an investor to a company or city or government for a fixed rate of return, say 10%. You loan the money, and, when the bond matures, you get all your money back. All the while you are being paid the interest—"clipping coupons"—at intervals and depositing it into the bank. Clear cut and sensible. How do they decline in value? One way to find out is to buy a bond paying 10% over twenty years, and sit on the bond until interest rates rise to 18%. Then try to sell that bond for its face value; after all, that's what you paid for it. But here is what the new potential buyer knows. Your $50,000 bond, paying 10% interest, will earn $5,000 per/year interest for twenty years, or $100,000. Add this to your original investment, now mature, and arrive at a total sum of $150,000. But the $50,000 bond which paid out at 18% interest, will earn $180,000 in interest, plus its original value, for a total dollar return of $230,000 at the bond's maturity date. That's $80,000 more for the 18% coupon bond. So, would **you** pay the same for a 10% bond as for an 18% bond? Clearly not. The 10% coupon is not as valuable.

Most bonds outstanding today were issued years ago at rates much lower than current rates. Take a bond that is ten years old and still has ten years to go before maturity. Want to know what the interest rates on most of those bonds are? If it is a municipal, city or state government bond, probably 3-4-5%; a corporate bond, likely

6-7-8%. How much would **you** pay today for a $50,000 bond paying 3% annual interest? Would you pay $50,000 for it, its face value, when you can currently buy a $50,000 bond paying 7-20%? If you would, there are plenty of sellers of old 3% bonds to accommodate you. But the other buyers are picking them up for less than 50¢ on the dollar. If you would buy the current bond paying 7-20% interest, then you already understand why bonds fall in value. As interest rates advance, bond prices fall because all outstanding bonds are paying less-competitive interest rates. No one will buy them for the same price they would have a few days, weeks, or months earlier. To give you an idea of this in the real world, I own a bond that pays 11.5% tax free interest, a school bond issued by the town where I graduated from high school, in order for that town to build a new high school building. Today I called my bond broker to see what I could get for this bond on today's higher interest rate market. The offer was 85.5%. It had fallen nearly 15% in value in a single year, and it pays 11.5% interest, tax free. It is difficult to make progress along the road to wealth if you, like the seven wives of St. Ives, are walking in the opposite direction.

Most of the rest of the shopping list is made up of other interest fields: money market funds, U.S. Savings Bonds, bank accounts, in one form or another. Young people like Rocky and Karen, pondering their first investments, will not be able to become rich off of interest-bearing instruments, as their parents once could. To make any money at all from these accounts and funds requires a great deal of money to start with. That money market account with the irresistible 15% interest will earn $15,000 a year — if you have $100,000 to start with — and of that $15,000, the government will take up to $7,500 in taxes. You will be lucky to conserve the money you already have from the damages of inflation by investing in money market funds. In addition, most young investors don't start with $100,000. They start with $1,000, or $5,000, or $10,000. A thousand dollars in a 15% money market earns $150. Wealth accumulation? Forget it.

Two other areas remain: real estate, the field of investment that has most recently been the start of the wealth show, and your own business, which has always been the means of wealth accumulation, yesterday, today and tomorrow.

Vancouver, British Columbia, Canada, is a lovely city, a city of green and gray in the soft climate of the Pacific Northwest. There are many home owners in that city, and while there are some imposing, show piece homes to be found, most of the homes in Vancouver are simply the frame, mom and pop three-bedroom houses that we all grew up in, with a basement, or a postage stamp yard, a brave garden, some homemade repairs. Homes to love, tidy homes showing a lot of care, but hardly something to cause Frank Lloyd Wright to come back from the land of the dead. The plainness of the real estate, however, did not stop these parcels of land and boards from making their owners ''wealthy'' during the real estate boom of the 70's. It was a raging fever, a real bull market. A $20,000 home rose to $40,000 overnight. Then upward to $60,000, only a step along the way to $100,000. In fact, a few $20,000 homes actually rose to the $300,000-$400,000 plateau, pushed by the pressures of the boom and utter optimism. Huge sums of wealth arose overnight for these owners, in a heady ten years.

Enter 1982. Houses that one year earlier had sold in Vancouver for $400,000 were on the market for $150,000, when a buyer could be found were actually selling for $135,000. The real estate boom was fraying at the top. It was a general boom for several years. All Vancouver homes were like boats tied to the floating docks of the marina; the incoming tide raised the dock and all boats with it, but the values rose so quickly, and to such heights, that when the tide recedes, as it appears to be doing, the boat owners are left seasick.

Fortunes are still to be made in real estate; it was a sure road to wealth for our fathers and grandfathers, and it still has that potential. But most of the fortunes have been made. To make it in real estate today, you will simply have to be lucky, **real lucky**. You'll have to pick a winner months or years in advance, just like in the stock market, and sit and hold for years and years. You'll be investing in hope and luck, not real estate, trusting that someone else will envision the shopping center you see in a field of weeds and marsh life. Nor will it be an inexpensive investment in hope and luck. I see in the newspaper this morning an ad for a "fixer-upper," i.e., a wreck, selling for $115,000. That is not a "fixer-upper"; that is an open mouthed furnace that burns only money. Yes, you may buy it with "creative financing" and no money down, but you will be buying a $115,000 hulk with a 16% mortgage and a five-year balloon payment down the road.

The only guarantee that exists for real estate of the future is hard work, huge debt, a market in which it will be increasingly difficult to sell, and problems in managing the property. If anyone guarantees you that real estate values will continue to rise, please write his name down also and mail it to me, I have a little list of these fellows that I am compiling.

None of these examined roads lead to wealth accumulation. To wealth preservation, perhaps, if you already have plenty, but none to the actual nitty-gritty accumulation of the stuff. There is only one example from our list left, just one. The single opportunity for wealth accumulation in the coming decades must be found in owning your **own business** — a new approach to a new era. Your own business, but a new kind of business, one that you never even dreamed existed. Not in your wildest imagination, not in a thousand years, not in ten thousand years. The new approach to super wealth accumulation involves taking on a new business enterprise, and staying with it until the end.

TODAY'S BUSINESS FOR TOMORROW

W HAT SORT OF ANSWER IS THAT TO ROCKY AND Karen Becket, who already own their own business? There aren't enough hours in a day to run two independent businesses, and not enough heads to hold all the headaches.

To which I must answer that I'm not suggesting that Rocky and Karen run two businesses. I'm suggesting that they run **ten** businesses. But businesses with rare qualities. Businesses that avoid normal business problems.

- Businesses with no organizational problems, no decisions as to whether to be a sole proprietor, corporation, or subchapter "S" entity.

- Businesses with no accounting problems.

- Businesses with no collection problems; no possibility of accounts receivable not being paid.

- Businesses with no inventory problems: businesses without inventory of any kind.

- Businesses without merchandising problems; no need to worry about sales or goods being returned.

- Businesses without distribution problems; no distributor to work with, to make or break your line of merchandise.

- Businesses without overhead problems; in fact you will have little or no overhead in your new business.

- Businesses without employee problems: no employees and therefore no problems with respect to unions, pension benefits, retirement programs, no strikes or walkouts.

- No bureaucracy problems in your business; nothing in triplicate, for no one will exist in your business except yourself.

- Businesses without legal problems: Few businesses have no legal problems, but you are about to learn of several that have no need for lawyers or subpoenas.

- Businesses without tax problems; the taxes in your new business will be cut and dried, easily calculated on a $50.00 adding machine.

- Businesses without insurance problems; you will have nothing to insure and thus no need for any insurance.

- Businesses without estate planning problems: business entity passes to heirs free and clear, with no debt or lingering threads to cause them harm.

Normal headaches and concerns, the countless details that fill the businessman's head and time, that dull the pleasure that can be found in work, all vanished forever. And yet these businesses **do** exist, not only do they exist, but they have some very special advantages:

- They are rarely affected by outside factors.

- They are almost entirely immune from governmental action, as much as anything can be in this new era.

- They are unaffected by the environment. They neither harm nor are harmed by the water and air, foul or pure.

- They are, and have proved to be, immune to bad times—like a crash or depression. You will never suffer from a depression while in these businesses.

- They are also immune to the symptoms of hyper-inflated times. If prices skyrocket, you have more opportunities, not less, and your merchandise will **never** be priced out of the market. Hyper-inflation proof.

These are businesses that offer you the greatest psychological advantages and, above all, the greatest financial reward of any venture in today's new era world. There is one overall principle that drives these new businesses, the same principle that is at the heart of virtually all fortunes made in these modern times — **momentum**.

To better define that momentum principle, I need to ask Rocky and Karen two odd questions about their nursery and flower shop:

Do you carry five trees and sell them for $2,500 each, or do you carry five thousand seedlings and sell them for $2.50 each?

And, if your inspection is lax and you allow one single egg cluster of spider mites on a single plant to enter your nursery, how long does it take before the nursery is infested with spider mites?

Queer as they might be, these two questions will start Rocky and Karen and you toward an understanding of the principle that can lead to the rewards we all so deeply seek.

It is a principle of remarkable force. Let's look at it, learn from it, and apply it.

Take a ball. Roll it across a table......

Chapter Three

TAKE A BALL. ROLL IT ACROSS A TABLE. YOUR HAND has given momentum to the ball; the amount of momentum determines how far the ball will roll before stopping. That is the simplest form of momentum.

Take a ball. Roll it down a hill. Your hand gives the ball momentum, but an additional force, gravity, will supply additional momentum. The ball will roll faster and faster, gaining speed until a counterforce acts against it: another hand, gravity, a barrier. The same flick of your wrist that rolled the ball a few feet across the table has started the ball down the hill, yet momentum has sent the ball rolling at 5, 10, 25 miles per hour: other forces can act on momentum.

If you build a water wheel on a stream to grind wheat, you have harnessed the momentum of the water in the stream. You've supplied no impetus to the water, but you can use the momentum to make your livelihood.

This sort of simple momentum is familiar to everyone. It is the force that moves something from the Starting Point to the Stopping Point. Momentum is the force that causes movement over time.

STARTING POINT — — — — — — — — — — — — — STOPPING POINT
(time)

But momentum is not limited to the physical and tangible. Wherever there is movement over time, there is momentum. If an abstract idea can be transferred to a line on a paper, the potential for momentum exists.

If you've ever watched a basketball game on television, you've probably heard a commentator say that one or another team "Really has momentum going for them now." That's a figure of speech, but the momentum really exists: it can be drawn.

It looks hopeless for the tired yet scrappy "Stoppers," down by ten to the stronger "Starters." Their coach orders them to win one for the Greatest Stopper of them all, or go down fighting.

The Last Quarter

		FINAL SCORE
	80	80
	75	75
	70	70
"The Starters"	65	65
	60	60
"The Stoppers"	55	55
	50	50

Time Remaining In Game 12 11 10 9 8 7 6 5 4 3 2 1 0 Minutes

The sportscasters may attribute the miracle comeback to one player on the "Stoppers" who got a hot hand and carried the whole team forward to victory. That may well be true. But the reasons for the momentum are not now important. What is important is that the "Stoppers" scored 23 points in the fourth quarter, while the "Starters" scored only 12. We draw a line from 55 points, across twelve minutes, to 78 points. The movement of that line is momentum, the momentum of the winning team.

STARTING POINT (55 points) — — — — — (78 points) STOPPING POINT
(time)

How it came to be momentum is beside the point: it happened. It happened in a simple progression of numbers, one or two at a time, two points followed by two points, and the line tracking those points moved over time.

That is simple momentum, an arithmetic progression. But it is possible to apply a **lever** to that step-by-step, point-by-point, plodding momentum, and use that momentum to produce results that can be **staggering**.

A FABLE

I T IS THE YEAR 2011 AND SIXTY-FOUR-YEAR-OLD slugger Reggie Jackson limps forlornly into the plush mahogany offices of one-hundred-and-four-year-old Gene Autry, still owner of the California Angels baseball team. The one-time singing cowboy scowls at the one-time Mr. October. "I'm surprised to see **you**, Jackson," croaks Autry. "Where are all your agents?"

"Dead. All dead," Jackson answers quietly and respectfully, coughing nervously. "I'll have to negotiate my own contract this time, I guess."

"I don't know what kind of deal you think you can make. I have all your statistics here from last season and they stink. They're rotten. They're vile. And that's the good part. I'm not even talking about your strike-outs."

"I know my statistics," Jackson protests, but Autry continues.

—23—

"Batting average, .025. Two RBI's. One home run all year, one crummy inside-the-park homer in the Yankeedome, and you wouldn't have had that one if that fan of yours hadn't held the outfielders at bay with his .38 revolver."

"I know, I know. I had an off year."

"An off year?" Autry roars. "You had no year. My own sixty-one-year-old grandson can outplay you. I can't imagine why the fans still come out to see you."

"I know I let you down and let the fans down last year," the white-haired star says, his head bowed, eyes downward. "That's why I'm asking you for just one more year. Then I'll hang 'em up." It is a poignant moment, almost sad.

"I don't pay .025 hitters a million dollars a year," fires the crusty old magnate, with the knowledge that he is on top of the relationship now, perhaps for the first time ever in their long and often bitter association.

"No. That wouldn't be right. No, all I want is to play, to play as best I can, to prove myself. I'll play next year for a rookie's salary, if you want. $39,500.00. Just give me a chance, Mr. Autry."

"A Rookie's Salary!?"

"The absolute minimum, just for the chance to play."

Autry ponders this. "That's all?" he asks suspiciously. He and Jackson have faced each other across the table too many times for Autry not to be wary.

Reggie has recovered slightly and smiles wanly. "Oh, maybe just a little incentive clause? Just to put some fun into it."

"Ha! I could smell it coming. You and your incentive clauses! I remember 1997 and that one cost me half the stadium. Okay, what is it this time?"

"It's nothing, really. All I want is to be paid a dollar for my first home run, in addition to the rookie salary. Just one dollar."

"And if you should be so lucky, what about the second home run? How much will I have to pay you for the second one?"

"If I hit two home runs, you'll pay me two dollars for the second. If I hit three, you'll pay me four dollars for the third. Eight dollars if I hit four. And keep doubling, as far as I go during the season. Just for the fun of it, for old time's sake. It'd mean something to me. Let's make a contest of it this year."

"A dollar for a home run? That's not much incentive."

"It's all the incentive I need. Just double it each time. Like a friendly wager."

Gene Autry counts on his ancient fingers, well worn from passing by the frets on his guitar. The last time Reggie Jackson hit more than five home runs was in the 1993 campaign, Autry remembers, and we drew 4 million fans that year. He remembers and smiles to himself. "It's a deal. I'll put it in writing this afternoon. Welcome aboard, Reggie. If you can show me some homers, I'll be glad to dig into my pockets for a few greenbacks. Just between friends. For old time's sake."

Spring training season arrives, and never has Reggie Jackson worked so hard; he is an inspiration to the rookies. Endless hours in the batting cage; aerobics; weight training; limitless running: he pounds his aged body into shape by brute determination, with a regimen that would exhaust a corn-fed all-star. He seems a man possessed. Clearly Reggie Jackson has something on his mind, something eating at him, driving him. Is it something he said? Was there more to his agreement than first blush would indicate?

The season opener, and Reggie Jackson, the slowest starter in the history of baseball, comes out swinging! Swinging for the fences! Trying to scald the ball, trying to turn it inside out, trying to hit the screamers, the towering drives, the tape-measure stretchers!

He isn't the supple slugger he used to be; the years have clearly taken their toll; every swing is a scream of pain and maximum effort. But still he swings, swings for the fences, ties himself into knots only to swing again. His body may be held together by scotch tape and corsets, but by early July he has sent ten balls over the outfield fences. Ten hits in total, and each a home run. The crowds go wild, the ballpark is jammed. Either a homer or a strike-out, no middle ground, just like the Reggie of old.

In his private, glassed in box high above the action in 150,000 seat Anaheim Stadium, Gene Autry ponders the bonus he has guaranteed Jackson. "Ten home runs means $512. Not bad. Quite cheap, actually." Then he looks at the size of the crowd that Reggie has drawn to the park by his heroics. "Yes, sir, the best deal I ever made with **any** player." But with all this thinking, the elderly grandfatherly Autry finds his energy level dropping fast, and he takes his seventh-inning nap, untroubled by the bonus, the simple one dollar for a home run, two dollars for the second.

By the end of the season our ancient star has, by grit and determination, belted thirty-one homers. Thirty-one. Thirty-one hits, thirty-one homers, as if there was no such thing as a single, a double, a triple. No, all season it was the far fence or nothing at all. Most of the time it was nothing at all, blue blue sky and a swirling gushing disturbance of the air, but on thirty-one occasions some lucky fan went home with a souvenir of Reggie Jackson's epic season. It was not enough to lead the league, but it had driven the fans batty and attracted them to the game in record numbers.

On the day after the season ends, it is a much younger and more confident Reggie who saunters into Autry's office. All his gray hair is gone; he looks sleek, even trim. "Hiya, Cowboy," Jackson jokes. "I guess it's time to settle accounts."

"With pleasure, Reggie, with pleasure. You earned it. We've never been more proud of you or had attendance like we did this year. Thanks, old man." Autry pulls the company checkbook out of his desk drawer, signs his name to the bottom line and leaves it blank for Reggie to fill in. Then he hands it to an open palm. "What's the damage? Fill it in, my friend."

Reggie calmly fills in the amount on the check and hands it back to Autry.

$1, 073, 741, 824.00.

One billion, seventy-three million, seven-hundred and forty-one thousand, eight hundred and twenty-four dollars.

Even the year 2011 bank account balance of Gene Autry was not to be found with that kind of money, a value exceeding all the property in the city of Cleveland, Ohio. Reggie Jackson had won again.

THE FORCE OF THE RETURN

T HE USE OF THE PRINCIPLE OF SIMPLE MOMEN-tum can produce **overwhelming** results. In our fable, Reggie Jackson applies a plodding, steady momentum—the mounting number of home runs (arithmetic $1 + 1 + 1 + 1 + 1$) — to a simple lever — the steady doubling of a single dollar (geometric $1 \times 2 \times 2 \times 2 \times 2$) — to earn over one billion dollars for his last home run. It is a numbers game you probably first saw in grammar school. Arithmetic progression looks like this:

```
                                    7   7
                                6       6
                            5           5
                        4               4    INCREASE
                    3                   3
                2                       2
            1                           1
STARTING POINT   ————— (time) —————   STOPPING POINT
```

But if you double each step up, each increase, you take the **same distance** and get a geometric progression, which looks like this:

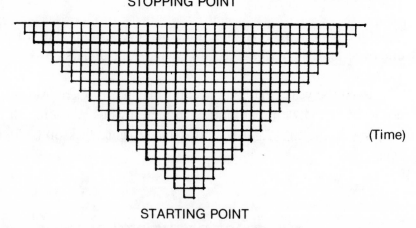

STOPPING POINT

(Time)

STARTING POINT

When run on a horizontal plane, the difference is obvious.

Value of Each New Home Run Hit

(1)   (ARITHMETIC INCREASE) —————————————

(0) STARTING POINT 1+1+1+1+1+1+1+1 STOPPING POINT (31)
                         (time)

—28—

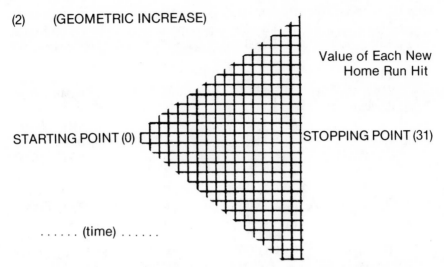

(2)   (GEOMETRIC INCREASE)

Value of Each New Home Run Hit

STARTING POINT (0)   STOPPING POINT (31)

. . . . . . (time) . . . . . .

In each case the length of the line from the starting point to the stopping point was identical—from zero home runs to thirty-one home runs. The line had identical length. Reggie made his $1 billion simply by taking this single line of arithmetic progression and turning it into a Momentum line by using the doubling sequence to maximize return. In actual numbers, the value of each home run arithmetically and dynamically looked like this:

HOME RUNS	MONEY REGGIE WOULD HAVE BEEN PAID IF HE GOT $1.00 FOR EACH HOME RUN	MONEY OWED TO REGGIE BY INCREASING THE PAYMENT TWO FOLD WITH EACH NEW HOME RUN
1	$ 1.00	$ 1.00
2	$ 1.00	$ 2.00
3	$ 1.00	$ 4.00
4	$ 1.00	$ 8.00
5	$ 1.00	$ 16.00
6	$ 1.00	$ 32.00
7	$ 1.00	$ 64.00
8	$ 1.00	$ 128.00
9	$ 1.00	$ 256.00
10	$ 1.00	$ 512.00
11	$ 1.00	$ 1,024.00
12	$ 1.00	$ 2,048.00
13	$ 1.00	$ 4,096.00
14	$ 1.00	$ 8,192.00
15	$ 1.00	$ 16,384.00

16	$ 1.00	$	32,768.00
17	$ 1.00	$	65,536.00
18	$ 1.00	$	131,072.00
19	$ 1.00	$	262,144.00
20	$ 1.00	$	524,288.00
21	$ 1.00	$	1,048,576.00
22	$ 1.00	$	2,097,152.00
23	$ 1.00	$	4,194,304.00
24	$ 1.00	$	8,388,608.00
25	$ 1.00	$	16,777,216.00
26	$ 1.00	$	33,554,432.00
27	$ 1.00	$	67,108,864.00
28	$ 1.00	$	134,217,728.00
29	$ 1.00	$	268,435,456.00
30	$ 1.00	$	536,870,912.00
31	$ 1.00	$	1,073,741,824.00

For his first home run, Reggie Jackson applied 195 pounds of sixty-four-year-old muscle and gristle to a ball traveling at ninety miles per hour, and propelled same ball in an arc for a distance in excess of 300 feet. It was worth $1 to him.

The next homer would be worth $2, but it would require the **same act** as the first: hit a ball over a distant fence.

The thirty-first home run required only the identical effort and result as the first home run which paid $1, yet, by his accumulation of home runs, and, working with the momentum of a geometric progression, that last homer resulted in a value in excess of $1 billion. Actually, Gene Autry owed Reggie the **sum total** of all the figures in the right column above, for a total of $2,147,483,647.00, instead of just the last figure in the column, which was owed only for the thirty-first home run. He still had to pay him the amounts due for the previous thirty. But it was a moot question, if Autry didn't have even the billion dollars for home run thirty-one, there was no need making him pay for the previous thirty also. The total cost to Autry per home run was $1 each, arithmetically, $34,636,833.00 each with Reggie's progression.

And how had Autry gotten into this, the worst business deal of his hundred-and-three years?

By Reggie's offer to play for "...a rookie's salary, with a small incentive clause, one dollar for the first home run and two dollars for the second." And by **Momentum**.

Take a ball. Roll it across a table......

ANOTHER STORY

YOU LIVE AT THE HEADWATERS OF THE GREAT Qwerty River. One day you learn that five hundred miles downstream is a lumbermill that will pay you ten dollars for each delivered log. So, with great enthusiasm, you fell ten trees and lash them together into a raft for the long trip south. The river is fast where you live, wild and narrow, laced with rapids, and you can barely hold your little raft of ten logs together through the treacherous water. But then, a few miles downstream, the river widens and the water becomes smooth. It is a long trip, those five hundred miles, but, after the rough beginning, there is little risk. For two weeks you float down the placid Qwerty, eventually reaching the mill where you sell your ten logs for a hundred dollars, not even enough money for passage home. Forced to hitchhike, you exhaust your profit on food and shelter along the way home.

You do make one pause on the return trip, by the banks of the Qwerty, about forty miles upstream, to stare in amazement at a man floating downstream to the mill with over one hundred logs. One hundred! How did he ever make it through those murderous rapids with a hundred log raft?

The answer comes slowly to you, but, because thumbing a ride goes slowly, you have plenty of time to think on the long journey home, and you arrive at the solution. There is an answer. Once home you begin again, in the same fashion, cut another ten logs and lash them together with rawhide into a crude raft. You hang on for dear life through the rapids, and make it. But this time, when the river widens, you cut ten more logs, lash them into a second raft, and affix it to the first. Farther down the river is wider still, and you cut twenty more logs. They are getting hard to handle now, so you hire a roustabout to help you cut and raft for ten dollars a day, payable upon reaching the mill. You and he cut sixty more logs, form a boom, hire another man, and head on, as the Qwerty gets wider and smoother still. You finally arrive at the mill and sell your one thousand logs for ten thousand dollars. This time you drive home in a **new** pickup truck.

STARTING POINT —————————————— STOPPING POINT
(Your Home)   (Movement of the River,   (The Mill)
                                flowing with time)

The river carried you along during both ventures. Discounting the time taken to cut and secure the logs, it took no longer to deliver a thousand logs than it did to deliver ten. The river flowed no faster, nor did it become wider or narrower. The only difference was that on your second trip you used the momentum of the river to maximize your dollar earnings. The river didn't earn you the ten thousand dollars, it was **your use** of momentum that did.

Momentum means movement with time. Profit is normally the movement of **value** from one price level to another higher price level. If you buy at the lower level, and the line of movement over time traverses to a higher price level, you have the opportunity to sell at a profit.

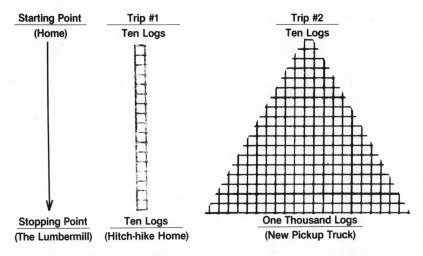

Starting Point (Home)	Trip #1 Ten Logs	Trip #2 Ten Logs
Stopping Point (The Lumbermill)	Ten Logs (Hitch-hike Home)	One Thousand Logs (New Pickup Truck)

Profit is simply momentum. **Momentum** is the principle by which profit can be turned into fortunes—into the super accumulation of wealth. In fact, **Momentum** is the essential principle behind virtually **all** personal fortunes made in this world. It is a means toward accumulation, the very accumulation itself drives the momentum, it feeds on itself.

This is not a complex principle. The factors that determine the momentum may be complex, but the momentum itself can be reduced to the simple movement of a line from a starting point to a stopping point over a period of time. As long as this momentum exists, it will allow you to maximize your financial return as the river carries you along.

THE FORCE OF DESTRUCTION

A DREAM IS ENDING. AS I WRITE THIS, THE AMERIcan people are worried about the prospect of billion dollar deficits in the Federal budget. The debate is stormy, and the possible consequences are unknown.

Less discussed is the fact that the unfunded liabilities, the debt owed to the American worker, of the Social Security System are growing at the rate of $300 billion **per year**. As things now stand, the Social Security Administration has $48,000 of unfunded, meaning no money in the bank, debt for every man and woman in America between the ages of 20 and 65. And the consequences of this one fact are unavoidable.

The total debt of the Social Security System exceeds $4 **trillion**. The total net worth of all Americans alive today is only $2 trillion dollars. If Social Security is to pay off, the cost will be twice the total net worth of all living Americans. The nation is bankrupt, and like Gene Autry, the obligation cannot be met. But Gene Autry acted in a fable. Social Security is real. There is really only one question any more with respect to Social Security and that is, "On what day will the Stopping Point be reached?"

STARTING POINT (1935)

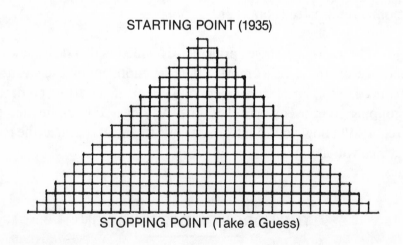

STOPPING POINT (Take a Guess)

What caused this mess? The answer comes quickly, take a ball, give it a shove......

With Social Security, each new year brings a larger dollar payout, an expanding number of beneficiaries, and recipients living longer than ever. Each year is like another Reggie Jackson home run; the numbers mount geometrically while the years pass arithmetically.

Social Security was designed so that small contributions from many workers could ease the burden of retirement for those who worked so hard to build this country. In 1945, there were 40 contributing workers for each Social Security recipient, the contribution from each could be small. In the year 2010, there will be only 2.2 wage earners for each beneficiary so small contributions no longer work. Over the next several years this demographic time bomb will lead us into higher and higher social security taxes, further reducing the net earnings of working men and women and, at the same time, draining away funds for business investment in America. By 2011, if the average Social Security recipient is receiving $1,000 per month, which is the projected cost of living growth rate, the monthly payroll taxes for each worker for social security alone will be $454.00. Each worker will have to pay $454.00 per month into social security just to meet the minimum monthly benefits of the recipients.

Social Security is an honorable and marvelous thing and 95% of those who receive monthly Social Security checks both need and appreciate the help. But this moral justification does not solve the financial dilemma. Here is the inescapable problem. Once the number of workers paying into the system began to shrink, while at the same time the number of recipients was expanding, the system was doomed. It is simple mathematics. Despite every stop-gap legislative measure designed to save it, Social Security, as we know it, will one day collapse. The only question is: "When will the Stopping Point be reached?"

The turn of the momentum in social security was due to an achievement that we all take a great deal of pride in. Our national average life span went up, and the retirement age went down. That was all that happened. But it was enough to make the momentum

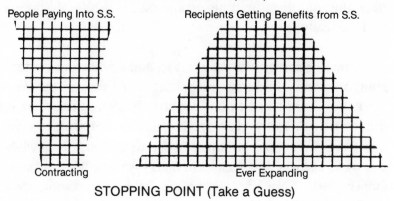

STARTING POINT (1935)

People Paying Into S.S.   Recipients Getting Benefits from S.S.

Contracting   Ever Expanding

STOPPING POINT (Take a Guess)

of the river shift to a contracting work force and an expanding number of beneficiaries. Someone once wrote that it takes almost **no effort** to switch the train track at any given junction, but the effect of that very little effort can be significant as the train rolls on. A thirty-second effort can put the engine and passengers in Milwaukee or Miami, in Dallas or Denver, in Chicago or Cleveland. Not much effort for the change effected. As payees into the system contracted and recipients expanded the change was almost imperceivable at the beginning, and yet, today, the result is certain bankruptcy.

Momentum is neither good nor bad. It is simply a force. It can be destructive retrograde, as in Social Security, or it can be destructive progressively.

Somewhere under sunbaked earth, in the nation we know as Saudi Arabia, there are 100 female locusts. When the warm summer sun follows the heavy Spring rains, each of those female locusts will lay seventy eggs. Of these, under the very best of conditions, only eleven will survive, only 15.5%. Weak momentum, an eleven fold increase per generation considering a seventy fold egg laying ratio. But Momentum is at work here.

Within the next five generations, only a few months, there will be 1.4 million locusts surviving from those original 100. Three generations later there will be 2 billion. Within ten generations the one-hundred will have grown to 236 billion. The simple momentum was the progression of one generation to the next, only ten steps in all, but the Momentum of expanding outward with time resulted in 236 billion flying grasshoppers. A moderate size locust swarm consumes the same quantity of food as 100,000 Egyptians in a total year. Each infant locust eats six times its weight **daily**. An adult eats only twice its own weight, but then adults weight much more than infants. Eventually this momentum will be halted, but in a destructive way: The land will be denuded, a wasteland. Only then will the locusts die off. But if, by chance, 100 remain deep beneath the desert sands, when the rains and the sun come again, the cycle will repeat itself.

Momentum is neither good nor bad, it is simply a **force**. It can work for you, or it can work against you. The force worked **for** Reggie Jackson, but worked **against** Gene Autry. There are limitless other examples. The purpose of this book is to teach you how to harness this incredible force to your **personal advantage**. It has been done, it is being done, and it will continue to be done.

Recall that I asked Rocky and Karen to consider what would happen if a single cluster of spider mite eggs escaped their inspection. They understand now that Momentum can move in both directions, both toward profit and toward destruction. I asked them a second question: "Do you carry five trees and sell them for $2,500 each, or do you carry five thousand seedlings and sell them for $2.50 each?" Within that question is the beginning of an understanding of how momentum can carry you down the stream where the river is wider, the going easier, and the profit waiting.

Chapter Four

HOW **ARE** FORTUNES REALLY MADE IN AMERICA
today, made not from inheritance, but from scratch? What
principle is behind **every** great American fortune? You know it by
heart now—it is momentum. Take a ball, and give it a shove.....

I have a friend, an extremely talented and dedicated woman,
who has for some years been the only teacher at an Inuit federal
reserve in Canada's Northwest Territories, near the Arctic Circle. In
many ways, she has chosen a life of extreme isolation. The village in
which she teaches is 500 miles away from any town with a population of more than one thousand; as far as she knows, she is both the
only teacher and only white person settled within 400 square miles.
Her only direct contact with the outside world is by bush plane,
and, during the eight-month Arctic winter, even that contact is
sporatic. In recent years the Canadian government brought in
satellite television and telephones, but she makes little use of either,
except to keep track of her outside businesses.

She loves the life; she does not consider herself isolated. Over
the years she has formed close ties with the Inuits; she is wholly of
the village. She is a superb teacher. During the winters, when the
average **high** temperature is minus twenty degrees, she is not af-
ficted with cabin fever. She reads 18th Century literature, her first
love; Fielding, Johnson, Walpole. She is very well paid by the Cana-

dian government for the hardships she does not sense. Her paychecks are almost beside the point; she probably has less opportunity to spend them than anyone in Canada.

This friend, this teacher in a one room school in the Arctic, operates one of the most successful businesses in all of Canada. It is a business without inventory, personnel problems or major capital needs. It is a business with a rate of return that can equal or exceed that of any business or venture in the world; a respected and conservative business; with no taint of hucksterism, or mail-order schemes or dishonest practices; no exploitation and no "insider's information." It is a business fueled and propelled by **Momentum.** In 1973-74, this woman quietly and carefully accomplished one of the greatest financial coups I have ever heard of; the return on her business was beyond comprehension. No matter how large the percentage or how great the dollar return extant now in your thoughts, she **exceeded** your guess many many times over. We shall return to her shortly with the full story.

She is a very wealthy woman. She started with nothing, less than $5,000 in fact, and built one of the largest fortunes of the 1970's, all the time never leaving her Indian village. Yet she contines to teach, even with the lifetime financial freedom to pursue whatever she wishes. For now, that is teaching. It is what she loves. Her wealth is the result of her selecting one opportunity for success out of several possible choices, and maximizing her return from that opportunity. When the momentum began, she knew how to apply a lever to it. Luck was not involved. Prediction was not involved. Financial expertise was not involved.

Her success was based on her ability to know when an opportunity was occuring, and her ability to move with that opportunity. That is the basis for **all** success.

TWO HOLES

A FRIEND TOLD THE STORY TO ME, SO I CAN'T testify in the first person that it is true, but that friend never told me a lie before.

"He drilled two holes. That was the sum of his great wealth. He didn't do much before those two holes and, as far as I know, hasn't distinguished himself since the drilling. But the effort that went into those two holes provided him with the foundation of the wealth he has today."

He tells the story often, so often that he has it down to a recitation, ornate and florid. He is proud of the man he once intimately knew, and makes the most of the seemingly absurdity of the story. But he always swore that it was true.

"Two holes, and my friend didn't grow up in the Dust Bowl of Oklahoma on a homestead near Clarion and Enid. He didn't put every penny he had into drilling two four-thousand foot wells and come up with oil," he responds rhetorically.

"Nope. Sorry. He grew up in Miami Beach, and his father was a life-insurance agent. If J. Paul Getty wanted to make his fortune drilling for oil, that is okay, but not my friend. No sir."

"This is how you get rich, so take notes." He starts the story each time in the same fashion. "First, you go to law school in Washington, D.C. and you get a job with a Washington law firm doing patent searches in the patent office. Now that can be very boring work, or it can be very exciting, it all depends on what you bring into it, and what you take out."

"Get married, that is important, you have to have a wife to come home to, if my story is going to work. So get married early in your legal career, and marry someone named Christine. People named Christine always make good wives."

"Now that you are doing patent research at the United States patent office, it is imperative that you find an item among those daily entries you will be examining that intrigues you. I recommend that you look for a brand new can-opener, with a brand-new patent application pending. That would be the best way to make your fortune, and a way to participate in the revolution concerning how tin cans are opened."

"Since every kitchen already has one of these gadgets today, it is hard to convey what a new idea a can-opener was back then, when you were just out of law school. You clamped this device onto a can, and turned the flat piece of silver metal, which turned the cutting wheel, which opened the can. Just a plain old can-opener. You have one in the kitchen drawer. But it was new then, brand new, patent-pending. So that is the item you are going to focus on to make you and Christine rich."

"The first thing you do is to take this new gizmo home and give it a test, and it works great, except for one little drawback. The part you twist, the silver flat piece of steel, that causes you problems. What problems? Your fingers keep slipping off, especially when your hands are wet. The mechanism works great when your fingers are attached, but when they slip off, it won't work at all. You ask your wife to try it, and she'll come in fast and start yelling because by this time you've opened just about every can of food you had in the house, all sitting open on the kitchen table. But Christine loves you dearly and never complains, and so she gives it a try. The problems are the same, her fingers slip off also, off the turner, especially when her hands are wet."

"Now comes the part that makes you rich. You think for a moment, about sixteen seconds, and then you start to drill, in the shop, in your basement. By dawn you are the first one at the patent office, the earliest you have ever arrived there, even your secretary is only pulling into the parking lot, but you are there. And what do you do? You file an overriding patent on this little device, known as an improvement patent. If the can-opener is **ever** sold with your granted overriding patent improvement, you get a royalty from each sale. The vendor doesn't have to use your improvement, but if he does, he has to pay."

"All you did was drill two holes. One hole at the end of that flat piece of steel and the other hole at the other end. Those two holes keep the fingers of the operator from slipping off, wet or dry, and make you a millionaire in the process."

"From then on, from that very day, each can-opener sold brings you one or more pennies. Just a penny or two, but there are tens of millions being sold. Now that is the way to get rich in this world, just drill two holes. Of course, my friend already did that, so I guess you will have to take another route. Sorry."

I think he likes telling that story, and I always enjoy hearing it.

STARTING and STOPPING and STARTING-UP

THIS IS NOT A BOOK ABOUT TWO HOLES. BUT IT IS A book about three points. And those two holes and three points have much in common. They both can make you very successful.

The first point is your starting point, the start of a horizontal line. That line is the line of your lifetime, a line of jobs and careers and opportunities and ventures. The line begins at the starting point, as all lines do, when you first seek out success, and runs to any number of stopping points, when you think you have found it, all the stumbles and chances met in your working lifetime.

STARTING___STOPPING___STOPPING___STOPPING___STOPPING___STOPPING
POINT   POINT #1   POINT #2   POINT #3   POINT #4   POINT #5

Consider our friend who drilled two holes in a piece of metal. Put his life on this line. His vocation did not start out to be a driller of holes. His vocation was that of a patent lawyer; even before that, he was likely to have had any number of summer jobs, perhaps a stint in the service. Any number of stopping points, any number of fields in which to succeed along the horizontal plane. He believed that his success would be in law, perhaps his tenth stopping point, perhaps his twentieth. But it was the next stopping point of drilling holes he came to, quite unexpectedly, that was the source of his success. He had the wit to know it when he came to it.

Very few of us start out certain of our destiny, knowing exactly what our schooling will be, what our vocation will be, what jobs we will take, and what opportunities we can challenge. You may devote twenty years of your life to school to earn a doctorate in History, and find yourself driving a bus in Chicago when there are no teaching jobs to be had anywhere. Or you might start out as a cop only to become a novelist, as Joseph Wambaugh did. Fidel Castro thought his life's work was to be that of a professional baseball player. The search for the "proper stopping point" is the elusive goal of us all. We're always looking to the horizon beyond that first horizontal line. That's what makes life such a treat. You can be certain that stopping point 35 is the key to success, heaven on earth, and yet you're never certain that stopping point 36 might not be just a little more suited to your needs and wants. John F. Kennedy had been planning, at the end of his terms as President, to found a great Washington D.C. newspaper. Even Presidents have yet another stopping point on the horizon.

I will put it as a maxim: **All great financial successes start with the location of a proper stopping point**. Momentum and all you will learn from this book are dependent on your understanding those few words. You must begin — as we all must begin — on this horizontal line and search for a point at which to stop looking.

The man who drilled the two holes found his stopping point at the federal patent office and in the basement of his house. Reggie Jackson found his on a baseball diamond. Clarence Birdseye found his in a barrel of frozen vegetables in Labrador. Steinway built pianos. William Levitt built thousands of identical houses. Henry Ford didn't like walking. Bill Boeing didn't like driving cars. Henry Miller liked sex, and said so. Walt Disney found his stopping point when he changed Mortimer the Mouse to Mickey the Mouse.

Go through **Who's Who** in your local library and pick out twenty-five names at random. Those names are a testament to the location of stopping points; behind each name will be the name of that point which brought success, and many of the other stopping points along the way. **Who's Who** is a book about locating one's niche in life.

If you have not yet achieved financial success, it is because you are still running along the horizontal line, looking for the proper point to end your sideways journey. You may have foregone the opportunities presented by a point of the past; most of us will not seize the first opportunity that comes our way. But the rule of the first line is still: **All great financial successes start with the location of a proper stopping point.**

And when found, it must be acted upon.

"BUY 'EM BY THE BAG"

I PASSED A McDONALD'S HAMBURGER STAND ON the way to my office this morning and watched as a young man perched precariously on a ladder to update the familiar "OVER 35 BILLION SOLD" sign. It now reads "OVER 50 BILLION SOLD."

It took me back a bit. I was a pioneer in the world of fast food. I ate my first McDonald's hamburger at the stand in San Bernardino, California in the early 1950's, when it was the only McDonald's stand in the world. The hamburger — no better than the ones they serve today — cost 15¢, and their promotion, instead of a nationwide advertising campaign pounding "You Deserve a Break Today" into our heads, consisted of an electric sign flashing "BUY 'EM BY THE BAG."

As I recall, the place was quite popular, the food more or less flavorless: just a hamburger stand, not much different from any of a hundred Southern California hamburger stands. But, then, I wasn't Ray Kroc.

In 1954, Ray Kroc was a travelling salesman, peddling a very fast and efficient milk-shake-mixer, when he met Richard and Maurice McDonald, who owned that thriving little stand. They seemed natural customers; their stand was run with assembly-line speed, and a better milk-shake machine couldn't hurt. But Kroc was fascinated with the operation itself, and lost interest in his milk shake machines. He liked the way that one stand was run. That was enough for him. He changed careers in mid-stream. He proposed to the McDonald brothers that they expand and build more stands; he, Kroc, would do the expanding, as a franchise salesman. They struck a deal. Ray Kroc began to build hamburger stands.

In 1960, long before McDonald's stands were becoming an American symbol, Ray Kroc bought out the McDonald brothers for a great deal of money. They were rich men, and would never have to pound patties again. They had found a stopping point, and they had sold it. They had achieved a large measure of financial success. They were happy men. But what was to happen in the next two decades must have broken their hearts. They knew the **first** rule of financial success — look for a stopping point — but they didn't know the **second**:

> *Once you find a proper stopping point, change the direction of your business line from horizontal to vertical.*

Ray Kroc pondered the lowly hamburger. There is not much room for profit on a 15¢ hamburger, yet the profits from the hamburgers from the few stands then in existance provided a steady, plodding, if unspectacular income. Kroc studied the stands: What was it that make it so popular? One reason, he learned, was the 15¢ price. The burger was cheap, it was served up quickly, it was eaten on the run. The stands were in heavily trafficed areas on the fringes of Southern California's burgeoning suburbs, and the suburbanites often fell into the habit of McDonald's, habits reinforced by their young, who **loved** the cheap burger. The profits per hamburger may have been infinitessimal, but as long as the hamburger sold, the profit was there. And the "fast food" concept of the McDonald brothers sold a lot of burgers.

Three points. The McDonald brothers understood the nature of the horizontal line, and they found their stopping point, sold and achieved their success. Ray Kroc also found his stopping point, but knew he wasn't **really** stopping. He was, in fact, just getting ready to move, only this time switching from horizontal effort to a vertical one. He was changing the nature of his stopping point from **stopping** to **starting-up**. And that is what made him a **billionaire!**

THE RAY KROC STORY

RAY KROC INSISTED THAT ALL McDONALD'S stands be run with an intimidating degree of efficiency. He demanded speedy service, standardized the cooking, ordered that the stands be kept immaculate, to avoid any "greasy spoon" stigma, to keep the families coming in, to sell hamburgers, to make the tiny profit. He refined the operation, made an art of hamburgers. The he began to use **rule number two**. He plowed his profits, and his own capital, into more stands, and more stands, and still more stands, franchising them only to investors whom he trained to uphold his rigid standards. He studied demographic charts and maps to pick the best locations for his stands, the busiest intersections of every town and hamlet; he built stands everywhere, first across the nation and then around the world, over **four thousand** franchises, each selling cheap hamburgers, one by one, with a tiny profit tucked into each one, just under the squirt of ketchup.

I know very little about what odd jobs and ventures Ray Kroc the travelling salesman may have followed at stopping points before 1954. But I do know something about what he did when he discovered his **start-up** point that year, and moved to the vertical line. Ray Kroc, within twenty years, accumulated a personal fortune large enough to pay off Reggie Jackson when he cashed the billion dollar check. His entire fortune was built on the profit he could squeeze from a 15¢ hamburger...multiplied by the "OVER 50 BILLION SOLD."

Ray Kroc found 50 billion hamburger enthusiasts to give him at least 15¢, or today's equivalent, for a thin beef patty, a roll, and a splash of ketchup. Kroc kept a penny from each. He didn't start with 50 billion hamburgers being sold. He didn't even start in the hamburger business. He was a traveling salesman looking for a proper stopping point. He found it to be the same stopping point that the McDonald brothers had, so he bought them out. He started with just enough hungry Southern Californians to give him just

—48—

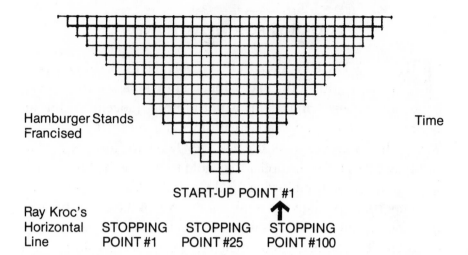

Hamburger Stands
Francised

Time

START-UP POINT #1

↑

Ray Kroc's
Horizontal   STOPPING   STOPPING   STOPPING
Line   POINT #1   POINT #25   POINT #100

enough profit to build a couple more stands. He financed his expansion one penny at a time — a patty at a time — and he never needed more than just that microscopic profit out of which to build his great fortune. He didn't try to make $1.00 out of a 15¢ hamburger: he tried to maximize the number of stands he owned, and thereby maximized the number of pennies he made each day. Each stand contributed to the **momentum** impetus leading to the next stand, which contributed to the next stands, and so on. He asked nothing of his buyer except to fork over the 15¢ (adjusted for inflation, a McDonald's burger is even cheaper today); he did not diversify the stands to sell sewing machines or insurance. He simply sold burgers for pocket change, and kept a bit of that change for himself. William Wrigley did it with chewing gum at a penny a **stick**; imagine what the profit can be on a stick of gum! Yet the Wrigley fortune is mammoth.

How have most great fortunes been built? By three points, and some rules. **First**, work from an initial **starting point** to find your proper **stopping point**. **Then** you convert that stopping point into a **start-up point** and turn your line from horizontal to vertical. **Finally**, you concentrate on that vertical expansion which, from the start-up-point, will spread outward like a branch. The guide to your growth will be our rolling ball of momentum.

LOOKING FOR WEAK HANDS

THE ACCUMULATION OF WEALTH IS BASED ON A hard and gritty principle. Money **always** passes from weak hands into strong hands. This is not a moral judgement, but an observation. That hands are weak does not mean the person is weak. The hands are weak because they falter for just a moment, just long enough for the dollar they hold to be snatched from their grasp. The reason for allowing the dollar bill to leave one's hands is not important: perhaps the weak hands give up the dollar because the mind behind those hands wants something, or needs something, or has made a bad bet, or has an itch to spend, or feels like eating a hamburger. Poof! — the dollar is gone to a stronger hand, a hand that won't give it back without a fight. Wealth accumulation simply involves finding many weak hands out of which to snatch your financial security. Great wealth involves finding more weak hands to pass those dollars into your wary iron fist. Super wealth accumulation requires finding the **most** weak hands out of which to take the single dollar, it is as simple as that.

If everyone in the United States was to wake up tomorrow morning with a crisp hundred dollar bill by their pillows, before the month was out 10% of the population would have 50% of those bills. There **are** strong hands out there, searching for the weak ones, trying to get those who have not yet given up their hundred dollar bills to do so, or their dollar bills, or their pennies. Economic activity consists of a search for the weak hands of the world, a simple if sad truth.

Why is this so? Because everyone makes money from someone else. Even the printers and engravers at the Treasury Department do not walk home with the sheets of money they have made out of paper and ink, nor pocket the chunks of cheap metal we call coins. They draw a salary, and that salary is paid out of taxes; they make their money from **us**. In order to obtain money, we have to find someone to give it to us. The grocer pays a dollar to the clothier and the clothier pays a dollar to the designer; both pay a dollar to the taxi to get them together for lunch; all pay a dollar in taxes. The person who is unable to work, or is retired, may have to get his dollar from the government, but that same government got it from its citizens. It should be printed on the back of dollar bills, replacing "Annuit Coeptis": If you want to make a dollar you have to find someone to give it to you.

All business activity consists of producing products that will cause weak hands to part with their money, to give you something they already have. You may sell furniture, you may sell flowers, you may sell ideas; you can sell whatever it is that the weak hands are buying. Economics at its most elementary level: you provide weak hands with goods and services and those weak hands will give you money. If you don't, you won't have any wealth.

Once you find your stopping point and convert it to a start-up point, **Momentum** will be the means toward the end of finding the **most** weak hands. Momentum is the power behind super wealth accumulation.

THE TRUE SUCCESS STORIES

A H, SUCCESS STORIES. THERE BUT FOR THE GRACE of God go I, We invariably think while reading these stories. Traditionally, financial success stories have to do with the little guy who, on a hunch or tip, invested in Polaroid stock when it was an unknown company selling at 25¢ a share, and held onto the stock for years with rock solid faith, becoming a millionaire in the process. How we envy that person; if only we were so insightful and lucky. Yet this is the **rarest** type of success; very few people make their fortunes that way, which is why it makes such a good success story, for the same reason that "Man bites Dog" is such a good headline.

Success stories lead to a basically **incorrect** impression of how most fortunes are built. We tend to think that they result from a coup, of buying a single item and holding on, like stocks or real estate. The success stories pass on the wisdom of a man buying some scrubby, alligator infested piece of land for pennies because the investor "smelled oil." That was much of the reasoning behind the great real estate boom in cities like Vancouver, British Columbia, Canada. People staked their future on the rising tide of real estate values because they know owners of $20,000 homes who had sold them for $120,000. Huge sums of money were made overnight, for a short period of time. So investors would buy the $20,000 homes now priced at $120,000 and wait for the price to advance to $240,000. But most of them couldn't even find a buyer at $100,000 when the tide started to recede.

It is a trap; and this trap is called trying to make a lot of money out of a single item. Own one house. Buy it for $20,000. Sell it for $120,000. Make a lot out of a single unit. Buy a Kruggerrand when the price of gold is $100 an ounce and sell it when the price has risen to $900 an ounce. Make a lot out of a single item.

History, however, tells us that this is **not** the way real and lasting fortunes have been made, not at all. Real fortunes are not made by making a lot out of a single item, but by making a little out of a lot of items, the exact reverse of the normal success story.

You make a lot by first making a little, making more of the little, making that little bit, over and over again. Ray Kroc did not sit and hold his handful of McDonald's stands, waiting for their real estate value to rise and then sell out. That's what the McDonald brothers did. Ray Kroc used the stands to pay for more stands to pay for more stands. He wasn't making a lot out of a single item. He was making only a penny at a time, from weak hands glad to part with that penny. Nine million weak hands a **day** makes a lot of pennies, and Kroc makes it easy for them to give up their money.

The main difficulty in trying to make a lot of money out of a single item is the type of people you have to deal with. If you plan to make a lot out of a little, you're going to have to find someone with a lot of money to buy your single item. And who has a lot of money? **Strong hands!** Only in strong hands is a lot of money condensed and the one thing we know about strong hands is that they won't give up a penny without a fight. They are certainly **not** going to pay you $240,000 for a $20,000 house, not pay you $900 for an ounce of gold they expect to decline to $300. By trying to get a lot out of a little, you are doing business with the stingiest, meanest-hearted, most miserly pair of hands you could possibly find, while Ray Kroc busily sells his burgers as fast as his teen-aged crews can flip them. You should take your lesson from that cagy strong-handed Ray Kroc; he'll give you a free lesson, but he won't give you his money.

How do you find weak hands? That is what this book is all about. The fast-food market is saturated, the gum market is chewed-up, and the holes have already been drilled into the can-opener. Obviously you must find **new** markets and **new** ways to take a little from a lot. Start out by understanding how it is done. It is done by means of woefully simple rules:

I. Find your proper stopping point.

II. Convert that stopping point into a start-up point and turn your line from horizontal to vertical.

III. Then use **Momentum** to maximize your returns. Take money from weak hands, a little at a time but stay with the momentum as long as it lasts and you are well on the path to **super wealth accumulation**.

Why do Rocky and Karen carry five thousand seedlings to sell for $2.50 each instead of five rare trees to sell for $2,500 each?

Because that's the way to make money.

"Bormann also did his bit to eliminate Adolph Hitler's financial anxieties permanently after 1933. He found one source of ample funds. Together with Hitler's personal photographer Hoffman and Hoffman's friend Ohnesorge, the Minister of Posts, he decided that Hitler had rights to the reproduction of his picture on postage stamps and was therefore entitled to payments. The percentage royalty was **infinitesimal,** but since the Fuehrer's head appeared on all stamps, **millions** flowed into the privy purse administered by Bormann."

Even Hitler understood. Make a little from a lot.

That's how money is made.

Chapter Five

IF YOU PLAN TO ACCUMULATE A GREAT DEAL OF wealth before your time is over, these are the steps you must take:

YOUR HORIZONTAL LIFELINE

STARTING POINT — — — — — — — — — — — — STOPPING POINT

(time)

First you need to locate a proper stopping point as you move along life's horizontal line.

Once found, you then need to shift your attention from a horizontal scan to a vertical view.

Upward Momentum
Upward Momentum
Upward Momentum
Upward Momentum
STOPPING POINT

Finally, you need to use that momentum in a fashion which will allow you to make a little from a lot. If you follow these three steps, you are on your way to making a **lot** of money.

UPWARD MOMENTUM

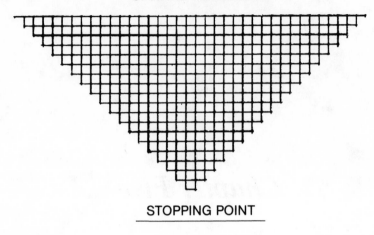

STOPPING POINT

Once you get this far, there are five more important concepts to have a grasp of:

1. *How does the tier system of outward expansion with momentum actually work?*

2. *Where are you located with any expanding tier you may be involved with?*

3. *Where does the momentum for the expanding tier come from?*

4. *How long will the momentum last, and when will it be time for you to get off?*

5. *Are there passive opportunities of momentum in which you can participate if you have the desire for wealth accumulation but have no interest in running a day-to-day normal business?*

HOW THE SYSTEM WORKS

HAVE YOU EVER RECEIVED A CHAIN LETTER IN the mail? More than likely, you have. Utterly illegal, ultimately fruitless and fraudulent, still, chain letters display an understanding of economic workings that many well-known economists laugh off as an absurdity.

Dear Friend,

God has blessed you. A friend has prayed for your good luck, and your luck is here. . . if you want it! This letter was first begun by Mr. Johnson in Amsterdam in 1911. It has gone around the world over 800 times, bringing luck to all who keep the chain alive. It has received official permission. To receive your good luck, send $1.00 only to the first name at the top of the list below. Cross that name out and put your own name at the bottom. Send the letter on to ten friends. When your name reaches the top of the list, you will receive at least $124,816.00 . . . as long as you keep the chain going. DO NOT BREAK THE CHAIN. Captain Welles broke the chain. Two days later his wife died. Mary Smith sent the chain to ten friends. In three weeks she was sent $186,272.00 in one dollar bills. Mrs. Peterson in England threw the letter away and lost her job, and her dog died. Then she found the letter and sent it to ten of her friends. She received $79,112.00 in one dollar bills in the mail. She also got a new job and a big raise. And a stray dog wandered into her front yard. DO NOT BREAK THE CHAIN. God Bless You.

1. *Bruce Gould, PO Box 16, Seattle, WA. 98111*
2. *Robert Spear, 1602 Hamilton Avenue, Palo Alto, CA. 94303*
3. *Bill Weinstein, 2735 Montlake Blvd., Seattle, WA. 98105*
4. *P.T. Barnum, 1 Grants Tomb, New York, NY, 10004*
5. *Charles Ponzi, PO Box 1000, Leavenworth, KS, 64002*
6. *Billy Sol Estes, Truth or Consequences, NM, 80303*
7. *Dr. & Mrs. Fred Pomeroy, PO Box 279, Chelan, WA. 98816*
8. *Ed Mader, EF Hutton, 1 Battery Park Plaza, NY, NY, 10004*
9. *Peter Pomeroy, PO Box 13, San Francisco, CA 94101*
10. *Your name - - - - - - -*

The entrepreneur who starts a chain letter understands the basis of momentum. The opportunity of getting a little from a lot drives him on. One dollar from a lot of people equals a bountiful harvest of one dollar bills. In fact, the amount of money you will receive if the chain remains intact is **greater** than the writer suggests. $124,816.00? Nonsense. By the time your name works its way up from 9th or 10th place to the top, you will be receiving millions, even billions, even hundreds of billions.

We saw that by **doubling** the quantity on each tier, Reggie Jackson was able to take $1 dollar and reach $1.07 billion by the thirty-first tier (or homers). What do you think happens when you increase the width of your expanding branch ten fold? Take a look:

Step #		Total Number of People Receiving A Request for $1 dollar bills.
1	Mail the letter to 10 persons.	10
2	Have **each** recipient mail to 10 more persons.	100
3	Have **each** recipient mail to 10 more persons.	1,000
4	Have **each** recipient mail to 10 more persons.	10,000
5	Have **each** recipient mail to 10 more persons.	100,000
6	Have **each** recipient mail to 10 more persons.	1,000,000
7	Have **each** recipient mail to 10 more persons.	10,000,000
8	Have **each** recipient mail to 10 more persons.	100,000,000
9	Have **each** recipient mail to 10 more persons.	1,000,000,000
10	Have **each** recipient mail to 10 more persons.	10,000,000,000
11	Have **each** recipient mail to 10 more persons.	100,000,000,000
12	Have **each** recipient mail to 10 more persons.	1,000,000,000,000

By the time you reach the twelfth step (12th tier), you have letters going out to 1 **trillion** people. That would be okay, except there are only 4 billion people on the planet earth. So, if you wish to contact new sources for your dollar bills you will be writing to everyone living, everyone dead, and all the inhabitants of the planet Dloug, fifth planet in the G-2 binary star system in the Andromeda galaxy. Think of the postage! Yet the people who sign up at the twelfth step and are waiting for their name to rise to the top will **start** with a trillion names already on the list and have to increase new sources a hundred billion fold.

Foolish as they are, if your name is at the bottom of the list, chain letters do explain how Momentum works. They are a valid example of the principle of momentum expanding outward through a lever fixed to that momentum. Each person enlists only ten other people for each new step, yet by **only twelve steps** you have exceeded the population of the entire earth two-hundred-and fifty times.

Chain letters are illegal. Yet the business practices of many well known companies are centered around variations of the exact same principle, companies like Century 21 Real Estate, Avon, Mary Kay Cosmetics, Amway, Shaklee Health Products, among others. "Get a little from a lot." "Take the ball, give it a shove, and then use the momentum to increase your wealth."

KNOCKERS KNOCKING

MANY YEARS AGO, A DOOR-TO-DOOR **BOOK** SALESman devised a way to reduce the risk of having his face flattened by slamming doors. This entrepreneur enticed housewives with a free bottle of perfume to get his foot in the door. He soon discovered that the perfume was more popular than his books, so he shut down the book business, rented an office in Cleveland, and began The Ohio Sales Company. No fool he; door-to-door sales are a tough way to make a living, and he was surely relieved to get **off** the road and into his new office. Now, however, he had the problems of getting salesmen **on** the road, to do what he once did, sell door-to-door, and convince these salesmen that they liked it. Gradually, he devised an ingenuous way to do this, changing his company name along the way.

We'll provide the products, his company tells newly enlisted sales staff, and, if you sell the product, we will pay you a sales commission. In addition (and this is the most important element), if you will enlist a friend of yours to **also** sell our products, we will pay you a bonus commission, and additional sum for getting one friend to sign up. A two-fold increase with each step down the tiers.

That's the system, the entire secret of success of this company now traded on the New York Stock Exchange. It is almost seamless.

Enlist your salesforce and make your sales, without having to pump your own capital into the company or pay anyone any salaries, without having to absorb any losses. Take a little profit from each sale; not a large profit, just enough. And you have a graph that looks much like Ray Kroc's graph for McDonald's... but with a crucial difference. Ray Kroc had to build real estate, build 30×50 foot buildings from which to sell hamburgers to obtain the profit to build more buildings to sell more hamburgers. Our company door-to-door has no buildings, only sales people, and it doesn't pay them anything unless they make a sale or sign up a new member of the expanding fraternity. It is as if Ray Kroc asked each member of his work force to put up their own money and open a new stand across the street from where they worked, and all Ray Kroc had to do was to keep the beef coming to each new outlet. Door-to-door sales expand within their own momentum and finance the expansion internally. Unlimited door-to-door expansion is simply a **human chain letter**.

Knockers (door-to-door) puts the momentum of its expansion in the hands of its sales force. "We're sorry about your loss in using gas to cover your territory. If you'd like to recoup part of your investment, get a friend to sign up. We'll even give you a bounty. For each new salesperson added to the growing beast, Knockers gets a start-up fee, and pays the recruiter a small piece of the action. Moreover, the recruiter will also get a tiny percentage of the take from the sales profit of his enlistee. Knockers always takes a cut. And the new salesperson is now encouraged to sign up a friend.

This is how Knockers wins. (1) Sign-up fee (2) sale of the product wholesale to itself (3) percentage of profit on each sale made in the field, and (4) momentum of expansion produced internally. All produced on an original investment of $0.

This is how the system works. **You** won't be starting any door-to-door company as your new business. But your business will operate with this rule in mind: Those on the upper tiers **always** get a little from those on the tiers below. Where you are situated within any expanding tier is vital.

BOTTOM'S UP

T HERE IS ONLY ONE PLACE TO BE ON A TIER SYSTEM such as Knockers. On top, or near the top. You pay a little to those above you, and get a little from those below you. There are many more below you to pay you a little (get a little from a lot). Sideways relationships mean nothing. It's the ups and downs that count. You pay above, and receive from below. At the top of it all, at the very top, sits the corporate headquarters of Knockers.

For human chain letter firms, the catbird seat is **always** at the top, looking down. If you are near the top of the Mary Kay Cosmetics tier, you will benefit greatly from the momentum constantly generated at the bottom tier, out in the trenches. But if you sell cosmetics yourself, then you're somewhere down the ranks. Most likely you will never make it to the top. The only way to be at the top is to form your own Avon, or Century 21, or Shaklee or Mary Kay Cosmetics. You are too late to join those already formed, except somewhere down in the ranks, somewhere in the tiers.

However, even if you form your own Knockers and operate from Corporate Headquarters, if you use the human chain as the main concept for your expansion, you are probably spending a great deal of time under your desk hiding from men in suits bearing subpoenas. For once you push the ball and start the momentum, the federal government will push its own ball and start examining your business entity as a potential "illegal chain letter." Such business concepts have been so declared and so closed down time and time again. Another problem, if you successfully avoid the first, is the limitation of your expanding sales force. If each person recruits ten new sales-people, by tier 12 you have one **trillion** ace drummers, and you're back to the planet Dluog.

For the established companies, those that make it past the first two difficulties by modifying their practices, a third problem emerges — what to do with all the money that is rolling in day by day and hour by hour. Take a trip to the public library and examine the growth history and balance sheets of some of the companies named, such as Avon or Century 21. A quick check at the business section documents will show you that Momentum made these firms a **lot** of money in a very short period of time.

BOOK SALE

Sponsored by
FRIENDS OF
THE PUBLIC LIBRARY

I know books, **you** know books, or you wouldn't be reading this one. I am going to show you how to recover not only the cost of this book, but many times its value through Momentum.

Run the ad, "**BOOK SALE**, Sponsored by Friends of the Public Library" in your local newspaper, that is after you have secured the rights to sell a book — write me and we can negotiate your rights to sell this book — and get the Friends of the Public Library to sponsor you, which could be your two neighbors. All your ad has to do is earn you enough to pay for the books sold **and** a return equal to twice the ad's cost.

If the ad costs you $40, and you sell ten books which cost you $3 each, you need to gross $150 from your experience to start you on the way to riches. Use the $30 to pay for the cost of the books sold (I am including shipping with this $3 per unit cost) and use the extra $80 to run **two** more ads in local newspapers, save nothing for yourself.

You started with $40 and you earned $80, net profit. Not too bad, a 200% return. But can an $80 profit make you a millionaire in a few weeks time? It certainly can, simply by the force of Momentum. Again, this is not the kind of business I recommend, especially if you doubt your ability to sell books. But watch how it works.

You initially invested $40 running the ad in a small weekly paper which returns an $80 net profit. You turn around and invest the **entire** profit in two additional ads, both of which again return twice your investment. You now have $160 net profit. With that $160 you can buy a larger ad in a magazine, such as *Arizona Highways*, or better yet a magazine read by the same kind of people who like to buy books. If history again repeats itself you should net $320 from your magazine ad. From that you put a full page ad in a **daily** newspaper — one that will run a full pager for only $320 — and, in our example, you net twice your cost or $640.

Now, and this is important, use the $640 to go back to step number one. But instead of placing **one** $40 ad selling books in a small weekly newspaper, place **sixteen** similar ads in sixteen similar weekly papers around the country. Each should return twice its cost: $1,280 net realized profit to you. Then use that profit to run two additional ads in each weekly, $2,560 earned, 320 books sold. Look again for regional magazines with circulations similar to *Arizona Highways* or whichever magazine you first selected and invest the entire $2,560 into ads in those magazines, for a return of

$5,120. that profit is used to place full page ads in **sixteen** daily newspapers. The result? $10,240 net to you.

Go back to step one. The $40 ad. But in 256 weekly newspapers. 256 people now on your sales force each calling themselves a weekly paper, 256 hamburgers, 256 units to make a little out of, each returning to you twice their cost. Then down the line again: two more ads in the weeklies, an ad in the magazines, the full page ads in daily newspapers. At the end of this time through you have a return of $163,840.00 off your initial $40 ad in the local paper.

Begin again. Invest the $163,840.00 in $40 ads in every weekly and throwaway circular in the United States and Canada. Repeat the ads twice. Place an ad in every magazine in the country, and finally a full page ad in every daily newspaper in America. All the momentum being generated internally, the cost of each subsequent ad and its partner being paid for by the returns from the previous single ad. Clones paid for by previous clones. And, when that is all done, you have a dollar return of $2,621,440.00. From an initial investment of $40 and no more. All by repeating our series only **four** times.

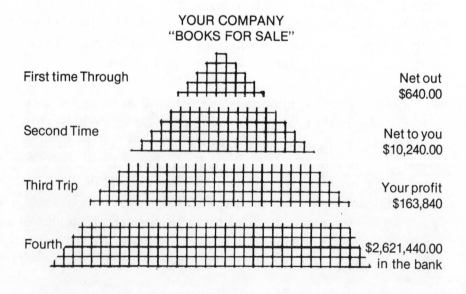

YOUR COMPANY
"BOOKS FOR SALE"

First time Through — Net out $640.00

Second Time — Net to you $10,240.00

Third Trip — Your profit $163,840

Fourth — $2,621,440.00 in the bank

The shape of the structure above should be getting very familiar to you now, all you have to do is to find a ball, start it rolling and let the momentum take care of itself.

But does this system of tiers **really** have any relation to the advertising business of today or how things are sold through the mail in the real world? Go to the magazine rack in a supermarket, flip through the stack of magazines, it doesn't matter which ones. You will find at least one and generally tens of ads being repeated in each and every one of those magazines.

That ubiquitous ad which hardly caught your attention before **had** to pay its way before it would be used on such a mass scale in so many magazines. Pay its way through test markets, selected markets, specialized markets; the return, measured and evaluated, is known, each step of the way. $40 billion a year is spent on the principle of Momentum in the advertising business, and every ad placed is expected to pay for its own expense **and** expansion.

Consider this about your company, "Books For Sale": You made an initial $40 investment and never put an additional penny out of pocket toward your ads. The $40 returned $80 returned $160 returned $320; the momentum of your rolling ball funded your campaign. You plowed your profits back into your business, and, in about 11 weeks times, you made $2.6 million. From a $40 investment.

That's Momentum in the real world.

However, this is not a field that I would recommend a beginner try. There are problems. First you have to design an ad that will return 200% of your investment with each placement. That's not easy. If it was, our magazines would be several times thicker. Secondly, there is a limit to expansion. By the last tier, I had my ad running in every newspaper, circular and magazine in North

America, the world was next and then I had to quit, just as you had to quit expanding Knockers when your sales force reached 1 trillion.

And again, your third problem: what do you do with all the money? $40 billion a year is spent on advertising, and every ad is expected to, and eventually must, pay for itself. That means advertising returns at least $40 billion in profits each year. But then, that is always a problem with Momentum: what to do with the profits.

It is a nice question to mull over in your mind. I recommend it to a few moments of your thinking time.

You may be suitably impressed by Ray Kroc's story, but there is no realistic possibility of your opening a chain of hamburger stands.

You found the idea of Reggie Jackson still in baseball at age 64 implausible, and you know that there is little likelihood of your striking a similar deal.

You can't really envision 800,000 Knockers knocking on neighborhood doors in order to get those dollar bills rising through the tiers to your strong hands. Not only is it a bit unsavory, but would require a lot of administrative work, and, as Rocky and Karen said, they don't have the **time**.

The logistics of placing 86,000 ads is staggering, and we can't be sure we can sell books or anything else effectively with the ads. We have the problems of placing ads, shipping the books, employee relations. It's simply not feasible.

These examples were used to teach some important facts about the application of Momentum. A tier, for the purpose of Momentum, is the point where one's holdings can be increased without the investment of further capital. And the only position in a tier structure that can be meaningful in terms of wealth accumulation is on or near the top. You can determine the potential of Momentum in any venture you will ever become involved with by asking yourself this question: **Where do I stand within the tier structure?**

The higher up the tier scale, the better off you will always be. It is a problem of looking up and looking down. The fewer people above you, the better off you **are**. The more people below you, better yet.

Everyone below you pays the dollar. You pay everyone above you a percentage. There are winners and losers, and if all you can see above you is a sea of wriggling rumps, it is "bottoms up," you're going to be a loser. Those at the very top see no one; nothing but blue sky. You may not be that person, but the closer you are to him or her, the better off you will be, financially speaking.

Remember, **momentum generates tiers**. You may be the only person who recognizes tiers when you see one but those tiers are going to be there.

If you are going to get on, it is best to get on early. The later it is, the farther down the tier scale you will be. There will be many rumps above you. If you bought a gold Kruggerrand at $800 an ounce, hoping to sell for a profit, you jumped on the bottom of a set of tiers that began forming at $35 an ounce. You are running out of people to pay you more for your single item.

If you bought a home in Vancouver, Canada, for $120,000, hoping to sell it for a profit, you are on that same crowded bottom tier. There are a lot of people on each side, but sideways views don't count. See that top tier, the very peak, way up there? That's where it all began. Those people bought their homes for $20,000, and sold it to you for $120,000. You paid them to get into the tier structure, but they don't have to pay you to let you out.

You can be near the **top** of the tiers. But you should never allow yourself to be anywhere near the **bottom.**

How do we get there so often then? Traditional investment and traditional programs are **designed** purposely to get us on board once it is too late. That is what everyone out there in the world of business is trying to accomplish, to get us on the bottom tier while they sit on top.

How do we get there so often?

By following the paths on which everyone else is walking.

SNOWBALLS

WHEN YOU ARE SEVENTEEN, YOUNG AND FULL OF life, the next age rapidly approaching, though not so rapidly as when you are 47 looking ahead, is eighteen, yes? Our definitions of time and numbers are all that make this age momentum meaningful. Eighteen has nothing to do with seventeen except as a definitional sequence. You cannot be eighteen years old without having once been seventeen, but the fact that you are now seventeen will not automatically mean you will make it to the next tier. Sad as it is, many people who are this year that age will not live to see their next birthday. The age seventeen does not **guarantee** the momentum to drive the age to eighteen.

But suppose that you were seventeen and on top of the highest peak in the mountain range in your home state, two thousand feet above an uninhabited valley. The air is clear and cold; it is the middle of winter, and the slope leading to the valley is blanketed with snow, clumping wet snow, the kind you love to make snowballs out of. It's the thin air, perhaps, but you get a wacky idea, though at seventeen it isn't as wacky as much as it is a normal thought: you're going to find out, once and for all, whether there is any truth in those old Bugs Bunny cartoons.

You pack together a solid round snowball, two feet in diameter, and, not without a grunt and some help from your friends, start it rolling down the hill. Give it a push and let it go. It rolls slowly at first, lurching, almost stopping; then it starts to move, carving a furrow in the snow, and the snowball starts to accumulate itself, doubling in size, doubling in speed, faster and faster, bigger and bigger, throwing a roostertail of loose snow behind it, a giant mass of snow moving as a blur, screaming down the hill, and smashing into the opposite wall of the valley with an explosion of white and a roar like thunder!

WHAM!

A good thing no one lives in that valley.

See the difference? In the progression from 17 to 18, you go from one tier to another, but the latter does not depend on the former for its momentum. But consider the monstrously huge snowball. The force of momentum is dependent on each successive tier. As the mass races down those 2000 feet, each foot it travels adds both to its speed and its size, added weight and added momentum. This is a **self-generating**, self-renewing momentum, through which each subsequent tier carries forward the previous tier and depends on it for its force.

Momentum can be applied to **both** types. The thirty-first home run hit by Reggie Jackson was entirely independent of home run number thirty; the only connection was sequential; Jackson had to hit thirty home runs before he could hit the thirty-first, a definitional problem. But even this momentum sufficed for Jackson to apply Momentum as a lever, in his bet with Gene Autry. The momentum of the snowball, however, is like McDonald's; it feeds itself along the way.

Remember this distinction. How you handle self-generating momentum may well be different from how you handle simple sequential momentum. If you are seventeen years old, all you have to do is survive and you will become eighteen. But to get that snowball careening down the mountainside, you're going to have to climb those 2000 feet, get the crazy idea, and give the ball a shove. It is tough to make money from sequential momentum. Self-generating momentum accumulates wealth as fast as the snowball is flying when it hits the bottom.

HOSTAGES IN IRAN

WITH ALL MOMENTUM, THERE IS A FINAL POINT, A point where the bottom of the valley will be reached and the momentum come to an end.

The force of return in Momentum can accrue holdings beyond that which can be safely or successfully handled. If the momentum is virtually limitless, there must be a point where you voluntarily get out. You had to do this with Knockers; before your sales staff exceeded the number of people on earth. Reggie Jackson had to quit when his earnings exceeded Gene Autry's ability to pay.

Momentum will **always** end, either through the exhaustion of the momentum itself, or the exhaustion of the force.

Remember the 444 days of captivity for the American hostages in Iran? For us at home, the little people, it seemed to be a cycle of hopelessness compounded by despair without end, and yet it **did** end.

At home we went through cycles of fear and bitterness, snatching at every rumor for a shred of hope. But all the while, the negotiators donned their suits and argued calmly for the release of the hostages. What held them together?

This simple fact: there has never been a hostage crisis throughout recorded history that did **not** end. Not one. All hostage crises end. Every one.

If you have that knowledge, you can negotiate.

We didn't think about that. We called the 444 day ordeal an "endless crisis." We have been in the midst of an "endless recession." The people who bought gold at $800 an ounce believed they were part of an "endless boom." Buyers of real estate in Vancouver believed the end would "never come." It came. Everything ends. Hostage crises, plane hijackings, economic cycles, toothaches, all end. We love to think in terms of "endlessness," "never ending love," "tomorrow will never come," but we are fooling ourselves.

All the momentum you will ever be involved with will end. So you must always plan for the end. It seems so simple, and yet so much financial activity is based on the idea that a trend will go on forever.

For every self-generated snowball, a valley is down below, it is not a question of whether the momentum will stop; it is merely a timing problem, **when?**

SO NOW YOU KNOW

A T THE START OF THIS CHAPTER WE PRESENTED five concepts that you would have to grasp if you hope to accumulate your just share of wealth as you pass down life's horizontal line.

The first: "How does the tier system work?" is now answered. It works by taking a little from a lot, a small piece from each of many weak hands. The more hands on the bottom of your tier, the better the system will work for you.

Second: "Your own tier location is important." The closer you are to the top, the greater the financial rewards. The more people you see on each side of you, and above, the worse off you are.

Third: "Where does the momentum come from?" It can be sequential or self-generating. If it is sequential, you have to design a program like Reggie Jackson to profit from it. If it is self-generating, the system itself will provide the profits along the way.

Fourth: "When will the momentum end?" It will end at a different time and place for each item examined. The crises in Iran could have lasted 443 days instead of 444, or it could have lasted 4 or 1400. But it could not have gone on forever. So you must practice your timing along the way, measure the distance from the top of the mountain to the bottom of the valley and after the half way point, or some point along the way, has been reached prepare for an exit. Remember, the snowball ended its journey with a WHAM! Be sure to get off your trip a few feet before that happens.

Finally, the opportunities: "Are there passive opportunities of momentum in which one can participate if a person has the desire for wealth accumulation but has no time or interest in mail order, baseball, door to door, or running a normal nitty gritty business?" The answer is a precise **yes!**

Several.

More than several.

And where are these several, more than several, to be found?

Read on, my friend, read on.

That is what the entire second half of this book is all about.

Take a ball.

Give it a shove.

And read on.

The End
Of The First Half

Chapter Six

IN THE AMERICAN MIDWEST, 1982 WAS A BRUTALLY cold year. Temperature records were shattered, to be broken again, on the following day. Cities were paralyzed. The weather monopolized the evening news; pictures of houses on fire due to faulty wiring quickly turned into video tape of frozen ice palaces as the water from fire hoses froze solid upon contact. Pedestrians, bundled like rag dolls, knocked to the ground by 70 MPH winds.

It came home to Rocky Becket, that cold chill, while comfortably watching a National Football League play-off game between Dallas and Cincinatti. The television commentators said that the wind-chill factor at Cincinatti was seventy-one degrees **below** zero. Rocky had no way to understand how cold that could be. He had lived in California all his life; the record cold temperature in Modesto was nineteen degrees **above** zero. But on TV he saw players working in pain, sliding on frozen turf, a stadium wreathed in the fog made by the breath of 60,000 troubled fans, doctors studying their frostbite manuals. It was a sunny day in Modesto in December, but, by osmosis, Rocky in jeans and a t-shirt, had never been so cold in his life.

The winter of 1982 was just another in a five year succession of bitter cold winters. Each predicted to be the last, each prediction broken. Meteorologists could speculate on the causes — a new ice age? Climatic cycles? Volcanic dust? — but their forecasts lacked authenticity. Rocky Becket, shivering in his warm living room, also made a forecast; a factual rather than scientific one: mild or harsh, long or short, early or late, there would be a winter of the **next** year, and people would have to prepare for it. Unless they were fools, they would have to plan for the worst, another bad year in a long string of tough winters.

It was a forecast Rocky could **act upon!**

It was time: for Rocky and Karen to enter the home heating oil business.

There is not much demand for heating oil in Modesto. The homes are newer, heated by gas or electricity; the winters are especially mild. Ordinarily, someone beginning a new heating oil business would confront that factor, and a plethora of other business problems.

There will be trucks to own, lease or rent, customers to acquire, invoices to send out, and the misery of dealing with the wholesalers: the notorious Shell, Exxon, Mobil, Atlantic Richfield, Texaco, and many others. There would be a need for lawyers; local heating oil distributors are forever suing the major oil companies for one reason or another, normally for refusing to deliver to the dealers the allotted quota during periods of short supply. And even a bland announcement from OPEC would affect the merchandise, make it scarce and prohibitively priced. The cost of beginning such a new business in Modesto should be all but unbearable, with overhead high and unrelenting, the competition fierce, the market minuscule. Profit was there, possibly, but only hidden behind a lot of business problems. For two quiet nursery owners used to nothing more threatening than a few flies or hot weather, taking on a life as heating oil dealers, part-time, would be close to lunacy.

But Rocky and Karen were far from lunatics.

They loathed business problems, but they had decided to get into the heating oil business for the profit. However, the way they are going to get into this field will demonstrate their complete sanity.

Their first step is to eliminate as many potential problems as possible, right off the bat. Before taking step number one, they will put limits on their new venture. Absolute limits from which they will **never** deviate.

They want no merchandising problems or marketing woes. Karen may be able to talk for hours about the advantages of key plants for the beginning home gardener, but she couldn't say ten words about the pluses of Becket's Oil Service. Her own home is heated by gas. They wouldn't change to heating oil on a bet. It is hard to sell a product you wouldn't even buy yourself. Not even from your own company.

They don't want any employees: no truck drivers, no clerks, no salespeople. No salaries to pay, no unions to deal with. If they are going to start this business, they absolutely plan to start it without any employees.

No organizational problems, either. The nursery is as complex a business as they can handle. They could not bear to be buried in bureaucratic paper. They do not want to calculate sales taxes, inventory taxes, payroll taxes, B & O taxes, or any of the other baffling taxes of small business. For most such businesses, taxes are the only growing part of the company and this is the type of growth they wish to avoid. The accounting situation has to be absolutely simple, first grade level stuff: they would have no accounts in or accounts out. They do not want to have to worry about collecting bad debts; they want no billings whatsoever. No billing means no customers, so they also plan to eliminate customers.

They want zero overhead, nothing in any physical tangible form so named. If you can see it, they don't want it.

Naturally, then, they must decide to do without inventory. They even have decided to have nothing to do with oil itself. It is a nuisance, and it is messy, it even stinks. Once you have it, you have to have trucks to deliver it, tanks to store it, or fill your swimming pool full of it. Since that would require overhead, which they have already eliminated, they have to eliminate heating oil itself. Nothing but problems, so no inventory at all in their new business.

What about money? The problem of capitalizing their new business could be pesky, so Rocky and Karen refuse to invest any more than $4,000 in it. That is the total sum. About one-third the cost of the cheapest used delivery truck on the market is the limit they place on their total capital investment. But since they don't need the money to buy one-third of a used truck, remember no trucks, they will have it available for other purposes.

So there you are, the limits Rocky and Karen see on their new venture, a business they **are** going to begin.

A new business, but a business without the problems of business, without inventory, personnel, or major capital needs. Rocky and Karen Becket are going into the home heating oil business in a fashion that none before them have ever gone into business. They are entering the venture as they have done many times before, as they will do many times again. They are not looking for oil, far from it. They are looking for momentum. Our friend, the rolling ball.

They will start this business as they have started all their previous momentum businesses, by study. Two pieces of information keyed them this time: the first was the fact that there would be a winter next year. The second was the price of home heating oil. A price that went up and down over time. Remember, momentum is simply movement over time. They had found their opportunity in heating oil.

*   *   *   *   *   *

In early March, 1982, Rocky and Karen sit quietly across the table from each other, in their spacious kitchen, examining the open graph in front of them intently. Finally, Rocky speaks. "It's definitely a tier three. What I am wondering is whether the bounce back will carry all the way down to tier four."

"We've never done a tier four," Karen says.

"If they give it to us, we've got to go. Enter at the 70¢ level and run the stop-loss at 59¢. No way can I see the price dropping 11¢."

"Will it come? Can we get in at 70¢? How far do these bounce back moves normally go?"

"If it comes, we'll take it, it's as simple as that. Otherwise, we'll handle it as a tier three. What do you think?" Rocky responds, bypassing for the moment the length of most bounce back moves.

"Okay. Let's give it a try," Karen says.

"A tier four. Wouldn't that be something?" Rocky warms with excitement.

A new business, about to begin with only $1,500 of the $4,000 capital that had been set aside. A new business, with new approaches, new methods, new goals, a business independent of the constraints of the past. New rules, new markets and new victories.

How did Rocky and Karen Becket comes to this new business?

If grass is growing in your front yard, someone planted the seeds. The business they are entering is growing faster than any plant that ever entered their nursery. By leaps and bounds this new business is growing, and there has to be a reason. And there is. An exciting reason. **The rolling ball**, momentum.

* * * * * *

TRADITION SPEAKS — LOUD AND CLEAR

FIVE THOUSAND DOLLARS REALLY ISN'T ENOUGH for **anything!** One summer, *Chicago Sun Times* columnist Andrew Leckey surveyed several famous financial writers. His question, which was syndicated nationwide, was blunt and to the point: "What's the best way to invest $5,000, if $5,000 is all you have to invest?" These are the answers he received, the answers for people like Rocky and Karen Becket, like you and me, who have worked hard to shepherd that sum together, and who are proud of the accumulation.

Frank Cappiello, Jr., president of Summit Advisors Inc. (one of those firms that like to manage other people's money), a regular panelist on public television's "Wall Street Week" said, "In my opinion, the only thing you can really do is put it into an aggressive mutual fund, since $5,000 really isn't enough for anything else. If you simply put the $5,000 into a stock or two instead of a strong fund that includes a **portfolio** of many stocks, you'd have to be awfully lucky to hit it just right."

In essence — give your money to someone else, and diversify. We remember those theories well.

Howard Ruff, a controversial "gold bug" and publisher of the well known "Ruff Times" newsletter favored stability. "First, put much of the $5,000 into a money-market fund, preferably one specializing in U.S. government securities because of their safety. The rest would be divided between silver and shares of a bond fund — the silver for long-term investment and the bond fund for short-term objectives."

Sound familiar? Assume you put $3,000 into the money market fund at 15%, you would earn $37.50 per month off that, of which the government would take up to $18.75 in taxes. The other $1,000 in silver and the bond fund, if each increase 25% in the upcoming year would return $250 respectively, which again would be taxed. Income items, diversification, a bond fund to let others make the decisions for you.

Gregory S. Junkin, executive vice-president of the Balcor Company, a real-estate investment firm in Illinois, suggested a real estate investment in the form of a limited partnership interest. However, he notes that the investor "shouldn't need the money invested for four to six years, when the real estate starts to be sold."

In essence, turn your money over to someone else again, buy high priced real estate, join all those others sitting on the bottom tier who are paying $120,000 for a $20,000 house.

Susan Richards, a financial advisor, suggested bonds. "Some of the really solid corporate bonds or zero coupon bonds are paying high yields and you can get them for $5,000 using a discount broker."

Bonds are interest rate items, except for the zero coupon bond which pays no interest until maturity allowing the issuer to keep your accumulated interest for his own purposes throughout the lifetime of the bond, all the while you keep watching the financial pages to make sure he is still around to make that final payment of principal and interest at maturity. There is no way that interest items can accumulate wealth for you, **none**, unless you start out with great wealth at the beginning.

Hank Struett, of the Harris Bank of Chicago, suggested depositing the $5,000 with a bank, he didn't mention which one though I assume he had one in mind. "The best bet is the new three and one-half year certificates. You can start as low as $500 in this one and, if you have any confidence at all that interest rates will go down, it offers an exceptional return for three and one-half years."

Assume you started with $500, and earned, once again, 15% interest for three and one-half years. That is the grand sum of $75.00 per year, or $6.25 per month, of which the government, once again, would take up to $3.13 (I assume they would round off the penny in their favor) in taxes. What could you do with your net of $3.12 per month? Possibly, just possibly, buy **one** movie ticket.

As columnist Leckey noted in his syndicated article, "unfortunately, $5,000 still doesn't seem to get much respect even as a building block..."

Yet all the financial writers were eager to supply answers, while not one of them asked Leckey the most important question of all, a question which **had** to be asked before any answer could be given, "What is the main purpose for investing this $5,000?"

Not much of a question, lengthwise, but a key question conclusionwise. Was the money, the $5,000, earmarked for wealth **preservation** or wealth **accumulation**?

If it has been set aside for preservation, then you will want to act in accordance with preservation guidelines. If it is money for additional accumulation, then the guidelines are entirely different. Preservation involves diversification, money management by others, interest rates and no risk. That is how our grandfathers preserve that which they have accumulated. But they didn't accumulate it the same way. They accumulated it by handling it themselves, making themselves the person on the top of the tier, by taking risk and by ignoring plodding interest rate returns. They are preserving now what they accumulated earlier.

But all the writers surveyed seemed to write off without comment the **possibility**, even the bare bones possibility, of using $5,000 to accumulate any real wealth. They only talked about how to preserve it, almost fearful of dreaming that a sum like $5,000 could actually double or triple or quadruple itself. Cloning $5,000 units, don't make me laugh. Or, as Frank Cappiello, Jr. put it, "$5,000 really isn't enough for anything."

The total sum Rocky and Karen had to work with was considered below contempt.

But then Frank Cappiello, Jr. hadn't been to the top of the hill. He hadn't heard about the snowball. He didn't know what momentum was. He didn't even know how to get the ball rolling. His main concern, as the president of Summit Investors, Inc., a major money manager of other people's money, was how to get more customers on the bottom tier. He was on top, the president, and if he planned to make a little from a lot, he would have to ask those down on the bottom level to scoot over a bit and make room for another $5,000 squeezing in.

Rocky and Karen planned to start their own business.

They planned to do it with the idea of wealth **accumulation** in mind, they would worry about presevation later. They knew, from experience, that they **could** do a great deal of wealth accumulating with $5,000, but they also knew, from experience, that they couldn't do it with **any** of the suggestions offered by the expert financial writers. A mutual fund would **never** make it for them, absolutely never. Nor would a money market fund or government securities, preserve, possibly, accumulate, never! Not even one bar of silver would do the trick. Wealth accumulation simply does not occur by making a lot off a single bar of silver. That isn't how it happens, sorry. Limited partnerships in real estate? "Scoot over a bit on the bottom tier, another sucker sitting down."

Traditional investment was **not** what Rocky and Karen **knew** would accumulate wealth for them. How did they know it? By experience. They already **had** tried bank accounts, mutual funds, stocks, bonds, government securities and real estate. **Tradition!** They were well familiar with tradition.

And they knew tradition was primarily good for one thing.

Just one.

Getting more people on the bottom tier.

SEARCHING FOR A START-UP POINT

ROCKY AND KAREN KNEW WHERE THEY WERE SIT-uated and knew how they got there, it wasn't by accident. They had traveled along life's horizontal line and they had found a start-up point. Not just any start-up point, but a very particular place at which to begin to accumulate wealth.

They had defined their location in advance, set out all the criteria, and they had found it. Many of us are **still** looking horizontally, but Rocky and Karen were moving vertically now. The criteria defined, in clear and precise terms.

Their start-up point had to offer freedom with success. They loved their nursery, but the business day was full of activity, from start to finish. Whatever else they got into had to offer them freedom and flexibility. It could not impede on their normal daily work.

With freedom came independence. Rocky and Karen would not hand over their money to financial advisors who thought the idea of investing only $5,000 was somehow amusing. If there is a single attribute that can underscore a life lived well, it is self-esteem. The Becker's overflowed with self-esteem; they would not allow it to be compromised.

They savored a challenge. They had fostered their nursery at the expense of eighteen-hour days in the beginning and they remembered those hard days with pride. They had pulled it off once; they could do it again. Pride was important. Perhaps they could accumulate wealth, but it would be flavorless if there could be no elation on thinking "We did it!" They wanted to imbue meaning into their venture, to have an end for the money, to take pride in watching the new business grow in its first and second and third years, like watching a baby grow, stand, talk. It would simply have to be an experience in its own right, whatever their start-up point came to be, even if that meant pitfalls. Yes, they could invest the money in three and one-half year certificates. But what would they have done by doing that? Could that **possibly** be a start-up point for someone like the Beckets. No. For them, life is worth the doing.

They wanted a start-up point that would teach them as they went. They were not in a position to learn all the complexities involved in playing the stock market, not equipped to study those 14,000 different stocks. It would have to be a start-up point that could be learned, a business in which their knowledge would clarify their decisions, rather than muddle them.

They wanted an absolutely private start-up point. They saw no purpose in amusing an advisor with their measly little $5,000 and allowing everyone to know about it. They took their money and their time seriously, and so for starting-up, they were serious.

But fun had to be involved also. It had to be a self-motivating point; it could not be a burden of constant care and worry. The Beckets had a good family and a good business. To make themselves miserable for a goal of wealth accumulation would be utterly foolish.

The Beckets believed these psychological needs could be met, if they could only find a start-up point within which all these elements could be fit. And, of course, they **had** discovered what they were searching for, right down to the dotting of the "i" and the crossing of the "t."

When **you** are looking for **your** proper start-up point, one essential element should never escape your consideration — the tiers. Plan to be near the top of the tier structure. Anything below the top is a dilution. In the middle of the tiers your $5,000 will simply be returning a portion to you and a portion to those above you. No one ever lets you in the tier system without paying a premium to those on top. And on top, or very close to it, is where you should plan to be, when you get to your start-up point.

In addition, always remember that if you plan to focus on accumulation, you must find **momentum**. Without momentum, you are dead in the water. You have no choice, if you plan to accumulate, than to seek out momentum. Momentum allows you to make a little from a lot, make the penny under the ketchup between the two hamburger buns, and then collect those pennies one by one until you have some real money. With their $5,000 of limited resources, Rocky and Karen have to find momentum within which to start their tier structure and from which to take a little from many weak hands. It was possible to buy an emerald for $100,000 and sell it for $120,000 and live for one year on that $20,000 profit, after paying taxes, if you don't plan to live very well. Possible, but not very likely. And even more unlikely if you don't have the $100,000 to begin with, and know nothing about emeralds. Not the start-up point for you, or Rocky or Karen.

Think back to the covered wagons. Many people **didn't** make it to Utah or California or the Oregon territory. It was a tough world then and it is a tough world now. Accumulating capital is never easy; if it was, then accumulated capital wouldn't have value. Value means scarcity, not super abundance. Accumulated capital has value because it is difficult to accumulate it, and especially difficult if you don't have any to begin with in the first place. That is why you have to set up a tier structure with yourself at the top and why you have to look for momentum to get your piece of the financial pie. Momentum is what makes it possible to locate all those weak hands. If you need $100,000 in accumulated capital, then you have to approach strong hands to part with $50,000 each, or weak hands to let lose of $1 each. It is much easier to get a pair of hands to give up $1, we all do it every minute of every day, than to let loose of $50,000, one hand at a time.

Thus the magnitude of your needs will force you to use momentum to accumulate wealth. In order to work with enormous numbers within a limited period of time, you must reach a lot of hands in a hurry. You can't do it knocking on doors, one at a time, all by yourself. If Rocky and Karen want to accumulate some money in this brutal business world, they will have to use momentum in one way or another. Brutal facts, but making it across the prairie wasn't a cinch either.

OVER PIKES PEAK

HOW WOULD OUR PIONEERS OF THE 1980's, 1990's, and 2000's know when they had passed Denver, pushed their wagons and goods up the Eastern slope of the Rockies, and were finally headed down the mountain to the green valleys on the other side? They would know when they found a start-up point that met their final list of criteria, a list that once again they would not forego, not even for the goal of accumulating wealth.

If they could find a start-up point which did not have an unquenchable thirst for money, they would know they were headed down the western slopes. Nine out of ten new businesses fail, and the foremost reason for these failures was a lack of capital. Rocky and Karen had it made, by one definition, but by another they were hanging on by their fingertips. They simply could not allow their new start-up business to drain them and all their resources. They had $5,000 to work with. That's all they were willing to commit. Any business they became involved with would have to be satisfied, forever, with that sum. If new capital was required, financing would have to come internally, like the snowball rolling down the hill adding weight and speed with increased distance. They wanted a start-up point with nearly unlimited potential, one of the problems with their nursery business had been the limited market in Modesto with seven nurseries serving a well defined territory, but the expansion had to be financed by the dynamics of the opportunity itself. The business would have to support the force of its return. When they found that, they knew they were on the other side of Pikes Peak.

There were other signs that they were headed downhill rather than up the slopes, wagon and oxen being pushed and dragged. If the business was one *where* sound business practices worked, they would notch another cut for movement downhill. If the business was very liquid, one they could sell out nearly immediately and use the proceeds for a trip to Hong Kong or Hawaii, then they would know the trail ahead was easier. The business had to be an active business, not a 'wait and see', 'buy em and hold em' business. They had tried that before, way back when Rocky had graduated from high school. Then his father had provided him with a share of FORD MOTOR CORPORATION stock, a stock to grow with, its value $44.80 a share. Right after his teens when the opportunity· came.

But eleven years later the 'wait and see' stock was selling for $23.80 a share. Rocky was still waiting, and he was seeing. And he didn't like what he saw. ''Our new start-up point will never involve

—88—

holding value for more than a single year," had been one of the early guidelines that Rocky had written down, and FORD MOTOR COMPANY was the name behind each word. If they could find a start-up point with less than a year's duration, they knew the Peak was behind them.

The start-up point must be ethical. No hucksterism or dishonest practices, no exploitation, no "insider-information" machinations. It must be an activity that was overt, open, above board, and totally honest. They would leave covert action and furtive responses to the CIA. On this they both agreed. Unless they could be proud, open, and honest about their activities, they would not enter them. That didn't mean they didn't appreciate secrecy, they did. But if the light of day ever entered the room, they wanted no cockroaches hurrying for the darkness.

Exacting specifications. Psychological needs. Sound business needs. Ethical considerations. All toward the end of wealth accumulation. Thank goodness they weren't asking for all this from the genie out of the bottle, he would have given up in frustration. "The business you want, exists," the genie would say, "but only in your head."

NO THANKS TO LADY LUCK

THERE WAS NO NEED TO GIVE THANKS TO LADY Luck. She played no part. This process, the thinking that Rocky and Karen went through before they even considered taking on a new venture, cannot be taken lightly.

To have a new business you have to plan like a businessman, use all the intelligence and skill you have within you and then proceed ahead with your knowledge, experience, planning and abilities as your guard rail. You have to look at everything concerning your needs, your goals, your risks, before you can consider opening the doors to a new opportunity. Those who don't are the weak hands who are parting with their money so quickly to those who do, the strong hands.

Once considered, then work to the utmost of caution and drive, achieve success, and the compliment will come to you in the form of, "Oh, they are so lucky." But no thanks to Lady Luck.

When you opened your business doors, Lady Luck was on a vacation. When you succeeded, she was still out of town. When you enjoy the fruits of your efforts, **that** is when you will need her. Someone will have to help you locate a good room in Paris at reasonable prices. Look for Lady Luck about that time.

ON THE DOWNHILL SLOPE

ONCE PASSED AND MOMENTUM BEGINS, WHEN the sight of the Pacific is just over the horizon, no one will vote to turn the wagon around and "Head back East young man." No one. Once you have passed the summit, once your criteria has been met, once all the clogs have filled all the niches, you can't return to yesterday.

Once Rocky and Karen took their first step, they knew they would never return to the businesses that had made their parents and grandparents successful. They might have liked to. It was familiar territory, the bonds, the stocks, the real estate, the insurance policy, the mutual fund, well trod, that had proven itself once and would now suffice to preserve accumulated wealth.

Before they located their start-up point, had you asked them, they might have liked to have been in the same pastures of their parents, might have but most likely not. There are more space shuttle flights today than covered wagons across Kansas, once crossed, new generations look for new horizons. As they had searched for their new business, their chance to accumulate some wealth, Rocky and Karen were astonished to find themselves so conservative, and realized that it was because they were facing a new world. The old ways were failing, they really **did** know this. They were searching for new businesses, new opportunities, new horizons, but not in a random helter skelter fashion. The new business they found, before they stopped the roving wagon, would have to meet all those conservative tests they had so carefully laid out and now referred to quite often.

In the process of discovery, inherent in fact in that process, they were undergoing a personality change, and in many ways they liked it. They were becoming independent types, entrepreneurs, instead of salvagers. They listened, but they acted alone. They knew they **could** succeed in a new investment world, using new investment techniques, adapting the successes of the past to the special needs of the future. Those who had enough nerve to move when they saw opportunity, who were conservative and cautious, who kept a good watch on their money and their risks, who would use the very structure of the opportunity to build upon it, would be a vanguard. Problem solvers, independent types, looking for security in a new world. Strong hands, using intelligence, knowledge and education to seek out that which would provide for that security, without risking all that made the search possible: these would be the successful people for the next generation and beyond.

And they would do it by themselves, or not at all. They would manage their own money, turn it over to no other person, they would decide their own risks, set their own limits, take their own winnings.

They would invest in the future.

Their future.

And that, quite literally, is what their business would become.

Their nitch, their start-up point, would be a business of the future, entered today.

A business built on no more than the assumption that the months of December, January and February would bring a phenomenon called winter;

Momentum and winter would be their start-up point.

First they found winter.

Then the records showed momentum.

All the rest they already knew.

The result?

Opportunity.

The success?

Unbelievable.

Take a ball, and give it a shove. . . . . . .

Rocky and Karen are on the move.

* * * * * *

Chapter Seven

ON MARCH 9TH, 1982, ROCKY AND KAREN BECKET
started their heating oil business. They opened the doors by
purchasing 42,000 gallons of refined petroleum through a local
dealer who, in turn, called New York.

They had no time to conduct opening ceremonies or cut any
ribbons. Rocky was scrambling to fill a flower order for the
Stephensons, whose daughter Bette had eloped to Reno the week
before with the son of the local baker. Karen had no time for cele-
bration; it was pediatrician day for Michael and Tanya. So no lines
formed at the front door of Becket Heating Oil, no free coupons
were given out, no opening day balloons, not even a tanker truck
pumping oil into holding tanks. In fact, the Beckets didn't even
know that they were in the heating oil business until the next day,
March 10th, when they received verification of their 42,000 purchase in the U.S. mails. There at the counter, at the local post office, when the envelope had been torn open and the confirmation of
their purchase examined and understood, the Beckets simply
changed hats. From nursery green to petroleum black they had
switched. They were not only the green house Beckets now, they
were also members of the club with Exxon; they were mini oil
magnates.

Rocky and Karen examined the slip of paper which had opened the doors of their new company. They had been through this before, many times. They knew how they would run this new business. They had, in fact, even designed the business to run itself on the basis of a few terse instructions and guidelines. There were no employees. Rocky and Karen were alone.

How well the business is doing will be monitored **daily**, much as a follower of the New York Giants determines his teams league standing by examining the sports page each afternoon. Other than that, this steady examination of the afternoon Daily Times—they will continue to sell house plants and flower, mail bonsai seedlings. There is nothing more they need to do. They have no inventory; no employees; no trucks; no accounts receivable and no accounts payable; they don't even have a front desk. No one in the entire neighborhood, and none of their friends even know they own a heating oil business, their children don't even know. But they **do**. And their home heating oil business stands to net them in two months what it would take them a year to net from the nursery business they really love.

Is it really possible for Rocky and Karen to get into a new business in this fashion, the home heating oil business? How can they open a business and have all the customers they need, while, at the same time, have no inventory, no overhead, no accounting department, no collection staff, no tanker trucks, no holding tanks, no marketing staff, no distributor, no retirement programs for employees, no legal problems, no tax problems, no insurance problems, no estate problems, no mounds of paper, and no merchandise? How many home heating oil distributorships in America can boast that they have no employees, overhead, or inventory? It would be like Gene Autry boasting he had no players on his California Angels baseball team. What oil companies can make this boast? Only the bankrupt ones; all the rest **must** have inventory, employees, and overhead, the rest **must** bitterly fight both business problems and the major oil companies for survival. Rocky and Karen are well acquainted with this process; they once tried to locate white roses in early March for a very special coming out party. Compared to that, an oil embargo is nothing. Rocky and Karen didn't plan to get into a second business to become a slave to it and all its demanding verities, never again. But yet they **are** in the home heating oil business, and they **are** avoiding all these major problems. It is possible. It can happen. It does happen.

And it is **easy!**

$$* \quad * \quad * \quad * \quad * \quad *$$

I am going to offer three guiding comments which you should keep in mind as you consider the balance of this book. They may well be guildines which will have a profound effect upon you and the rest of your business and investing career.

> *There is no quicker or easier way to get into an active business than by investing a small sum of capital in a unit for that business as offered on a government regulated futures exchange.*

> *This type of activity involves none of the normal problems associated with businesses you are acquainted with, and yet offers greater potential benefits than any of the normal businesses you know.*

> *Traded with Momentum these markets offer profits beyond your wildest dreams. Nothing you have ever known about in the world of finance or business comes even close. Not even close.*

Once the momentum exists, you can maximize your return. You can do this in **any** business, even your own. If you sell insurance, you can try to enlist two sales people under you to enlist two more each, to enlist two more each, and so on down the line.

You can try, but you won't succeed. Momentum can be used to maximize the returns in any market and business where momentum exists, but of all the opportunities in the world of finance and business, well known or not known at all, the buying and selling of units of business for delivery at a **future** date offers the most extraordinary returns. For the purpose of wealth accumulation, there is nothing to compare it to.

On March 9, Rocky and Karen Becket bought one unit of home heating oil for delivery the following winter on the New York Merchantile Exchange, for $1,500 cash margin. It is their intention to use the momentum of the market to generate their expected profits. They have done it before. And by the simple act of buying a unit for future delivery on a government regulated exchange, they have accrued advantages, from the start, that are not available in real estate, or the stock market, or in money funds, or mutual funds, or in limited partnerships, or in insurance, or municipal bonds. Consider the advantages; they led Rocky and Karen into their new business; you should consider them carefully:

- Units of goods for future delivery can be bought and sold with very little initial capital.

- Such units offer the investor almost total liquidity, they can be sold with little difficulty in most cases.

- Normally the investor can place a limit on his risk in these units at the very outset and know his approximate total risk with each unit.

- These units of goods for future delivery involve holding periods which only rarely exceed one year.

- The growth potential offered in this form of business is virtually without limit.

- Each investor can apply his own business principles to his own units and succeed or fail on his own skill.

- Near total privacy is the general rule.

- No employees, no organizational issues, no accounting problems, no collection problems, no inventory problems, no merchandizing problems, no distribution problems, no overhead problems, no bureaucracy problems, no legal problems, no tax problems, no insurance problems, no estate planning problems will ever surface in this field of activity, at least none that you can't handle with a minimal amount of effort.

- If your units increase in value, you can finance your growth internally without needed outside capital.

- This new business field is not subject to outside manipulation or influence.

- It is a field which is relatively free from government interference.

- It is a field almost totally free from any environmental problems.

- It is a field 100% free from slow enconomic times, there is no depression, or recession, or even moderation in this field of investment.

- It is a field which is 100% immune to hyper-inflation.

- It is simply a field of momentum where momentum advances and declines with time, the reason why being of little importance.

- Finally, these units of goods for future delivery offer **you** the unparalleled opportunity to use Momentum to make a little from a lot by self-generating virtually unlimited growth and profit potentials. They are, in fact, the snowballs rolling down the hill.

If you have already decided to use your money for **wealth accumulation** rather than wealth preservation, nothing remotely compares to the opportunities offered by buying or selling units of future delivery on the nation's futures exchanges. There is no wait and see, sit and hold, preserve capital and clip coupons syndrome in this business. 99% of all futures units require less than $10,000 capital; some, much less. 99% of all these transactions allow you to limit your dollar risk right from the outset. 99% allow you to expand your holdings based on value, rather than out-of-pocket capital, permitting the snowball-down-the-hill effect. And 100% offer unparalleled profit opportunities.

Perhaps most importantly, this new field of business allows you as a businessman or woman freedom of movement, the ability to come and go, flexibility of working hours, pride in success, and an opportunity to learn and profit from your growing body of knowledge and experience.

It is not by accident that these markets are attracting some of the brightest minds in America. The new businessman has found that these opportunities offer the greatest growth potential in business today and the new path to wealth accumulations in a tough and modern world. They are a challenge: challenges attract the vanguard, attract those who want to succeed. And for that, these businesses were born.

There is no certainty that Rocky and Karen will succeed at their new business of wealth accumulation. But they weren't asking for certainties. They were looking for opportunities. Certainties they could get. They could get a savings account insured to the teeth by the federal government that only lost 7% of its value every year, instead of 13%. Certainty was the $5,000 bond they could buy from a discount broker, certain to pay a fixed interest and lose value. Certainty was FORD MOTOR COMPANY stock, purchased eleven years earlier for twice today's price. They knew all about certainty and tradition; and sitting on the bottom rung of someone else's tier structure.

No, there was no certainty that Rocky and Karen could accumulate wealth in these new markets, the non-business-like businesses that function different from any they had examined before; no certainty at all. That's why Christopher Columbus stayed home and sold fish at the Genoa market and never set sail. The lack of certainty was the reason Neil Armstrong refused to leave the platform and set foot on the surface of the moon, afraid the dust might be too deep. Louis Pasteur felt obligated to let the little boy die, a victim of a rabid dog; rather than test out his new vaccine which had no certainty of success.

Opportunity, freedom, challenge, pride in success, growth in knowledge, enhanced privacy, achievement: these are not certainties. They are achievements out of opportunity and experience. There is little that offers wealth accumulation that is certain; I wish that there were, for such would be a path even I would follow. But never in history has accumulation been the pot of gold at the end of a certain road. If it were, the road would be overflowing and the returns exhausted by the time you bullied your way to the end. Opportunity, even implying the chance of failure, is the paved journey to accumulation. It is opportunity's path that you must seek out, not certainties.

There are risks in buying and selling units of goods for delivery next winter, or next spring, or even next fall. But the extent of that risk can be determined by you. There will be no excuse and no reason to suffer a financial reverse beyond that which you can bear to lose. The mechanics to minimize your risks are freely available and easy to use, as easy as entering the business itself, and I will show them to you. Such mechanics are not available to someone who bought a $20,000 house for $200,000 and now awaits for a buyer to knock on the door. That person has no liquidity, no chance to get out "even for a $2,000 loss", he simply has to wait and see, and hope. The risks in units of goods for future delivery are modest, and must be modest, and you can **always** keep them modest, if you use good business judgment and sense. It is up to you, solely.

While the risks can be limited, the opportunities are awesome. The opportunity is that of wealth, great wealth. Not certain wealth, but achieveable wealth. Not as a long shot. Not dependent on luck. Wealth acquired by applying a lever to opportunity, to momentum. It **is** being done constantly. It is being done now, as you read this very page, it has been done for over one hundred years, and it will be done for decades into the future. When man next lands on Venus, his second venture on a new planet, that very day someone will have accumulated a sizable sum through the purchase of a unit of goods for future delivery. All it requires is the trying. If you can learn from experience, practice, education and application, the chances are good that you will succeed. If you do not succeed, there is no reason for you to be hurt, and the opportunities to try again tomorrow will reappear with the dawn.

Is it an opportunity for you? Think back for a moment to the second chapter of this book, about the failure of the traditional means of investment to provide for wealth accumulation any more. Then answer your own question. Flip through the yellow pages and make your own inquiries into the means of taking a small sum of accumulated cash, $1,000, $5,000, $10,000 and working with it to accumulate $2,000, $10,000 or $100,000. Put the question direct to those in power: The banker, the insurance salesman, the stock broker, the money manager, the consultant; Ask them **directly** how they plan to manage your money so that it has the opportunities to realistically return real value within a few years. Don't let them waffle, pin them down direct and refuse to leave their desk until they answer this question, if they desire to handle your money:

Considering inflation, taxes, and effort, outline for me your step-by-step approach, using history as a guideline, for accumulating real wealth with the sum I have to give you.

Your question will trip them all, all the traditionalists, for they have no step-by-step approach to accumulate real wealth. Preserving current wealth? Perhaps. Accumulating new wealth? They will not be able to answer your question.

No one of tradition can make you wealthy following traditional approaches. Remember that each time you sit down to do business with them.

No one of tradition can make you wealthy.

But you can accumulate wealth for yourself.

By using non traditional paths.

THE MECHANICS

MOMENTUM IS MOVEMENT OVER TIME, NOTHING else. This is the graph of the price of heating oil in New York City two years before Rocky and Karen decided to enter the heating oil business by buying a unit for future delivery.

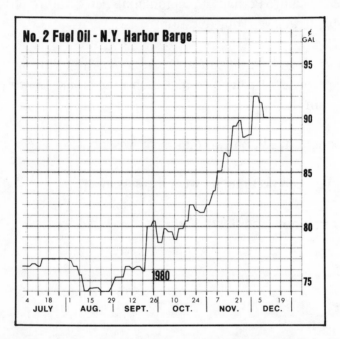

The graph above reflects the actual price of heating oil as paid by wholesalers in the marketplace when the oil was unloaded from barges in New York harbor. The graph on page 103 reflects the price of the identical product, but with delivery delayed a few months, in this case until March of the following year.

The graph above reflects actual nitty gritty pump and dump oil business. That is real life.

The graph on page 103 represents opportunity. It is the price of the product, the same product, with delivery postponed a few mon-

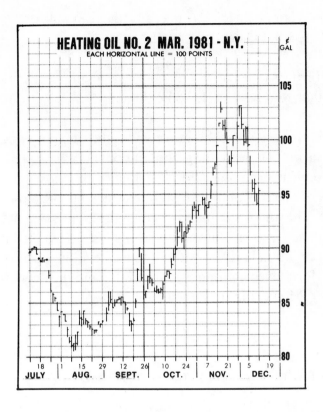

HEATING OIL NO. 2 MAR. 1981 - N.Y.
EACH HORIZONTAL LINE = 100 POINTS

¢/GAL

ths. The graph on page 102 is known as a graph of **cash prices** for a product. The graph above is called the graph of **future prices** for the same product. The product is identical in both cases, only the delivery of the product is different. One is immediate delivery, the other is postponed delivery. Would you pay the same price for oil delivered to your business today as for oil delivered three months or three years from today? You would have to think about that for a while. If you thought prices would skyrocket in the upcoming three years, you would gladly pay today's price good for three more years. If you believed the oil glut would appear and that prices would drop again, then why would you want to pay today's price three years from now if supply is abundant then? The price of today is known. The price of the future will always vary depending on what **you,** and hundreds of thousands of other people like you, think will happen tomorrow.

Today's price is an idiot's price; any idiot can walk down to the dock and see what the current rate is.

Tomorrow's price, ah yes, that is the thinking man's price. To arrive at that, you have to do some thinking.

But both prices have this in common: they are both prices for the identical product, and, the graphs of both prices reflect **momentum,** movement over time. For you that is the most important observation. The why of the price is interesting, but the momentum is thrilling. The who won't make you rich, the momentum may well do exactly that. It is the movement of the line across the piece of paper that returns all profits; without movement, there is no profit. You look for movement opportunities first, and then concentrate on the why. Momentum means the rolling ball.

HEATING OIL NO. 2 (NYM) — 42,000 gal.; $ per gal.								
Sept	.8850	.9010	.8850	.8989	+ .0154	1.0850	.7025	2,581
Oct	.8900	.9080	.8885	.9074	+ .0194	1.0950	.7175	5,275
Nov	.8995	.9160	.8990	.9156	+ .0196	.9830	.7300	3,068
Dec	.9090	.9255	.9080	.9241	+ .0181	.9965	.7450	7,869
Jan '83	.9195	.9310	.9195	.9310	+ .0200	1.0040	.8200	1,848
Feb	.9220	.9325	.9220	.9325	+ .0175	1.0050	.8970	272
Mar	.9125	.9125	.9125	.9275	+ .0180	1.0200	.8895	62
Apr	....	....	....	.9040	+ .0115	1.0200	.8900	13
May	....	....	....	.8940	+ .0090	1.0550	.8680	32
July	....	....	....	.8890	+ .0090	.9050	.8875	1
Est vol 6,175; vol Wed 2,484; open int 21,021, —85.								

We will be using these charts of price momentum by which you can visualize the momentum as it is occuring throughout the remainder of this book, and you will be using such graphs throughout your career, if you enter this new field of business. These are professional graphs readily available by subscription. You can also make up your graphs of momentum from the listing of prices that occurs daily in most newspapers in America, as provided above.

These mysterious numbers are not mysterious at all, when you look behind them. They are simply today's price — or the date when the price was printed — for a product to be delivered at the month specified.

Take the fifth line, January of 1983. 42,000 gallons of heating oil to be delivered that month had an opening price of 91.95¢ per gallon (the figure to the far left), a high price of 93.10¢ per gallon (the next price), and a low price of 91.95¢ per gallon (the third and same as the opening price), and a closing price of 93.10¢ per gallon (the last price of the day's business). That price was .02¢ higher than the previous day's price, meaning price momentum was upward, prices were advancing that day. The highest price for the year so far in units not to be delivered until January of 1983 was $1.00 and .40 cents, and the lowest price for the year for these same units was 82¢. There were 1,848 units bought and sold on that business day of units for January 1983 delivery. The total volume for all months of delivery is given at the bottom of the listing, est. volume 6,175 units, the previous day's volume had been only 2,848 units, and the total number of units currently being owned by people like Rocky and Karen came to 21,021, down 85 units from the previous day. From this explanation you should be able to work out the figures for all the various months of delivery, and even graph it on a piece of paper if you like.

Most graphs simply take the highest price for the day and connect that to the lowest price for the day by a single line, and then draw a horizontal line to the side to indicate the last price of the trading day.

Day's High 93.10   Day's Last 93.10

Day's Low 91.95

On paper, any given day of business looks like this. This is what it looks like for January 1983 heating oil. Naturally, if you were examining the price for another period of delivery, say December of 1982, the figures would be a little different, as you can determine by re-examining the previous listing.

All the graphs used in the balance of this book will reflect that little line above, daily high, daily low, daily last. The momentum of a single day of business activity reflected in a vertical line with a nitch out horizontally. Over time the accumulations of each day's line form a line of their own, and that accumulated line indicates the **general momentum** of the force of price. It will be that general line that will determine many of your actions, that will determine to which degree you apply the principle of Momentum to your business enterprise and at which point you wish to place an order limiting your financial exposure.

It doesn't look like much, that little line, but it will be all you ever need to accumulate a substantial sum of wealth, if you are successful.

Not much until you remember it represents **momentum.**

The line isn't anything but a representation. But what it represents can be more explosive than any stick of dynamite or roaring waterfall. The little red button on the President's desk is only a piece of plastic, itself, but if he ever pushes it down in anger, watch out. It doesn't look like much either.

Both represent power.

THE REMAINING STEPS

T O BECOME ACTIVELY INVOLVED IN THIS NEW BUSI-
ness activity you have to start with a brokerage firm to do
business with. Most stock or commodity brokers are listed in the
yellow pages and I have given you an address to start with at the end
of this book. If you want to learn first about home heating oil, ask
your broker for information, and tomorrow's mail will bring it.

Within that literature will be a form for opening an account
with the firm that mailed you the literature. You may or may not
decide to do business with that firm, but whatever firm you select,
opening an account is realtively easy. Today stock and commodity
brokers are the main firms handling such activity, but tomorrow. . .
banks, bond dealers, and even Sears may be entering the field. By
the time you read this book you may well be able to call your financial advisor at Sears or American Express or your local bank and request him to order you a unit of home heating oil, and his response;
"Done," "At what price?"

To open an account you simply need a moderate credit rating,
some references, investment money and, perhaps, a little business
experience. If you have these ingredients, it takes just a few steps to
fill out the forms, all nice and tidy.

Once the account is open, you will be required to deposit a sum
of money into that account so that when your order to buy a unit of
home heating oil is transacted, you will have the $1,500 or whatever
it costs per unit handy. Normally, you should be able to start in this
business for $5,000 to $10,000 capital. If the firm requests more, I
would make my beginning steps at another firm. Some will allow
you to get your feet wet for as little as $2,000 of initial capital. The
firms that want $20,000 and up to open an account are more in-
terested in their welfare than in yours. I would look for another firm
and start small. Once you have made your bundle, then you can

consider bigger things at bigger places, but initially, keep your capital and your risk at a minimum.

My own personal rule is that $5,000 is sufficient to be successful in this field of activity, and if you cannot succeed with $5,000, you cannot succeed with $50,000. Why? Because success is the end result of skill and caution; success is not a factor of money being thrown at an object. We threw a lot of money at poverty during the Great War of Lyndon Johnson and there still seems to be poor people around. Money is only part of the problem, usually the smallest part. Hard work, knowledge, effort, goals, rules and regulations, polished experience all play a major part on the road to life's successes. With $50,000 to plunge into home heating oil you can be sloppy and careless; you'll hardly notice the money being nibbled away. With $5,000 you will know quickly if you have made a mistake, and the pain will force you to learn. Why don't we put our fingers on a hot stove element to make sure it is really hot? We did, once, many years ago, and that experience forced us to learn not to use that technique again in the future. $5,000 forces you to learn, $50,000 does not.

Once an account is opened, and a moderate sum of money is deposited, you now have an account. But having an account does not mean you have to get into business; don't ever begin until **you** are ready. The firm that opened that account may like to see you start some activity but always remember this; that firm has its tiers and you have your tiers. That firm wants you to sit on their bottom step, and you want to sit on your own top peak. Don't let their eagerness for getting you into their game prevent you from slowly slipping into your own program. It is your life you are running, control it from the outset. The firm works from commissions, they profit when you buy and sell, regardless of how well you do. You work from profit, you only profit when you profit, just like Reggie Jackson only made a home run when the ball went over the distant fence. He couldn't make a home run by simply swinging, and you won't make a profit by simply buying and selling. The firm has activity as its motive, you have profit as yours. Don't ever confuse the two and enter this new field only when **you** are ready.

Once you have gone this far, you have to decide a few more things, none overwhelming but each important.

Decide what product it is you wish to buy or sell a unit of, there are several choices.

Then decide what particular month of delivery you wish to be involved with, one month away, six months away, eleven months away.

Then decide the price you are willing to pay for your units.

Once that is decided, how many units do you wish to buy or sell? One, two, twenty?

Compute the amount of risk you wish to assume with respect to your units, a dollar amount, be it $1,000, $1,500, $5,000.

Finally, decide when you wish to do all this, today, tomorrow, or next Wednesday?

The last touch involves considering the exit point for your investment, do you want to get out after you have made $1,000, $1,500, or $5,000, or do you simply want to watch the momentum and decide at a later date.

These are the main decisions you have to make, and just about all the decisions you will ever make. The rest simply involves the execution of those decisions by giving the firm you are doing business with the appropriate instructions. After all, if you decide to insure your home there are several steps you have to take even in that single decision. For how much? Is liability coverage to be included? How about theft? Fire, rain and earthquake damage added? Do you want replacement costs or simply a fixed dollar amount? Business requires decisions, even the **American Apple Pie** business involves some nasty turns and decisions. Business is not without problems.

Business

Owner of Best Pie will fight off bankruptcy

By Bruce Ramsey
P-I Reporter

Dr. Paul Chilton, owner of Best Pie Co., intends to fight the attempt by three creditors to take the company away from him and force Best Pie into Chapter 11 bankruptcy reorganization, said company spokeswoman Stephanie Chilton, Dr. Chilton's daughter, in a telephone interview yesterday.

On Monday, three creditors of the pie company, led by American Conserving Co., a Seattle-based supplier of sliced apples, petitioned federal bankruptcy court in Seattle to declare Best Pie bankrupt, and appoint a trustee to run it. A hearing on the issue is scheduled for today.

Stephanie Chilton said Best Pie will ask for more time, because bad publicity about the company's finances has hurt its ability to retain a lawyer.

She said that the picture painted of Best Pie Co. by the creditors' petition — which basically charged Dr. Chilton with running the company into the ground — was not true. She described extraordinary cost-cutting measures, undertaken by the company, including hard tactics with unions that were accepted because the company was financially strapped.

The biggest problem

"We bought the company just before it would have gone under," she said. "It was losing $60,000 a month." Since its long-time owners sold it in 1972, she said, the company has had six different owners.

"The biggest problem is that there were five unions in the building," she said, adding that the work rules increased costs compared to the company's major competitors, which are non-union.

Clean-up by union staff was costing $16,000 a month, she said. The company contracted it out at half the cost, was taken to arbitration by the union, and lost. It then defied the arbitrator's order, she said.

"We didn't have the money," she said. "We said tough, come after us."

Since buying Best Pies, she said, company employment has been reduced from 66 to 25 and the unions from five to two, in one case simply by firing all the members of a union and hiring them back. The remaining unions are the Teamsters No. 227 and the Bakers No. 9.

"The employees here are really trying hard. They are already making $9 an hour instead of scale, which is $11," she said. She added that payments to the union pension plans haven't been made in six months, because the company is trying to renegotiate the payment levels.

Not a big deal

In their legal petition, the suppliers made an issue of some moldy pies which were being kept in cold storage by Dr. Chilton as evidence in a lawsuit. The petition argued that storing the pies is a waste of money, and implied that it was a bit eccentric.

Stephanie Chilton replied that the previous owners had guaranteed in writing that all the inventory was usable, and that the moldy pies were evidence that it wasn't. Refrigeration on the pies cost the company $200 a month—not a big deal.

The three suppliers charged in their brief that the company's elimination of its own drivers and its arrangement to sell the pies to Gai's is profitable, and that Best Pie can't raise its prices because of aggressive competition from Vern's Pie, a Spokane company.

She said Best Pie could not afford its own delivery fleet. "We penciled it out last year and it cost us $437,000. By eliminating that, we feel we are at a break-even point with the company."

In sum, she said, "we are baffled why three minor creditors are trying to push us into a Chapter 11, and run the bakery." The legal action, she said, surprised and shocked other creditors, who supply the company with sugar, spices, and other ingredients of pies.

But it is normal nitty gritty American pie businesses that have so many problems, not the business of buying units of goods for futures delivery.

How then do you take the steps to follow through on your decision of what product to buy, for what month, at which price, in how many units, with what dollar risk and potential gain, and **when** do you want to do all this?

Rocky and Karen had been in this new business field for two years before they got into 42,000 gallons of home heating oil. To answer the questions you have about how to follow through, we will see how they, with their two years of experience, did just that. Remember, however, they **do** have two years of experience on you, you may wish to start a little slower with a toe in the water before a full foot.

One trade, one couple, one product — home heating oil. Even one unit purchased. Just one.

One unit, but then it was only one snowball that started down the hill. It was only one pair of locusts that began the swarm, it was only one fruit fly that cost Governor Brown the presidency.

One may be a small start.

But one can grow. With momentum and one principle.

Momentum!

"We've never done a tier four," Karen says.

"A tier four. Wouldn't that be something?" Rocky warms with excitement. "If they give it to us, we've got to go!"

The game had begun!

Momentum!

Chapter Eight

THREE-HUNDRED-POUND GIANTS SLIDING ACROSS an icy field in Cincinatti while winds carried the chill to seventy degrees below zero. That was enough to convince Rocky Becket to watch the price of home heating oil closely. In the two years that he and Karen had been buying units for future delivery, they had tried to keep an eye on patterns and emerging profit opportunities; they knew some deserved special attention. The cold football game brought the price of home heating oil to the fore. Rocky went to the library, looked up the history of heating oil prices, made a copy to take home, and then left. He was about to begin a new business career.

Rocky had served his time, spent those days in the gas line trenches, as had we all during the oil embargo years. He still remembered that gas and oil — the petroleum product out of which gas is made, of course — prices had gone through the same wild price gyrations. As gasoline shot through the magic $1.00 per gallon barrier like a hot knife through butter, oil prices by the barrel had soared also. Now he noted, prices for heating oil were dropping. Why, he asked himself.

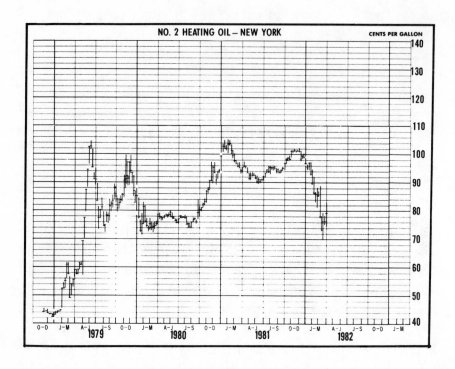

NO. 2 HEATING OIL — NEW YORK

CENTS PER GALLON

The answer was as close as the front page of the evening newspaper. It was the time of the great oil "glut." Through planning and conservation, the nation's oil supply became plentiful; ships were sitting in the harbors loaded, the oil producing nations of OPEC and Associates had over-produced in their skyrocketing need for the American dollar to finance their internal development and external wars; the effort had been made to exploit the high price, it had failed. For a while, at least, supply was exceeding demand. It was economics at the most simplistic level.

Rocky immediately keyed on one factor; **nothing lasts forever, not even oil gluts.** Indeed, by the time most of us came to learn that a glut even existed, it was starting to dry up. People who buy units for future delivery are people who think and plan — ahead, not for today. They stake their sums of capital on what the price of an item will be — in the future, at the time it reaches the consumer, at the time their unit calls for delivery. They are not trying to guess who will be ahead when the first quarter of the game is over, they are using business judgment to decide who will **win** the game, when it is all over, all four quarters.

Rocky and Karen began to discuss the current state of events. Prices were dropping, heading to levels they had seen only three years earlier. Nothing else was selling for the 1979 price in early 1982, why oil? Perhaps because of new discoveries? Each new find at some distant point on some far and distant shore would effect today's price of petroleum **and**, more importantly, tomorrow's price — the futures price. But an embargo, perhaps due to Israel successes in the Middle East, would have a reverse effect on price, that of today's oil and tomorrow's needs. Even a threat by OPEC could advance the price. Shortages, even contrived, meant higher prices, abundance meant lower; there was no shortage of economic news or views, on which Rocky and Karen could have based their opinions, their decision to buy or not to buy, their judgment of the value of oil in the future.

People lose more money by trusting outside advisors than any single other cause; Rocky and Karen were willing to lose money, if they were wrong, but it would not be due to allowing others to make their final decision for them. They would decide the final go or not. They were not insiders, but they were people with experience, knowledge, analytical abilities and they had their own outlook. They could not make a diplomatic assessment of the clout of a Sheik from Arabia; they could not determine the break-even point for a barrel of petroleum made from pure shale rock. But they did know what gasoline sold for at the corner station, and they understood history. They were intelligent people who could read road maps just as their forefathers had read Indian signs on trails headed West. Their grandfather made it to a new horizon. They believed they could also. Their own knowledge would have to suffice, they wanted it no other way.

Rocky and Karen did not buy home heating oil for their own home, but they used gasoline every day and it was the price of gasoline that they now keyed upon. For all the talk of an oil glut, they knew that the price of gas had not dipped below $1.00 a gallon; $1.00 had become a barrier on the downside of price, no station was selling below that figure. While this barrier held, the price of home heating oil was dropping continually, heading toward 70¢ a gallon, a price it had not seen for several years. "If gas stays above $1.00, how can oil drop much further?" Karen asked. Neither believed it could. Nothing lasts forever, not even declining prices for oil.

There were many possibilities open to the unknowledgable person, that is with respect to the price of oil. But for Rocky and Karen, they knew only **three**. Oil prices could continue to decline. They could stop dead in their tracks; or, the decline would end and an advance occur. There were no other choices, only those three. And neither Rocky or Karen believed the price would stop dead still; so there were really only two options — up or down.

Two years of experience had not been devoted to heating oil prices, but it had been devoted to the possibilities of momentum of the line of price across a piece of graph paper. That line had momentum — it moved. And when Rocky and Karen saw a line, they were in business. They could work with a line, it didn't matter what it represented. Home heating oil was nothing; a **thousand** things could happen to affect the supply and demand of home heating oil, and out of that thousand they would be lucky if they were aware of twenty. But only **three** things could happen to the line. Up, down, or sideways. And history had taught them there was really only two, up or down. Sideways for very long was the

Dodo bird of prices, such movement became extinct in the 70's.

Besides a line moving sideways has no profit momentum, only stability. No one profits when the selling level is the same as the buying level, three years earlier. You need up and down motion with that line in order to profit. Should the line move from the bottom of the piece of graph paper toward the top of the same piece, it meant that prices were rising, the time to buy was at the bottom and the time to sell was at the top. If the price was moving from top to bottom, like a rock sinking in the ocean, you certainly didn't want to be a buyer. Stand aside or sell, those were the guidelines to follow.

They were not gamblers by nature, our two nursery owners. They did not enter the heating oil business gambling on the hope that the price would move as they wanted it to, to hope that their guess and gamble was a correct one. They didn't enter on guesses or gambles, but on business judgment, and that is why so much time during the previous two years had been spent watching, and learning, and then watching some more.

They entered these new fields of business when their expectations were the highest, when experience and history told them price should move in a certain direction. They made this business judgment, decided how much they were willing to risk on that judgment — just as they decided how many bonsai plants to order in the expectation that sales would equal purchases — and then entered. "Buy here, and if the price moves against us $800 get out," was the essence of their strategy. Decide when to buy, at what price, and how much to risk. Enter the field and then sit back and watch, quietly, without fanfare or flags, but with confidence. Confidence their knowledge and experience meant something. **It meant they were learning, bit by bit, how to accumulate some real wealth in this new world of ours.**

"With the possibility of another cold winter," "And prices already down 35¢ from last year's level, a 40% decline." "With war fever strong in Iran and Iraq, the possibility that their refineries will be bombed." "With gasoline refusing to drop below $1.00 a gallon." "I think it's worth the buy," said Karen.

"At the 70¢ level, with the tiers," replied Rocky.

"Naturally," responded Karen.

It was all so very natural to them both by now.

They were pioneers on their return trip across Kansas. For others the trip might be new, but our travelers had been there before, in theory and in fact, during those two years of travel.

And then they found it. Not an oil well. Not the oasis in the desert. Not the winning ticket to yesterday's lottery. But something just as good.

They had been on a horizontal journey these past two years, but now, for very precise reasons had stopped. They were traveling sideways no more. From now on the action would be vertical. They weren't looking for another Kansas; they were looking upward toward the skies.

They had found their **start-up point**.

TIERS

REMEMBER OUR MOMENTUM AND TIER DIAGRAMS of earlier chapters, and how most wealth accumulation comes from the dynamic use of that force. I assured you than that the discussion would shortly focus on the use of momentum in the world of passive investment and how the tier lever could be used as a force for massive accumulation of wealth.

We are there.

Tiers in passive investments define the way you increase your opportunities using the internal forces of the momentum.

A tier is defined, for our purposes, as that level after the initial entry level which enables the participant to increase his investment without additional capital.

A tier 1 market is the initial entry level, there is no expansion, it is the single unit. A tier 2 level takes the initial entry position and increases it, perhaps doubles it, possibly triples it, maybe only a fifty percent increase. The element that is important is this; a tier 2 level has more units in it than a tier 1 level, and those units are financed not by out-of-pocket money, but the profits of the units entered at tier 1. A tier 2 market simply uses the profits which have been generated from the original investment to increase the investment.

By the time you get to tier 3 you have made an additional expansion. The entry level tier 1, the expansion at tier level 2, and further expansion on tier 3; with that further expansion financed internally by the growth in value of the units purchased at level 1 and level 2. Internal financing. Tier 4 takes the process one step further, it uses the profits that have accrued by wise investment made at level 1, level 2, and level 3 to make additional investments at level 4

How did Rocky and Karen begin in this process? At the tier 4 level? Sorry, remember they are intelligent **and** cautious. If you have these attributes, you don't start at the fourth step up, you start at the bottom, and that is where Rocky and Karen started, tier 1. In time they would graduate to investing on the second tier; still later they advanced to level three. It was only now, after two years of experience, that they were about to encounter a four tier market. This hadn't come overnight, it had come over two years, of **successful** experience. If the success had not come, tier 4 would not have come either, for it was only by success at each level that the intelligent and cautious person would move, one further step up.

Theoretically, there is no limit to the expansion possibilities of a tier system. The Beckets had never been higher than a tier 3, now they were considering a tier 4; other businessmen who had been in this field for years went higher, some as high as a tier 7, some even higher. There is no limit, really, on expansion, as long as the dynamics of each situation continue to supply the momentum. It is up to each particular business and the room for expansion within that business. Ray Kroc of McDonald's advanced to tier 14; it made him a billionaire. But the returns on tier 2 and tier 3 can be substantial; at tier 4 or tier 5 extraordinary. Rocky and Karen have no plans to every go beyond tier 5, but who can say. It has been done; it is being done. Like the mountain, it is there for the climbing.

The why behind the reason that Rocky and Karen have decided not to advance beyond a tier 5 is mainly an issue of expectation. They want expectations within limits. It is nice to plan for winning the race, but if there are five entrants and you hope to come out in the top three, that is something to be proud of also. If you plan to win each race, you may, but you may not. Rocky and Karen plan to succeed at levels they can handle; and succeed they **do.** It works well for them, it is not up to us to offer different challenges. Each must run his own race, each must march to his own drummer.

The tier structure can be likened to the beginning construction of a suspension bridge. All suspension bridges begin in the identical manner — a single line is shot across a river, by a rock or rocket, and is secured to the other side. What is done next depends on the width of the river and the requirements for the bridge. If it is a narrow flow and the bridge is to take a single hiker across, that one line will be adequate for the journey, hand over hand, never to be used again, one man dangling for a few seconds over a rushing stream. That is a tier 1 market.

But suppose the river is a little wider, and the bridge is needed to support both man and mule. Then a shuttle must be attached to the first line — already in place, supporting the second phase of construction — and a strong cable woven in to support the walkway. Tier 2: it could not be built without tier 1. Add a jeep to the man and mule and you increase the construction activities, the thin line remains; so too the second cable, but now you need to construct a roadway and that will require steel as thick as a man's girth, steel on which the Brooklyn and Golden Gate bridges are built. It can be done, it has been done. But that doesn't mean that **you** can do it, nor does it mean that to get the donkey and the man across that narrow gulch you need to build a second Golden Gate Bridge; it may not be necessary. Each tier increases the complexity of the business; each tier increases the risks involved; the greater the structure the louder the crash, should it ever fail. All bridges like all tiers begin with a single cord of line across the valley within which the water lies; consider the labor involved, the complexity of your needs, and what is expected of the structure before you add any additional rope to that single piece.

For Rocky and Karen, if the chance ever came they hoped one day to go to tier 5. But in two years, opportunity never knocked on their door beyond the tier 3 level. They hadn't minded; they liked to start slow and learn; and they liked to profit, which they had done along the way. Now a new start-up point had emerged and they were ready to take the vertical steps necessary. They quietly sat and worked out their organizational chart. Their new company would be the Rocky and Karen Becket Home Heating Oil Trust Ltd., Inc. and Registered. Of course, they hadn't incorporated it, and they hadn't registered it, but they **had** limited it, limited it to the fourth step.

The initial capital, the $1,500, would be entered on level 1. Any additional levels would have to be internally financed; they would invest no more money than the entry fee. If the line ran in their favor, if momentum returned profit, they would use that profit to increase their expansion. If it never came, they remain steady with the unit until a loss occurred, or it came time to get out — the following winter. On paper, if everything went according to plan, their tier structure looked like this:

The No Employee Heating Oil Company
(Owned by Rocky and Karen Becket)

OPERATING PLAN

Tier 1 Invest $1,500. Buy one unit of heating oil for future delivery.

Tier 2 If the value of that unit ever rises to the level where that increased value can be used to finance a second unit, buy a second unit. Do not add any additional out-of-pocket cash.

Tier 3 If the value of the unit purchased at tier 1 level and the value of the unit purchased at tier 2 level ever rises to the level where that increase in value can be used to buy two additional units, use that increased value to buy two additional units. Do not add any additional out-of-pocket cash.

Tier 4 If the value of the previously purchased units at levels 1, 2, and 3 ever rises to the level where that increased value can be used to finance four additional units, use that increased value to finance those additional units. Do not add any additional out-of-pocket cash.

They would make the initial investment of $1,500 and then depend on momentum to increase their ownership of units. If no momentum ever came, no additional units would ever be purchased. If the momentum came, additional units would be added. Why? What was the purpose of this plan; a plan they had arrived at after two years of successful experience? **Remember our weak hands?**

A tier 1 level involves having only the initial unit as a customer paying you the weak dollar bill, or whatever the amount is to be paid. If you stay at tier 1, you have only the single unit (whatever the size of your unit) purchased at that tier around to distribute dollars to you when payday comes. But if you go to tier 2, you have **twice** the quantity of tier 1 giving you those weak dollars. And if you advance to tier 3, you have **quadruple** the quantity of tier 1. By tier 4 the line in front of you waiting to pay those weak hands dollars is **eight** times as wide as it was at tier 1. By tier 4 you have advanced only four steps, but width wise you have expanded outward eight times. If you had one customer on tier 1, you have eight customers by tier 4. Go one step further, as Rocky and Karen planned to do one day, and you have sixteen eager customers. More customers mean more weak hands means more money to you, if you are successful in your plan. That's the **why**; more money for you, and Rocky and Karen.

How much is being paid in? Really only pennies, especially in this home heating oil business. Only pennies per gallon. But the key question is not how many pennies are involved, it is how many **gallons**. Wrigley made millions off sticks of gum, it wasn't how much per stick that mattered so much as it was how many sticks were sold. Hitler got less than $1/100$th of a cent on each postage stamp with his likeness, but a lot of stamps were printed in Germany those terrible years he was in power. Ray Kroc didn't hide much under the ketchup, only a penny or two, or even part of a penny. But he sold 50 BILLION hamburgers. He didn't have to have much hidden away. It is not the little bit that is being paid, it is on how many units are they being paid on that accumulates the great wealth. There is one other question that is important to you also; how close to the top of the tiers are you sitting. In home heating oil, a business with no employees, Rocky and Karen were right on top. **And**, they liked the view.

ZONES

IT HAS BEEN WELL WRITTEN, "THAT IF WE WISH TO understand everything, we must do one thing thoroughly." Rocky and Karen took an early interest in price zones in the expectation that by understanding one thing well, they would be able to grasp the entire picture also. It was a very successful approach.

Michael and Tanya Becket, Rocky and Karen's toddlers, love peanut butter; they rank it right up there with Disneyland, on the top tier of their preferences. But there was a year in their short lives in which they never got a teaspoonful of the gooey nutty stuff. That year began with the price of a jar of peanut butter at about $1,80; a price that meant a full pantry and an abundance of PB-J sandwiches. That was how the year **started** out, but not how it ended up. In the course of a few short weeks the price of a single jar ran to over $4.00. That was a lot of money for a product which, at one time, had sold for 59¢. Why the increase? Simple economics, a world-wide shortage of peanuts, bad weather in the South, and heavy demand; peanut butter had become a luxury item, right there along with mink coats, and Karen Becket balked at paying $4.00 for one glass jar. She simply wouldn't do it, tuna fish sandwiches became the rule. No goober paste. It was out of the price range that Karen would pay. She understood **price zones** well.

Prices move in ranges. The rent on an apartment used to be $150.00 a month, then it advanced to $250.00, upward even to $350.00. Finally, luxury apartments and houses were going for $1,000.00 and up per month. As price moved, various zones were established. When the standard rent was $150.00, an apartment for $100.00 was a "buy". When rent became $900.00, the "steal" was located at $650.00. Price ranges and zones established by the forces of the market place.

Sometimes these ranges are wide, sometimes narrow — the outer limits being the maximum that a buyer or consumer can/will pay and the minimum limits being the least the seller will offer the goods at. Quite often, however, special conditions will occur which will force the price right out the top, or through the bottom of these zones. Peanut butter racing toward $4.00 a jar involved a special condition forcing prices upward. "Two tickets, half price, fifty-yard-line," indicates the efforts of a fan whose girl friend never showed, who doesn't want to go to the game alone, it is three minutes **after** the opening kickoff, and these special conditions have forced the price down to 50% their original cost. Eventually, the price of an item will move up and down within its normal price zones, but for a few short seconds, minutes, days, weeks, or even months — sometimes years, price can work its way out of well defined limits.

"If you wish to understand everything, we must do one thing thoroughly." Rocky and Karen watched for prices that, due to special conditions, were moving to the outer limits, or even outside of, their normal price zones. They were learning one thing thoroughly.

Detroit is not unable to sell cars. General Motors, Ford, American Motors, even Chrysler could sell cars by the hundreds of thousands, even millions. They could sell twice, three times, ten times as many cars as the Japanese. They could sell the big gas guzzlers, the convertibles, the Winnebago Campers, even the Mack Trucks. They could sell them by the millions. Any time they wanted to. What is keeping them from these record sales? Only one thing, one small item, just a five letter word stands between Detroit and the most magnificent sales year in their history. That word is **price**. When price is at the top of the zone, there are few buyers. If price slips to the bottom of the range, buyers crawl out of the woodwork like mosquitos in an Alabama swamp. The cars would sell, if the price came down, but no one wants to lower the range, in fact they even raise it each year just to add insult to injury, and then, in great deliberation and with frowned brows wonder what it would take to get Detroit moving again. Let the price slip a little, my friends, and see what happens. Your cars **will** sell, but not with price at the top edge of the zone.

Heating Oil Prices — A Four Year History

High Level
$1.05

Mid-Range

Low Level 40¢

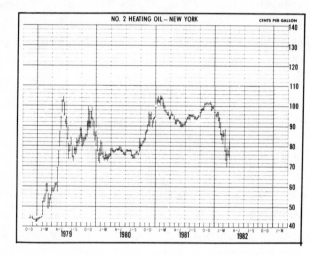

There were 100,000 reasons **why**. 450 million automobile owners using gasoline and 250 million home owners using heating oil, all making independent decisions which, coupled with the needs of the OPEC countries for an influx of cash to finance wars and internal development, affected the price of oil and gasoline in the years 1978 to 1982. Rocky and Karen knew this. But they saw only one thing when looking at the graph of new York heating oil, Number 2 grade. The price was heading toward 70¢, it had not been that low since April of 1979, nearly three years earlier. Gasoline was firming while oil was plummeting.

Maybe, just maybe, this was one of those "**special conditions**" which forced price out of its normal zone for a while and offered an opportunity for profit. Perhaps, just perhaps, this graph represented not the price of petroleum, but the price of a new AMC Gremlin. Add two zeros and you get $10,000 as the top range and $4,000 as the bottom. Price was now heading toward $7,000. No way would price get down to $4,000, no car dealer would offer a 60% discount off sticker price, but $7,000, a 30% savings? Now that **was** possible. The $10,000 car was now available at $7,000 and Rocky and Karen started getting itchy fingers to twist an aluminum key in the brand new starting mechanism of a brand new car — at a 30% savings. Price had moved to the bottom of its three year zone, the very bottom, they didn't believe it would drop to the 1978 level. 70¢ looked like a very good time to come on board. They were about to get into the home heating oil business.

Rocky **didn't** know, when he first considered heating oil as a start-up opportunity, that 70¢ was a low level. He didn't really know anything about heating oil prices. Ferns, yes, he bought them by the thousands, heating oil? His home used gas. It was only by the trip to the library where he had sought out the history of heating oil prices from the business librarian — he would later learn that one book covering all such prices is available for about $30.00 and is updated each year — that he began to show some interest. Karen? "What do you know about heating oil prices, dear?" Rocky had asked. "Nothing at all," came the response. Neither of them knew anything about the heating oil business, or current prices, but they **both** knew how to make money, and that was more important.

The plan this couple used was to divide any given price into five main zones. Zone 1, 2, 3, 4 and 5. Each zone would represent 20% of the price range of the previous three years. If the price had moved between 1¢ and $1.00 during the previous three years, then zone 5 would be a range between 1¢ and 20¢. Zone 4 would be the range between 20¢ and 40¢. Zone 3 would be the mid-range between 40¢ and 60¢, like the fifty yard line on the football field. Zone 2 would be the 60¢ to 80¢ range, and Zone 1 would be the top of the price momentum, the 80¢ to $1.00 range. Zone 5 represented the bottom 20% of the previous three year price momentum, Zone 4 the next 20%, Zone 3 the third 20%, Zone 2, 20% higher and Zone 1 the top 20%. Automobiles were selling in Zone 1. Heating oil was heading toward Zone 4 and 5 — they didn't have to know much about the heating oil business to see that. Price was collapsing to a zone 4, and headed toward zone 5, the bottom 20% range. All the while autos remained at zone 1 and Detroit pondered; "How come no sales?"

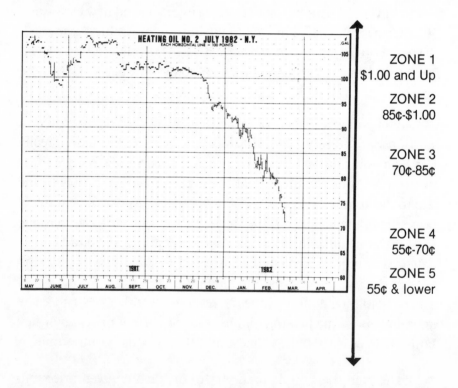

Not only was heating oil headed toward a zone 4 price range, 55¢ to 70¢ level representing the 20 to 40% price level of the previous three years, but something else was **very** strange, they both noticed it **immediately.** The price of heating oil to be delivered in the future was heading toward 70¢, but the price of heating oil for immediate delivery at New York harbor ports was resting comfortable at 85¢, zone 3, actually even at 85.75¢, a zone 2. The future price of heating oil was headed down toward zone 4, while the present price was holding firm at zone 2. Strong hands were holding onto current supplies, keeping price at 86¢. Weak hands were selling future supplies, forcing price down to 70¢, 16¢ **below** current price. If you found future supply at a 16¢, or 18% discount from current price, wouldn't you think seriously about buying the future right? **Yes,** and so did Rocky and Karen. It looked like a steal! It was.

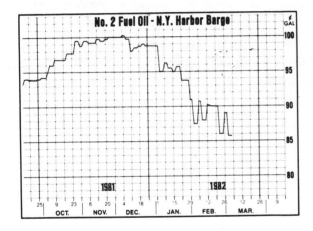

While the future price of heating oil headed toward 70¢, **the day-to-day cash price refused to drop below 86¢.** A 16¢ price advantage for those who bought the future supply.

If there was one rule Rocky and Karen had learned in those two years of watching and waiting it was this:

If you ever get the chance to buy the future right to a product two zones below the current cash price; consider it very very seriously.

There were 100,000 reasons why oil prices were dropping, but Rocky and Karen really cared about only two observations. Cash prices were holding in zone 2. Futures prices were headed toward zone 4. The difference was two zones. They **had** to seriously consider buying heating oil units for future delivery. The opportunity was too great, they had **no** choice.

Zones have another **special significance** for Rocky and Karen, zones help them decide how many units to invest in. This procedure, too, has been the product of watching and waiting; trial and error, during their two years of apprenticeship. The larger the number of the zone, the greater the potential of momentum, so they have discovered. If a market is in zone 1, at the very top of its range, don't bet on it going much higher. You may buy a house for $200,000 and make money on it, but don't bet too much that you will. A house bought in zone 5, the $20,000 range, will have less downside risk and greater upside potential, history has taught Rocky and Karen. Price in a zone 5 means that it has lost 80% of its previous value — it should be a **buy**. Price in a zone 1 means it is in the top 20% of its value range — not so hot.

To help them with their decision of how fast to expand the momentum of their money, how far to use the Momentum of any general price opportunity, Rocky and Karen adopted this general guide:

When price is in a zone 1 phase — be very careful going beyond a tier 1 investment.

When price is in a zone 2 phase — be very careful going beyond a tier 2 investment.

When price is in a zone 3 phase — be very careful going beyond a tier 3 investment.

When price is in a zone 4 phase — it is time to consider a tier 4 investment.

When price is in a zone 5 phase — it may be a good time to consider a tier 5 investment.

Guidelines; not absolutes, but guidelines given a great deal of credence. Experience had taught them that buying at the top of a price range, in the top 20% of prices for the previous three years, was difficult and involved risk of general price declines. If they were going to buy in that range, and they sometimes did, they generally entered only on a single tier. The original unit purchase and no more. As price slipped down the zones, the more eager they became to expand their holdings, until, at zone 5, they would seriously consider — they had never actually tried — a tier 5 level investment. Remember, a tier 5 looks like this. Initiate action at a starting point, move horizontally until you locate a start-up (stopping) point, and then advance vertically in five steps from your start-up point. Horizontal, then vertical, five tiers up.

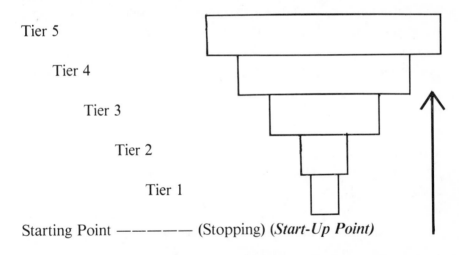

Tier 5

Tier 4

Tier 3

Tier 2

Tier 1

Starting Point ————— (Stopping) (*Start-Up Point*)

Zones do not correspond to tiers even though the numbers are the same. There are only 5 zones, each reflecting 20% price increments. There is no limit on the number of tiers one can participate in. But since Rocky and Karen had limited their activities to a maximum 5 tier level, for them, at least, the zones and the tiers were viewed with similar lenses. If the market was in zone 1, they would consider a tier 1 and no more. If the market declined to zone 5, the very bottom, they would consider a tier 5 investment, **guidelines,** not absolutes, and whenever any benefit of the doubt had to be given, it was **always** given to take the more conservative position, the lesser tier investment. They were conservative; but aggressive. The two are not incompatible.

There is a reason behind increasing the tiers with the zones and this reason is known as the **'bounce back'** effect. It is a common phenomenon in price movement, price momentum.

A price that has drastically moved at least 2 zones within a six month period of time, has the tendency to 'bounce back' at least one zone within the next six months.

Not an absolute, but a good guideline. The more dramatic the price momentum, the greater the zones that are passed, the more likely the 'bounce back' will happen. You have seen it, again, in sports or in your own activities. One team rushes ahead by 40 basketball points, the other team closes the gap to 20, then the original team surges ahead and wins by 50. The lull, the closing of the gap, was the 'bounce back', the pause in momentum, perhaps momentum in the opposite direction, and then the surge again. You start to clean your garage, you go like blazes, then you relax for a half hour, a pause, a lull, and then — if not exhausted — full speed ahead again. The lull, the change in momentum, is known in price terms as 'bounce back'. Watch for it and expect it; for, like the swallows at Capistrano, it is a regular occurrence.

Rocky and Karen noted all their observations; gasoline holding above $1.00 a gallon while heating oil plummeted, prices at the local harbor 16¢ above the future price of gas at that same harbor with delivery delayed a few months, a drop in the price from a zone 1 to nearly a zone 4 within six months time, the likelihood of 'bounce back', at least from zone 4 to a zone 3, a high zone 3, or zone 2 level. Add to all that common sense. The last time the price of heating oil had been in the low 70's was back in 1978, **nothing** else they knew about was selling in 1982 at the 1978 level.

There was another winter coming on, possibly another cold winter, another seventy-below-er, just waiting to happen. Only maybe this time it wouldn't be just in the Midwest, this time it could be nationwide, and what would happen to heating oil prices if that occurred? They dared not imagine. And war, war between Iran and Iraq, the on-going 1980 version of Europe's Hundred Years War, in year number two. What would happen if that continued, if the planes managed to bomb some refineries, if it spread to Saudi Arabia or the United Arab Emigrants, it was a crises ready to happen, a mouse trap set with the cheese waiting for the visitor or pitter patter by. With all this in mind, with the chance to reflect, with the opportunity to discuss their investment, with total agreement that it was very **unlikely** that oil would ever drop to pre-1978 levels, Rocky and Karen made up their mind. They made two major decisions:

They would buy heating oil units for future delivery investing $1,500 of their set-aside-cash, specifically earmarked for 'wealth accumulation' purposes.

And, they would buy, if the price would so let them, on a tier 4 level. Something they had never done before. Tier 3, a successful tier 3, had been their previous record.

It was heating oil for future delivery that they were buying units of, but Rocky and Karen didn't so visualize it. Rather, they saw only a **line,** a line moving across a piece of paper, a line which had dropped from a zone 1 level to a zone 3 level and was rapidly approaching a zone 4. A line which could only do three things, advance, decline, or stay steady. There was no indication that it would stay steady, so that left only advance or decline. Since it has already declined two zones and was headed toward a third zone decline, for Rocky and Karen the decision came easy. Price **should 'bounce back'** and when it did they planned to be on board.

Owners of a heating oil business? Yes, they would be that. A business with no employees? Yes, there would be no strikes or bargaining sessions. A business with no overhead, inventory or delivery trucks? Right, they would have none of these. They were opening the doors to a new business, the heating oil business, but for them it was a business they **had** been in before — **the line business.** They had been in it many times, by different names, but always the **same** business; a line moving across a piece of paper, sideways, upward, and downward. It had a new name, but it was the old game. Buy when it is low, sell when it is high, maximize the momentum in between those two levels and accumulate **real wealth** in the process. It wasn't life insurance, it wasn't bonds, it wasn't a savings account at the local bank, it wasn't Ford Motor Company Stock, it wasn't even a money-fund. It wasn't tradition, that is true. There was **nothing** traditional about it. It was just a line, a line of price momentum, with a little salt and pepper added for the spice. Not **just** a line; but a lifeline. The first line across the river valley, the line of opportunity, the chance line of one's life, the possibility — just the possibility, not the certainty — to accumulate some **real wealth**. It was a **wealth accumulation line** that Rocky and Karen saw when looking at the graph of prices. They didn't see heating oil, they didn't see any zones, they didn't see any tiers. In the last analysis they saw only one thing. The chance to make some money.

And they took that chance.

The very next day!

They weren't stopped any longer. They were **Starting-Up!**

OPENING DAY

ONCE THE DECISION WAS MADE TO CATCH THE momentum in this line, the steps required for opening day of business were quite routine, normal and easily understood.

The opening of the business account; had been accomplished a couple of years earlier with a firm in Modesto. Like you, the Beckets called a couple of firms, and after some trial and error and personality decisions — they had selected a firm. They had signed the normal two or three pages of forms, been given an account number, and they were in business. It took no more than twenty minutes, ten of which were spent talking about their nursery.

Transferring money into the account; had been just as simple, they had started with a $5,000 opening balance and, since their efforts had been successful, had never had to add more money. In fact, they had transferred a significant sum out of the account, as profits had been built up. They originally agreed to limit their investment to $5,000 and had never invested any more. When the account ran to a $25,000 balance, they decided to keep that sum permanently on deposit. If more than $25,000 ever *exists* in the account, they requested that the firm mail it out to them, which it did promptly. All very simple.

Deciding what product it is you wish to buy or sell a unit of; they had, of course, selected heating oil for all the reasons cited. Heating oil had become their start-up point. On another day, another time, it would be a different business, they weren't particular as long as they could find momentum, or possible momentum. It was this potential movement of the line that intrigued them, not the name on the line itself. This time they found the potential in heating oil, not for immediate but future delivery.

Deciding what particular month of delivery you buy; is primarily a question of how long you wish to hold your investment and what you expect will happen. If you expect the price momentum to come "within days", then you may wish to buy or sell a month very close to the current date. If you expect the momentum to come, "within six months", then you may wish to buy a unit for future delivery six months away. In Rocky and Karen's case, they were looking for a 'bounce back' to occur in the near future —

within three to four months. Why? Because just as lulls in basketball games occur quickly, or not at all, because the game had ended, so too in price momentum does 'bounce back' happen within a relatively short period of time. It was late February when Rocky and Karen started watching the price of heating oil, a price heading toward the zone 4 level of 70¢. They decided to give 'bounce back' five months — March, April, May, June, July. They would buy delivery in **July.** If prices hadn't bounced back by then, they probably wouldn't.

What about the cold winter that Rocky was expecting in the following January-February period? That was a factor, and that would be a key element in forcing 'bounce back'. If a brief price rise came in the July delivery they were buying, they would then transfer into December or January or February after July was over. By buying July they were giving themselves five months for 'bounce back' price momentum. They felt that was sufficient, and experience had taught them it would be plenty of time. They could have picked any month, and at other places on other dates they would pick different ones. This time they selected July.

Deciding on the price to pay; was easy. They planned to do a tier 4 investment and that required price to drop to zone 4, which was 70¢ or lower. They didn't expect price to drop to the bottom of zone 4, it had already declined all the way down from zone 1 in the previous six-seven months. Deciding price was easy. They would buy if the opportunity came at 70¢ a gallon. 40¢ and 36% below the high of the year. They would have bought a new Chevrolet also, had GM lowered its prices by 36%. But GM didn't, only heating oil offered the opportunity. 70¢ would be their purchase price, if the market offered it, of which there was no guarantee.

Deciding how many units to purchase; that question was easy also. They would buy at 70¢ a gallon and they would buy one unit. They were anticipating a tier 4 investment program where the first level was a single unit, to be added to if the momentum of price turned out favorable. What is one unit of heating oil composed of? 42,000 gallons. Why that amount? Because the New York Mercantile exchange has established each unit as 1,000 barrels. There are 42 gallons of oil in a single barrel, therefore 1,000 barrels contain 42,000 gallons.

Could each unit just as easily have been 84,000 gallons? Yes, had the New York Mercantile Exchange so decided, but they seemed to think a unit composed of 1,000 barrels was a nice figure to deal with. If you wish to buy 84,000 gallons, you simply buy two units. Why so many gallons? Why not have each unit worth only one gallon? Because a 1¢ price rise would only return to you one penny per unit. You would have to buy 42,000 units to equal today's single unit. The units are made large enough so that a small increment of price appreciation returns real value to you.

It is just like buying a car. You could buy 4 tires, 2 seats, 1 hood, 1 rear bumper. But no, when you buy a single unit — the car — you get all those thrown in. With heating oil, when you buy a single unit you buy 42,000 gallons. It could have been more, it could have been less, but the Board of Governors of that exchange decided that 1,000 barrels was a nice round figure to deal with, and it is.

On other exchanges with other businesses the quantity in each unit varies. This will be explained to you shortly. For now, simply remember each unit of heating oil is 1,000 barrels, 42,000 gallons. Why? Because if prices rise a little, 1¢, and you own a lot, 42,000 gallons, you are going to make a little from a lot — wealth accumulation. And, because the Board of Governors so voted.

42,000 gallons is more oil than 90% of all heating oil dealers in America pump in a month's time. On the New York Mercantile Exchange it is the **smallest** unit you can buy. The road to super wealth accumulation.

What will it cost to buy the quantity you have selected, is the

next question; and that involves two answers. The first answer is that if Rocky and Karen buy one unit of heating oil at 70¢ per gallon, and there are 42,000 gallons, the total cost will be (70¢ × 42,000) $29,400.00.

But their actual cost will be $1,500.00. Why the difference? I will answer you by asking you a question. How much did your own home cost, $50,000? $100,000? $150,000? $500,000? And how much did you initially pay? Most likely you did **not** pay the entire sum, whatever it was, you paid only part, and so will Ricky and Karen deposit only $1,500 to control $29,400 worth of heating oil. The amount they deposit with the firm they are doing business with is called "margin", and it is the dollars required to purchase and control a unit of goods for future delivery. Think of it not as a fixed price, but as a "guarantee". An insurance policy for the firm you are doing business with that if you should lose $800, or $1,000 or even $1,500 on your investment, they will have some money "on hand" out of which to cover those losses. When you have a loss, it is like writing a check from your bank account. The bank, like your new firm, wants to make sure you have enough money "in the account" to cover any checks written, any losses suffered. Margin money is simply a reserve to be used if any losses are suffered. If you never lose, no penny of your margin money will **ever** disappear. It is like a pile of poker chips in front of you on the table, there for the betting, but until you bet **and** lose, the chips remain in your control and ownership. We will have more on margin later, also. For now simply remember the amount of money required to control 42,000 gallons of heating oil at 70¢ a gallon with a value of $29,400 in February of 1982 was $1,500. At different times, with different firms, for different products, it could be more or less. **You are not buying anything with margin, you are simply setting aside an insurance policy that will pay off any losses.**

Remember one thing else about **margin.** It is this ability to use a small amount of money to control a large value that makes successful decisions so lucrative. Momentum works extremely well within the tier system of these new businesses because of your ability to control large value with small sums. You can remember that for now. You won't forget it shortly.

The actual buy order for the unit; follows naturally.

"Buy one unit of July delivery home heating oil for us at 70¢ a gallon, if possible."

That is it, and I don't know how much easier it could be. You are telling the firm the type of product you wish to buy, heating oil, how much of that product, one unit, what month of delivery — how far into the future — you are interested in, July, and what price you are willing to pay, 70¢. It couldn't be any easier to understand. If you have ever ordered dinner at a restaurant, you experienced a more complicated request; "hold the mayonnaise, dry toast please, egg over easy, salad dressing on the side, no dessert, two rolls for the lady." Ordering dinner can be complicated, yes. Ordering a unit for future delivery, a snap!

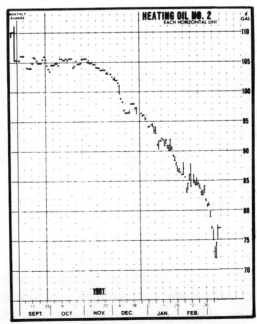

If the price ever drops to 70¢ or lower — the firm can buy for you at a cheaper price than 70¢ but never at a higher price — you will be the owner of one unit of heating oil for July delivery, 42,000 gallons of oil, 1,000 barrels.

Once in, or better yet before you get in, calculate the risk of loss you are willing to assume; buying a unit of heating oil for future delivery is just like buying a home. If you buy at $29,400 and sell at $29,000 you lose $400, whether it be house or heating oil. All that counts is the buying level and the selling level, boiled down to numbers, nothing else matters.

So, one of your first steps in entering this new business is setting a limit on how much you are willing to risk. If you buy a home for resale, and are willing to risk $5,000 on your transaction, that is your (hopefully) limit, provided you can find a buyer to take your home off your hands with that limit intact. It is the same for a unit of heating oil, or any other unit for future delivery. Assume you are willing to risk $5,000 on this business transaction, how would you go about protecting yourself to that extent?

First find out the quantity of individual units in your total ownership, here you have 42,000 gallons in your one unit of ownership. **Next** multiply the individual units by the price designation the units trade in, here 1¢. Multiply 42,000 gallons by 1¢ per gallon and you get $420.00. (42,000 × .01 = $420.00). This means a 1¢ price advance or decline is worth a profit or loss to you of $420.00. If your unit involved only one gallon, a 1¢ price advance or decline would return a profit or loss of 1¢, but since you have 42,000 gallons, it returns a profit or loss of $420.00. If you bought at 70¢ and sold at 71¢, you would make a profit of 1¢ per gallon; $420.00. If you bought at 70¢ and sold at 69¢, you would suffer a loss of 1¢ per gallon; $420.00. Subtract from your profit the business commission you have to pay your firm for handling your transaction, and add to your loss that same commission, and you end up with your total profit or loss. **Just like real estate,** buying price minus selling price including commission equals net profit or loss.

It couldn't be any simpler.

And just as simple is the determination of the risk of loss you wish to assume. For this example, suppose it was a risk of loss of $4,200.00. If you buy at 70¢, at what level would you suffer a $4,200.00 loss? That's easy. If 1¢ equals $420.00, then $4,200.00 equals 10¢. If you bought at 70¢, you would have to sell at 60¢ to lose $4,200.00.

The answer is **correct.** To keep your loss in that range, simply tell the firm when you buy at 70¢;

"If the price ever drops to 60¢, get me out."

This is called a **"stop loss order"** and it is an instruction to your firm to limit your loss to the amount you have specified. If you buy at 70¢, and you sell at 60¢, you will lose 10¢. Multiply ten times $420.00 per 1¢, and you get $4,200.00. The stop loss order does not **guarantee** that a buyer will be available at 60¢ to buy you out, but 95% of the time one will be found there or very close to that level. You may not have a 95% chance that someone will buy your house if the price should drop similar limits, but here the odds are 95% to 99% that a buyer will be available at your specified level or within that vicinity. The firm you decide to do business with will discuss handling stop loss orders in detail and explain in depth how they work. Ask them, if you have any questions or worries.

What about Rocky and Karen? They have $5,000 to work with in this heating oil unit and so they have decided to place a stop loss on their unit 11¢ away from the entry level. They will enter at 70¢, and place a stop loss at 59¢, they are limiting their loss to about $5,000. The order they give the firm is again, easier than telling the waiter how you like your steak cooked:

"If prices ever drop to 59¢, sell our unit at the market price."

Very easy, just like buying IBM stock at $70.00 a share with an order to sell if prices ever drop to $59.00. Easier than telling your son why you want him in by 11:00 p.m. on a Wednesday night.

Why would Rocky and Karen risk nearly $5,000 on this single unit of heating oil? There are a couple of answers. The first is that they normally don't risk this much, but they don't normally trade on a tier 4 level. Since a tier 4 offers a greater potential for gain, they are willing to subject themselves to a greater risk of loss. Second, this is not their first month of experience, they have been gaining knowledge, profits and skills during the past two years. The $5,000 they are now risking is not their original $5,000 that they opened their account with, it is $5,000 of accumulated profits that have been built up during the previous two years, part of their total profits which have been significant. They are not risking their initial start-up money, they are risking a portion of their accumulated profits. Third, they do not plan to keep this same risk forever. If their order to buy at 70¢ is executed, and they do buy heating oil for July delivery at 70¢ a gallon, and **then** if prices move upward, above 70¢, they plan to also raise their stop order. Perhaps from 59¢ to 61¢, and then to 62¢, 63¢, hopefully all the way up to 70¢. As soon as they can raise it to 70¢, meaning the market is well above 70¢, they are home free. Their stop-loss instruction is at their initial purchase level, the worst that can happen is that they will approximately break-even on their investment, and so they can relax and let the money accumulate.

The initial stop loss risk of $5,000 is thus the **maximum**. As soon as their unit is purchased, and they can reduce that risk, they plan to do so. And they regularly do. They will **never** increase the risk beyond the $5,000, but as soon as they can reduce it, they will act immediately.

Deciding when you want all this to happen, comes next; you have to tell the firm when you want your initial entry level order to be effective, next Wednesday, a week from tomorrow, on August 5th. For Rocky and Karen it was an easy decision. They don't care when, it is price they are interested in. "Buy a unit of July heating oil at 70¢ a gallon **whenever** it is available at that price." The price level, the top of zone 4, is what is important to them. Not the precise date. They are movement activists, looking for price momentum not days on the calendar. Momentum is what drives them on, and for momentum to occur in heating oil, they believe the price must drop to zone 4, 70¢, and then they will look for a 'bounce back' to zone 2, or the upper zone 3 area. When? Hopefully before July, because they are giving themselves five months for this to happen. If it doesn't, they will sell their unit come July at whatever price is available, provided they owned a unit. Prices have to drop to 70¢ first, before they are even the owners of a no-employee heating oil business.

The last touch involves the exit order, when do you want to get out if you have a winner by the tail; we saw that Rocky and Karen plan to buy at 70¢, with a stop loss order at 59¢. Suppose that 70¢ is reached, they are the owners of a heating oil unit, but that 59¢ is never reached. That price never drops that low — do **you** believe heating oil is headed down from above $1.00 to 59¢ a gallon? Neither do Rocky and Karen. Suppose rather than having a loser by the tail, they are sitting on board a winner. When do they get out? Remember, if they buy at 70¢ and sell at 81¢, they have **made** 11¢ rather than lost 11¢, and 11¢ equals $4,620.00. Should they sell at 81¢? If they wanted to, they would simply say:

"If our buy order at 70¢ fills, and price never drops to our stop at 59¢, then sell our unit at 81¢."

Very easy instructions, like taking candy from a baby, if the market rises 11¢, get them out for their $4,620.00 profit. That is the way they **could** handle it, but not the way they **plan** to proceed.

Remember this is a tier 4 trade, not one unit bought at 70¢ and sold at 81¢. This will be a go-for-it Joe tier 4. If tier 4 is ever reached, they won't have **one** unit of 42,000 gallons, they will have **eight** units totaling 336 **thousand** gallons.

Tier 1 is one unit. At tier 2 you add another. At tier 3 you add two more. At tier 4 you add an additional four. One plus one plus two plus four equals **eight**.

No sir, buy at 70¢ and sell at 81¢ was the way they did it on the one tier level, a couple of years earlier. It is the way they **could** do it now, but not the way they **plan** to proceed. They could have only one unit, but they plan to have eight. They could say get us out at 81¢, but they plan to make a little more. They will willingly tell us all the things they could do; it is a little more difficult to get them to admit their precise plans.

WITHIN THE TIERS

THE SECRET OF ALL WEALTH ACCUMULATION CAN be found within the tier structure. If you paln to accumulate real wealth, and you are starting with only a small amount of money, you **have** to use the tiers. There is no second alternative. This then is how Rocky and Karen planned to proceed.

If, there is always an "if", the price of heating oil declined to 70¢, they **planned** to buy. One unit, 42,000 gallons, 1,000 barrels at the price of 70¢ a gallon. That was their first step; but only the first.

For protection, they would place a stop-loss sell order at 59¢. If the market dropped straight from 70¢ to 59¢, they were out, an 11¢ loss, $4,620.00 of previously accumulated profits out the window. That was the second step. They never planned for the second step to happen; and it never did.

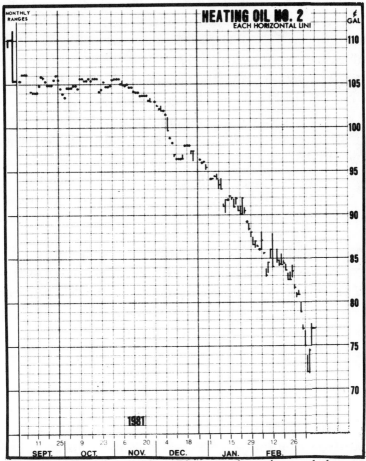

If the market dropped to 70¢, got them in, and then rose in price, step three went into effect. At 74¢ a gallon they would have a profit of 4¢ on the 42,000 gallons purchased at 70¢. That profit would be worth $1,680.00 (4¢ times $420). At 74¢ step number three would be to use this profit to purchase an additional unit at that level. The firm where they did business, and all other such firms, would allow them to keep their original unit purchased at 70¢, but use the 4¢ profit it now had to finance **internally**, without any additional out-of-pocket cash, a second unit. By the 74¢ level they had accumulated $1,680.00 in profit, they would not sell, but they would use that to buy a second unit, another 42,000 gallons; the price for the second unit? 74¢. Tier 2.

The next step involved tier 3. If the home heating oil price continued to advance, if it climbed another 4¢, they would have an additional profit of $3,360.00 ($1,682 times two units). At 78¢, 4¢ up the ladder, they would take tier 3 positions. They would use the accumulated $3,360 in profits to finance the purchase of **two** additional units, at the 78¢ level. No out-of-pocket cash involved, they would use the profits that were accumulating by having purchased a unit at 70¢ and a unit at 74¢ to finance two additional units at 78¢. They would now own four units, with each tier they had doubled their holdings. They were like Reggie Jackson starting with a single home run worth an individual dollar bill. They had **one,** then they had **two,** and now they had **four.**

Meanwhile, quietly, they moved their stop loss up to 70¢. And they placed a new stop loss for the additional units purchased at 70¢ also. **They were protecting themselves as they quietly advanced with the increased momentum.** They were conservative, yes, but they were aggressive also. They were putting the squeeze on, one twist after another, one tier after the other, every time price advanced a little, they squeezed some more. Conservative; but firm; they squeezed hard.

Four more cents up would see tier 4, the highest level they had ever been. 4¢ up meant the 82¢ level, a 4¢ profit for all four units purchased at lower levels, 4¢times 4 units equals $6,720.00 of profit. They could have sold their units and taken their profits, could have but didn't. Instead, they bought again, four more units at 82¢. Now they had expanded outward to **eight,** eight times the initial entry level, like Reggie Jackson their home runs were no longer worth only a single dollar, they were worth **eight** times the original level, for they had eight times as many units. They were using the momentum of price to establish their tiers, to increase the lot from which they would take a little. Price was moving in one straight line, they were moving upward and outward. They had found their start-up point, and they were expanding with time. They were at tier 4 and it looked like this:

Tier 4		8 units owned
(82¢)	1 − 1 + 1 + 1 + 1 + 1 + 1 + 1	
Tier 3		4 units owned
(78¢)	1 + 1 + 1 + 1	
Tier 2		2 units owned
(74¢)	1 + 1	
Tier 1		1 unit owned
(70¢)	1	

START-UP POINT
(70¢ a Gallon)

And how would they finance each of these steps? Like this:

Tier 1 — $1,500 out-of-pocket money.
Tier 2 — With profits from purchases at tier 1.
Tier 3 — With profits from purchases at tier 1, and tier 2.
Tier 4 — With profits from purchases at tier 1, tier 2, and tier 3.
Total out-of-pocket cost $1,500.

Take a ball. Give it a shove. The snowball was starting to pick up mass and speed as it started roaring down the slope toward the valley. It wasn't the distance that was creating the day by day accumulation of wealth; it was Rocky and Karen's use of that distance that was making them richer, day by day and hour by hour. They hadn't pushed a rock down the hill in the middle of summer, they had built a snowball and it was getting larger and going faster with each passing inch. The tier system was responsible for the added dimensions, not the distance from the top of the hill to the bottom of the valley.

Tradition? Ha! Tradition, yes; but a new tradition, a tradition of accumulating wealth in the 1980s and 1990, not the 1940s or 1950s. It was tradition, Rocky and Karen's tradition, but it was tradition like none before them had ever seen. It was the tradition of taking $1,500 to control one unit of 42,000 gallons of heating oil and expanding that unit with momentum into 336,000 gallons of petroleum. Now each 1¢ move down the hill of price didn't mean $420.00 in profit on a $1,500 investment, it meant $3,360.00 in profit on the **same** $1,500 investment. Each 1¢ move in their favor now returned **225% profit** for Rocky and Karen.

15% in money funds, the banks scream, put your money away for three and a half years. Buy our municipal bonds for 12% tax free interest, the cities roar, this way you can nearly keep up with the cost of living. Sit on our bottom tier, the real estate promoters beg, and in two or three years, maybe, just maybe, you can sell out for a profit; if real estate has risen in that time; and if you can find a buyer.

Tradition, ha. All the time tradition was knocking on the door, a new tradition kept that snowball rolling down the hill, each 1¢ returning 225% profit, more than a money fund pays in **15 years**, more than stocks pay in 20 years, more than real estate might ever pay, if you bought that last $20,000.00 house for $200,000.00

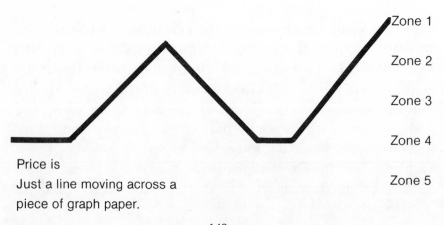

Zone 1

Zone 2

Zone 3

Zone 4

Zone 5

Price is
Just a line moving across a
piece of graph paper.

Tradition, yes, but a new tradition, triggered by a line moving across a piece of paper from one price zone to the next. Like the Mississippi, the line keeps moving, and like the steamboat owner, each trip offers the opportunity for profit.

The secret of wealth accumulation can be found within the tier structure, **no where else**; unless you start off wealthy, and then you don't need to find a secret. The first tier had given the ball a shove, the second tier had increased its size, the third tier had expanded it again, and the fourth tier had rounded off the final weight. The die was cast and the button pushed — now only price would ring the bell. If the market turned; if 70¢ was reached, if the 'bounce back' came, if 74¢, 78¢ and 82¢ were all levels on an upward momentum curve of exploding price, then, and only then, would our traditionalists of the future know they were successful.

Where to get out? Rocky and Karen made two decisions along the way. The first involved reducing risk; they would keep their stop loss 10¢ below current prices, raising it with momentum. If price advanced 3¢, they would raise their stop loss 3¢. Additional profits meant less risk, it was the way they operated. And the exit point, they had selected that at the very beginning. Not at 81¢, 11¢ up from the initial entry level of 70¢ as they might have selected their sell point. But at 81¢ they were just getting ready to buy again. They weren't selling at 81¢, they were buying **more** at 82¢. **The selling point? 92¢.** Ten cents up from the last entry point, in the precise middle of zone 2. Rocky and Karen were betting that if the market dropped to 70¢, to the top of zone 4, it would 'bounce back' to the middle of zone 2, at least. That was 92¢ and that was where they wanted out.

Tier 1, 70¢, tier 2, 74¢, tier 3, 78¢, tier 4, 82¢, and sell it all at 92¢, if momentum ever lasted that far?

They didn't **have** to play this game, but they **loved** it now and

couldn't resist. They were building their own tradition, a tradition of wealth accumulation, a **tradition of success**!

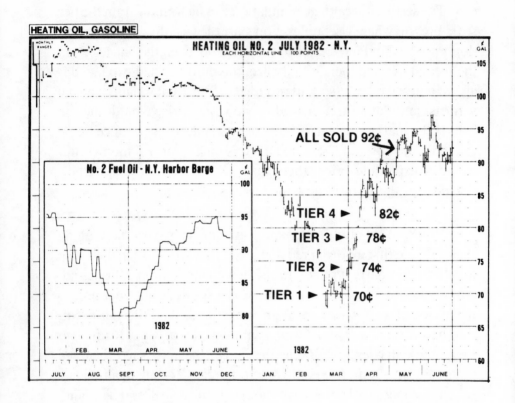

HEATING OIL, GASOLINE

HEATING OIL NO. 2 JULY 1982 - N.Y.
EACH HORIZONTAL LINE   100 POINTS

ALL SOLD 92¢

No. 2 Fuel Oil - N.Y. Harbor Barge

TIER 4 ► 82¢
TIER 3 ► 78¢
TIER 2 ► 74¢
TIER 1 ► 70¢

1982

FEB   MAR   APR   MAY   JUNE

1982

JULY   AUG   SEPT   OCT   NOV.   DEC.   JAN   FEB   MAR   APR   MAY   JUNE

They bought at 70¢, and again at 74¢, and again at 78¢ and again at
82¢, and they sold all their contracts when prices rose to 92¢.

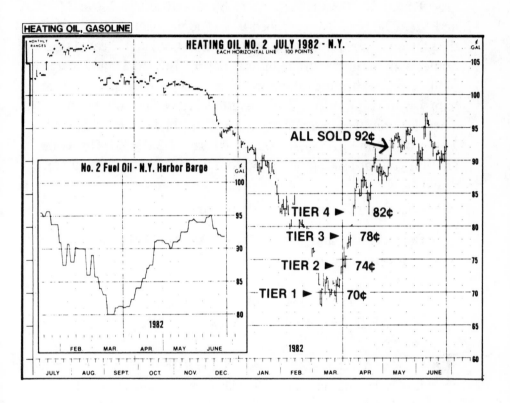

—151—

It took 34 days from the time their last tier filled on April 6th until they sold their eight units on May 10th. **"Bounce back" had come**. It had dynamically come. Price had dropped to zone 4, and then bounded upward almost to zone 1 again. They **were** right, the momentum in the line was there, heating oil would not collapse to pre-1978 levels, 70¢ was the time to buy. And so was 74¢ and 78¢ and 82¢. The price even reached 97¢. The momentum **had** come, the glut was over, prices were rising, and nobody who heated their homes with number 2 grade oil was happy. But Rocky and Karen didn't even use heating oil in their home; they used gas. They were happy with rising prices. They invested $1,500.00, nothing more. Their last units were purchased on April 6th. 34 days later they sold. The profit came to $45,360.00. A return of **3,024%**. The same amount you earn sitting on the bottom tier of a money fund in 201 **years**!

Rocky and Karen had found their tradition.

Take a ball — and give it a shove! And watch the momentum unfold. It **can** be exciting.

ONLY THE AIRPLANE PILOT
AND THE AERONAUTICAL ENGINEER

ROCKY AND KAREN BECKET **DIDN'T** BET ON THE football game between the Dallas Cowboys and the Cincinnati Bengals, they had no money riding on the outcome. And yet, that game triggered their thoughts, resulted in a trip to the library, allowed them to think a bit about the price of gasoline and heating oil, and was the first step in their decision to buy a unit for future delivery of number two petroleum. Their first step in a four tier program.

No, Rocky and Karen didn't bet on the football game, but by watching it they **did** bet on heating oil; and in the process made $45,360.00. An amount exceeding the annual salary of every blue collar worker and most white collar workers in America; except for the Airline captain and the aeronautical research engineer. But then Rocky and Karen made their money in **two** months; these people had to work all **year** for theirs.

	Airline captain	$142,800
	Engineer (aeronautical research)	48,800
	Foreman	37,800
	Plant Manager	37,800
	Ironworker	37,523
	Electrical Lineman	36,275
Rocky and	Data Processing manager	32,800
Karen made	Tunnel miner	32,739
$45,360.00 in	Garbage truck driver	32,676
two months	Sales manager	32,100
	Personnel director	31,600
	Auditing manager	31,100
	Accounting manager	30,900
	Newspaper reporter	30,815
	Beer truck driver	28,870
	Warehouse manager	27,600
	Engineer (SPEA scale)	26,750
	Meatcutter	25,646
Average	Credit manager	24,600
working	Branch manager	24,500
man's salary	Baker	22,776
for	Programmer	22,044
twelve month	Buyer	18,800
working	Legal secretary	18,144
period.	Word processing supervisor	17,100
	Word processing operator	16,848
	Computer operator	16,740
	Accounting clerk (senior)	16,272
	Payroll clerk	15,548
	Bartender	14,768
	Secretary	14,460
	Switchboard operator, receptionist	12,636
	General clerk	11,544
	Clerk-typist	11,388
	Photocopy machine operator	10,812
	File clerk	9,672

These salary figures were compiled from an area survey by the U.S. Department of Labor.

To calculate the profit in this new world of business, you use the same steps you used in the old world of business.

1. *Sales Price of Units Sold—multiply by Total Units Sold*
2. *Purchase Price of Units Sold—multiply by Total Units Sold*
3. *Subtract the bottom figure from the top to get your profit.*

Same old formula you learned in grade school; how much did your goods cost you, what did you sell them for, the difference is your profit.

For Rocky and Karen it worked out like this.

1. *Eight units equalled 336,000 gallons of heating oil*
$$(8 \times 42,000)$$
   336,000 gallons **times** *sales price of 92¢ per/gallon*
$$= \$309,120.00.$$

2. *One unit purchased at 70¢ cost*
   (42,000 **times** *70¢)* $= \$\ 29,400.00.$

   One unit purchased at 74¢ cost
   (42,000 **times** *74¢)* $=\ \ \ \ 31,080.00.$

   Two units purchased at 78¢ cost
   (84,000 **times** *78¢)* $=\ \ \ \ 65,520.00.$

   Four units purchased at 82¢ cost
   (168,000 **times** *82¢)* $=\ \ \ 137,760.00.$

   Total Cost $= \$263,760.00.$

3. *Subtract costs of goods from sales price*
$$= Net\ profit\ \$\ 45,360.00.$$

A grade school student with a good pocket calculator could calculate the net profit in five minutes. There are no commissions added to this figure, or subtracted from the net profit, since different firms charge different commissions; but the total commissions for the eight units should have come to no more than $80.00 per unit. Subtract that from the profit, and you end up with your final net.

They invested $1,500 out-of-pocket cash; actually it was previously accumulated profits they were using, they weren't even using any of their savings. They initially placed their stop loss at $4,620 potential; they were willing to risk about $5,000 on this tier 4 structure. Why so much? Because they were experienced, because they had built that $5,000 up from previous trades; it was accumulated profits they were risking, not baby milk money, and because of the **Rule of Ten!**

Rocky knew that if he could risk $5,000 and one time out of ten make $50,000, he would, under the **"Rule of Ten"** only have to succeed 10% of the time to make a net profit overall. He could be a loser 90% of the time, a winner only 10%, and yet if he managed his money well under the **"Rule of Ten"** he would end up ahead. It looks like this on paper.

Investment Number 1	*Lose $5,000.00*
Investment Number 2	*Lose $5,000.00*
Investment Number 3	*Lose $5,000.00*
Investment Number 4	*Lose $5,000.00*
Investment Number 5	*Lose $5,000.00*
Investment Number 6	*Lose $5,000.00*
Investment Number 7	*Lose $5,000.00*
Investment Number 8	*Lose $5,000.00*
Investment Number 9	*Lose $5,000.00*
Total Losses	**$45,000.00**
Investment Number 10	Make $50,000.00
Total Profits	$50,000.00
Minus Total Losses	-$45,000.00
Net Profit from Ten Decisions	$ 5,000.00

Under the **"Rule of Ten"**, Rocky and Karen knew they only had to be successful one time out of ten, 10% of the time, to end up winners. Even **they** could pick one winner out of ten; they believed, and they were able to prove.

For the **"Rule of Ten"** to work, all Rocky and Karen had to do was make ten times as much profit on the single winning investment as the average loss on the other nine investments. If they lost nine times in a row, and the losses for those nine averaged $1,100 each, they would be ahead from the series if the next investment made $11,0000 profit. **The winning decision must be worth ten times the averaging losing decision, and every series of ten trades, even though you lose on nine of them, will make you a winner.** And Rocky and Karen were able to do a great deal **better** than losing 90% of the time.

THE PERCENTAGES AGAIN

WHAT WAS THE ACTUAL PERCENTAGE RETURN for their $1,500.00 investment held these several weeks? How much did they really make when one looks at their profits straight on, sideways, and from the top? **A great deal!**

Overall, not including commissions since that would vary depending on which firm they did busines with, they netted 3,024% on their $1,500.00 **Three Thousand Plus** percent, in months. Individually, they did as follows:

The first unit cost $1,500.00. They bought 42,000 gallons at 70¢ and they sold those same gallons at 92¢. They netted $9,240.00 profit from the first unit. The return was 616%. They held this position 64 calendar days.

The second unit cost nothing. They financed it with the profit of their first unit. They bought another 42,000 gallons at 74¢ and they sold those same gallons at 92¢. They netted $7,650.00 profit from the second unit. What was the return? How do you calculate a return of $7,560.00 from zero out of pocket cash? They held this second unit 46 days.

The third and fourth units also cost them nothing. They financed them with the profits of the earlier two units. The third and fourth units consisted of 84,000 gallons purchased at 78¢, which were later sold for 92¢. The net profit for these two units was $11,760.00. What was the percent return? How do you calculate a return of $11,760.00 in profit from a **zero** out of pocket investment? What percent is that? They held these units **40** days.

The fifth, sixth, seventh and eighth units also cost them nothing, out of pocket. They financed them from the profits of the previous four units. These four units consisted of 168,000 gallons of heating oil purchased at 82¢ per gallon. These same gallons were later sold for 92¢ per gallon. They made a profit of $16,800.00 on these units.

What was the percentage return of $16,800.00 in profits from zero out-of-pocket investment? How do you calculate a return on zero investment? They held these units **35** days.

Overall, they invested $1,500.00 out of pocket cash, and they made an overall profit of $45,360.00. This amounted to a total return of **3,024.00%** considering the out-of-pocket cash involved and the total amount of profits. **But**, the longest they owned any of these units was 64 days, 64/365th's of a year. They only held the positions for two months at the longest, and on the average for 41.25 days. Assume that they held all units for 2 months. The return for those 2 months was 3,024.00%. Based on a calendar year, that was an **annual** return of **18,144%!**

They were making 18,000% interest on their money. The same yield as you would receive on the bottom tier of a money-market fund in **1,209 years.** There is a great deal of difference between sitting on top of a tier structure, and sitting on the bottom. The difference between **18,000%** and **15%.** A great deal of difference!

How do you calculate the return on a zero out-of-pocket investment returning you $7,560, $11,760, or $16,800 in profit? The same way you calculate how much **effort** it took you to get the snowball to roll the middle five feet of its downhill momentum. It took you no effort for the momentum of the middle five feet, none at all, the mass moved that distance **by itself**. Your effort was at the top, the thinking, the planning, the rolling and the pushing. There was no effort on the way down, the rolling ball did that all for you — free of charge!

In the year 1982, Ronald Reagan, President of the United States, by heroic efforts and mass unemployment reduced the inflation rate from 20% to under 10%. It was quite an achievement for inflation is the most cruel to the poor and the elderly. Wealthy people can cope, new workers can ask for a living wage or refuse to work; and the employers will pay that sum, whatever it may be. But the poor and the elderly have no means of increasing their income to combat inflation. Ronald Reagan, critized by the poor, by lowering inflation had done more for them than they might realize. And Ronald Reagan, by starting to consider the death trap that social security is in, without help or cooperation or even a simple 'thank you,' would one day help out the elderly also.

Rocky and Karen though, in 1982, decided to **help themselves**; knowing that the Lord would be on their side if they succeeded. They understood that inflation had been reduced from 20% to under 10%, but they were still worried, inflation **could** come again, and so they decided to invest "for inflation and a little plus". They made an annual return of **18,000%**, inflation with a **big PLUS!**

In the process they didn't pollute any air or foul any water; they didn't have to fire any employees when business was slow, or even buy a delivery truck for their petroleum business. They operated a business with no invoices, no books, no accountants, no lawyers. They didn't care if prices went up, down, or sideways. If a boom was on, a depression, or stagnation. All they would see when they looked at that piece of graph paper on the kitchen table was a line, a line moving across the paper, bottom to top, top to bottom, very rarely sideways. If it was moving up, like heating oil did, they wanted to be a buyer. If it stayed sideways; they hadn't seen that very often; they stayed at home watching TV and out of business. If it moved down, they wanted to sell at the top, or stand aside. They really didn't care what was happening or why. There were 100,000 reasons behind each tick in price; but they **only saw a line,** day by day, creeping quietly across a piece of paper. That was **all they saw,** even when they made their 18,000% return.

TIERS AND MOMENTUM

The Tiers made them do it.

Tiers and Momentum.

Out of a price movement of 22¢, when heating oil rose from 70¢ to 92¢, they netted a return of 108¢; 22¢ plus 18¢ plus 14¢ plus 14¢ plus 10¢ plus 10¢ plus 10¢ plus 10¢. Out of a 22¢ movement in the line, they made 108¢. It was a bit like the football player who took the opening kickoff of the game, ran the hundred yards from goal post to goal post and scored **eight** touchdowns. In football, you can't take any more distance out of the hundred yards than 300 feet. Through Momentum you can make 22¢ give you 108¢ by using the tier structure.

Rocky and Karen needed a little from a lot. They knew that this was the method whereby all wealth is accumulated. But they had all they could handle with their nursery, and there was no growth in Modesto for eight more such businesses. Besides, eight more nurseries meant eight more buildings, eight times as many employees, eight times as many plants to sell, and sixteen times as many headaches; headaches always seem to multiply faster than anything else. They needed a little from a lot, but they couldn't expand their own business. They needed a **new business.**

But McDonald's had already been taken, and there was Jack in the Box, Shakey's, Pizza Hut, Mr. Burger, Burger King, Arctic Circle and Dick's already crowding out the fast-food tier system. It would take too much effort to start a new tier there. And they weren't up to chain letters, even human chain letters, they liked to open the front door without meeting a postal inspector. What about selling books by mail, sponsored by a friend of the library? Nope, that wasn't their field either. It meant too many ads, too many newspapers to deal with, too many books to stock, too much shipping expense. The only mail order that Rocky and Karen would do was the shipping of their Bonsai plants to out of town customers. All the normal tier systems were taken, impractical or illegal; it looked hopeless.

Until they discovered a **new tradition**; a **tradition for their generation**. The opportunity, possibility, chance, potential, dream, call it what you like, of sitting on top of their **own tier** in a business which could earn them 100, 1,000, even 10,000 percent. They already knew how to make money for **others**; they had been doing that all their life, now they were learning how to accumulate some wealth for themselves. They liked the challenge. They liked the opportunity. They even liked the excitement. But most of all they liked the view. For the first time ever; really their first time ever, Rocky and Karen were sitting within a tier structure at the very point they wanted to be. **On top!** And the view was overwhelming.

Rocky and Karen made it; in heating oil, but also in numerous other activities we will cover shortly. **You too** can join them. In the search for momentum; in watching the line; in buying and selling; **and,** in sitting. Sitting right where you belong, **at the only location which will ever help you accumulate wealth**. Right on top, the very top, at the very peak; of your **own tier structure!**

NEW CAR PRICES

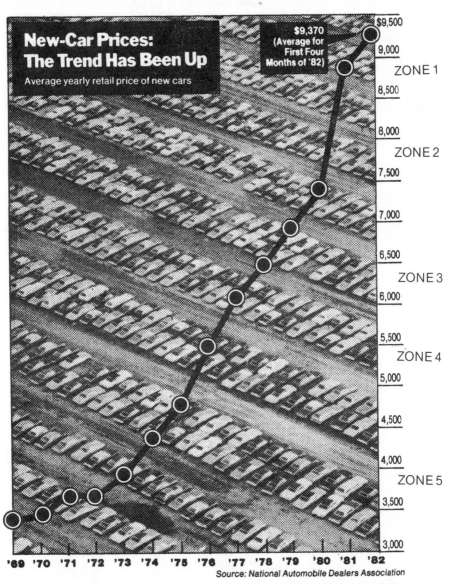

**New-Car Prices:
The Trend Has Been Up**

Average yearly retail price of new cars

$9,370
(Average for
First Four
Months of '82)

$9,500

9,000

ZONE 1

8,500

8,000

ZONE 2

7,500

7,000

6,500

ZONE 3

6,000

5,500

ZONE 4

5,000

4,500

4,000

ZONE 5

3,500

3,000

'69 '70 '71 '72 '73 '74 '75 '76 '77 '78 '79 '80 '81 '82

Source: National Automobile Dealers Association

The New York Times / August 5, 1982

AND THEY WONDER WHY NO ONE IS BUYING CARS ANY MORE

ROCKY AND KAREN BECKET
THEIR NEW BUSINESS

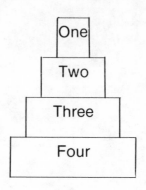

YOU
AND YOUR TIERS

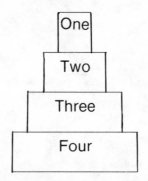

EARNING INTEREST ON YOUR MONEY
A Checklist for Savers

Savings Instruments	Minimum Deposit	Maturity	Yield	Pros & Cons
Passbook savings	None	None	5¼% at banks; 5½% at thrift institutions.	Money can be withdrawn at any time. Low interest rate.
NOW accounts	Varies	None	5¼%	Checks can be written. Many banks require large minimum balances.
Money-market accounts	$20,000	7-31 days	Thrifts to pay yield equal to current return on 3-month T-bills; banks will pay 0.25% less.	Market yields paid on accounts of short duration. No checking privileges; penalty for early withdrawal. Available Sept. 1.

91-day certificates	$7,500	91 days	9.633% at thrifts; 9.383% at banks. Tied to 3-month T-bills.	Short-term certificates offer market yields. No checking privileges, penalty for early withdrawal.
Money-market certificates	$10,000	6 mos.	11.614%. Yield pegged to average return on 6-month Treasury bills.	Savings earn market yields. Hefty penalty imposed if funds are withdrawn early.
All-savers certificates	$500 or less	12 mos.	8.96%. Yield tied to return on latest issue of 52-week T-bills.	Individuals can deduct up to $1,000 in interest from taxabale incomes. Married couples can deduct $2,000. Cannot be purchased after Dec. 31, 1982. Substantial penalty for early withdrawal.
IRA certificates	Varies	18 mos.	Current yield average 14%. Banks and thrifts may pay any rate of interest.	Both deposits and interest income are exempt from federal income taxes until withdrawn. Yields may vary. Annual contributions are limted to $2,000.
Small-savers certificates	Varies	2½ to 3½ years	13.45% at thrift institutions; 13.2% at banks. Yields based on returns paid by U.S. securities with 2½-year maturities.	High yields for small deposits vs. lengthy maturity.
Longer-term certificates	$500 or less	3½ years or longer	Yields vary, depending on maturity. No ceilings on rates.	Investors can shop around for best yield. Savings locked up for long periods of time.
Sweep accounts	$1,000-$5,000	None	Set by money-market rates — now averaging 10% to 13%.	Amounts exceeding minimum balance automatically swept into uninsured money-market fund. Check privileges. Banks may impose service charges.
Money-market mutual funds	$500-$10,000	None	Determined by market interest rates — now averaging about 11.89%	High yields paid on funds that can be withdrawn at any time. Checks can be written. No federal deposit insurance.
Bond funds	Varies	None	12.9%	Shares in these funds can be easily resold but could lose value if interest rates rise.
Tax-exempt bond funds	Varies	None	10.1%	Interest income is exempt from federal taxes. Shares decline in value if interest rates rise.
Stock funds	Varies	None	6.3%	Small investors can diversify their holdings. Shares will lose value if stock prices decline.
Treasury bills	$10,000	6 mos.	10.671%; varies weekly.	T-bills offer both market yields and safety and cn be easily sold.
U.S. savings bonds	$25	8 yrs.	9%	Maximum safety but lengthy maturity.
U.S. savings bonds	$25	8 yrs.	9%	Maximum safety but lengthy maturity.
Top-quality corporate bonds	$1,000	10-30 yrs.	13.83%, on average	Market yields plus liquidity. Investment will lose value if interest rates rise.
Common stocks	— —	None	6.48%, on average	Potential for dividends, long-term capital gains. No protection from capital loss.

Note: Yields as of early August.

USN&WR—Basic data: U.S. agencies, Donoghue's *Money Fund Report*, Standard & Poor's Corporation, Wiesenberger Investment Companies Service

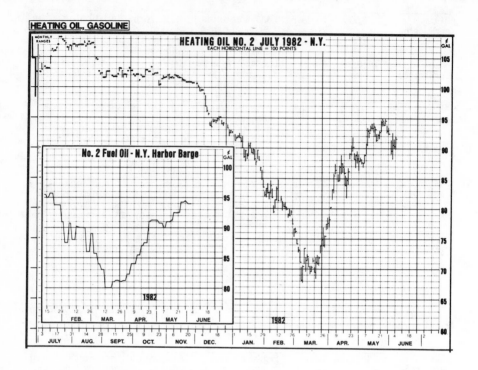

NOTE that the cash price for heating oil soared from 80¢ a gallon to 95¢.

AND the futures price moved from 70¢ (the buying level of the Beckets) to 92¢ (their selling level) and above.

The move from March to May took 2 months, and made them **18,000%** on their money. Not much of a move, but an **18,000%** **return.**

Chapter Nine

ROCKY (ROCKWELL ROCKEFELLER THE THIRD) and Karen Becket did quite nicely in the heating oil business; splendidly, in fact. But it was not their first business. They had operated many such businesses over the past two years, though this was their first experience in heating oil. It was also their first experience with a tier 4 opportunity. Their trading had begun first on paper; **they traded with no actual money invested for a considerable period of time.** Once they had mastered success "on paper"; if you can't succeed on paper, you will never succeed with real money, they moved on. The next stopping point was a Tier One trade.

Their program was the essence of simplicity; master "on paper" trades first, then try Tier One trades, then move on to Tier Two, finally work up to Tier Three, and their ultimate goal, Tier Four — maybe one day Tier Five. **Each successive step required continual success on the previous step.** Not blind success, but skillful, knowledgable, sustained success. Never advance until you can continually succeed on the previous level became their guideline for growth, a guideline that worked very well.

TIER ONE

THEY REMEMBERED THEIR TIER ONE TRADE WELL, it had happened many months earlier after continual "on paper" success. The name of the actual business they were in was either forgotten or no longer important. They were making money from momentum, not particular businesses, and it was the momentum that they now remembered. A line that moves forward, upward, sideways and top to bottom with time. The momentum was what returned profits to them, not any name attached to a particular business.

How had their first Tier One opportunity begun? It started with everyting looking **bad,** really bad. Terrible, in fact, so terrible that price was cascading downward in a never-ending-race to absolute zero. There was, however, one small factor that Rocky and Karen kept in mind: **Nothing** last forever, and absolute zero is rarely reached as a price level. All the bad news looked like a **great** opportunity for them. A terrible situation offering a terrific opportunity. They liked it.

The past was known, it was a fact. Price was collapsing, in that never-ending-down-cycle, heading toward absolute zero. But Rocky and Karen knew a couple of things about this business, from their studies and "on paper" experience.

*1. It was a business that had **never** reached absolute zero before. No reason to suspect that it would this time.*

2. The current price level of 8¢ was very low, in the zone 5 area. The price in this business was normally in the double digit range.

3. This was a business which historically saw price move in sharp "V" patterns. Sharply downward

EACH HORIZONTAL LINE = 10 POINTS

The Future?

The Past.

for several months, and then sharply upward for an equal number of months.

4. Finally, they knew that never-ending does not exist in the world of price. **All** price momentum comes to an end. The question is not "will it end?", the unknown is simply "**when** will it end?"

Arm yourself as you walk out the front door to face the world of the future, with swords, pistols, a baseball bat and screwdriver, but **never** forget knowledge. Arm yourself with knowledge first, forget about the others if you must, for the knowledgable person will always succeed where the fanatic fails.

This amount of knowledge; absolute zero had never been reached before; the price of 8¢ was a zone 5 price; this business historically experienced "V" pattern price fluctuations; nothing in price is ever never-ending, was all the knowledge they needed for their first "real live" Tier One adventure.

Rocky and Karen had developed their checklist by now, and for this first Tier One trade they went through the items one by one, cautiously and conservatively, but fighting to keep the excitement under control.

The opening of the account had been accomplished. They had deposited money into it, so the first two steps were behind them. The third step involved deciding what business they wished to buy or sell a unit of in expectation of profit. This too was decided, they would buy a unit of the business whose price had *passed 8¢* and was dropping drastically toward 7¢.

What particular month to buy became the fourth item on their checklist, and they decided to buy one six months away from the current date. Why six months? To give the business a little time to recover from this drastic price drop, if an increase in price came within six months, they would be overjoyed. If it didn't come in six months, they would rethink the opportunity.

Step five involved deciding on the price to pay, and they selected 7¢ a pound. Again, why? Because the price was in such a downward momentum it looked certain to hit 7¢, and since 8¢ was in zone 5, 7¢ was even a better buy. In addition, if price ever did approach absolute zero, 7¢ was one-cent closer to the bottom and thus

1¢ less risk of loss. They both agreed, unanimously; "Seven cents it is."

How many units were they willing to buy for this, their first real life experience? Step number six required an answer and their answer was one. A Tier One investment would be their first actual experience. Mastering "on paper" business was one thing, now they would work with actual money," but only on the Tier One level. If, and only if (the biggest two letter word in the English language), they could master Tier One investments would they move further down the road to Tier Two. There wasn't any hesitation here, they would buy at 7¢ and they would buy only one unit. Simple and settled.

What would it cost them, what would the firm they were doing business with charge for the purchase of this one unit at 7¢? They knew this might vary from firm to firm and that the cost, margin, was unrelated to actual profit or loss. It was just like one seller of a $40,000 home requiring $4,000 down and the other seller requiring $8,000 down, both houses still cost $40,000 and assuming all cash was to be paid on closing, the buyer would be out $40,000 in both cases. What the seller required at the time of the earnest money did not affect the total cost of the houses for sale. In the case of this new business, the firm they were doing business with required only $1,000 per unit for this field of investment when prices were below 10¢ a pound. Other businesses required from $750 to $1,500 per unit. This "margin money" was simply extra money to have in the account should it ever be needed, just like having a credit balance in one's checkbook. Until the checks are written, the balance remains untouched. And until the new unit of business was purchased and sold, none of the original $750, or $1,000 or $1,500 would be used. Only if there was a loss, would a portion of that sum, or perhaps all of it, be needed. In the case of a huge loss, more than that sum might be needed. But first you had to both buy and sell to sustain a profit or loss, and Rocky and Karen hadn't bought yet. They were **planning** now, and planning isn't doing. If the market dropped to

7¢, they would buy, and the cost to them would be $1,000 per unit. Since they would buy one unit only, their total out-of-pocket investment would be that $1,000 dollar bill; the same bill that Bret Maverick used to keep pinned inside his jacket lapel, and which he was forced to use for emergencies about every other week.

Their checklist showed step number eight as giving the actual purchase order for this new business to the firm they were doing business with. They simply picked up the telephone and made the call:

Buy one unit for us at 7¢ a pound, or lower.

If there was a simpler way to get into a new business, Rocky and Karen had certainly never discovered it. "Buy one unit for us at 7¢ a pound, or lower." That single sentence left no room for ambiguity. Please do it, if possible, at this price or lower, and thank you very much. Checklist step number eight accomplished.

Calculating the risk they were willing to assume was checklist item number nine, and they selected $2,000. A **huge** risk on a $1,000 investment, **two hundred** percent. Yes, that is true. But price was collapsing drastically, they doubted if they would be able to pick the "absolute bottom" of the price drop, and it was quite possible, should they buy at 7¢ that price could work itself lower. They offered to buy a unit at that level, but if the market dropped $2,000, "sell them out." Was this a wise choice? **Remember,** Rocky and Karen had been trading "on paper" for some time, they were not beginners. They felt it was a wise decision and it is not up to me to second guess them. But I can tell you this; the $2,000 initial risk was the maximum risk they were willing to assume. If they bought at 7¢, and the market moved to 7.5¢ or 8¢, I know they would quickly move that "stop loss" order, their risk limitation order, closer to current prices, quickly reducing the maximum risk fom $2,000 to $1,500 to $1,000 to $500 to zero. But they initially gave themselves $2,000 leeway. "If price moves against us $2,000, get us out", was the essence of their order to their firm.

When did they want this to happen? Step number ten on the required checklist? They didn't care, just so long as it was in the somewhat near future. They told the firm they were doing business with to leave their order "open" until it was changed or cancelled. This meant they would watch prices, and if they never dropped to 7¢ in the next 10-20-30 days or so, Rocky and Karen would reconsider the situation. Perhaps leave the order "open"; perhaps cancel it altogether; maybe they would raise it to 7.5¢ or 8¢. For now it was simply an order to happen — whenever it happens, until we tell you differently. It is like having an employee, they will know when they are fired when the time comes, but in the meantime report to work each day. The order was effective immediately and "open" until notified otherwise.

The exit order was step number eleven, and it was a step that could be taken or ignored. They could decide now at which price they would exit from this market, should their "stop loss" level never be reached and should the market move in their favor, or they could simply wait and see what happened. Rocky and Karen decided, since this was their first actual money investment, they would get out when they had a $2,000 profit. They would risk $2,000 and get out if they made $2,000. Not a unique approach, a one-for-one ratio. But it was the approach they decided to adopt. The "stop loss order" had said, take us out if we lose $2,000. The "stop profit order" now said, get us out if we make $2,000. They were OCO orders (one cancels the other); which happened **first,** the other was automatically cancelled. If they lost $2,000 right off the bat, there would be no opportunity to sell for a $2,000 profit. If no loss came then they would sell for the profit figure. Whichever happened first, OCO, cancel the remaining open order, please.

The final step in their decision making process involved step number twelve; working with tiers. But step number twelve would never be taken this time around, for they were buying only a single unit. If the market moved $2,000 in their favor, they would sell that single unit, if it collapsed and went $2,000 against them, they would take thir $2,000 loss and reconsider their approach. But in neither case would they go on to invest in tiers — make a little from a lot. This time there would be only one unit; whatever they made, a little or a lot, it would come out of that single square in their tier structure on which they were now seated. Later, as we saw in heating oil, they would use tiers to increase returns, but on opening day of their first real money trade, they would never go any further anyway.

So Sorry! Now you know they **were** successful on tier one, for without that success they would never have been in heating oil. By establishing a condition for advancement, and then by telling of their heating oil experience, you already know without reading fur-

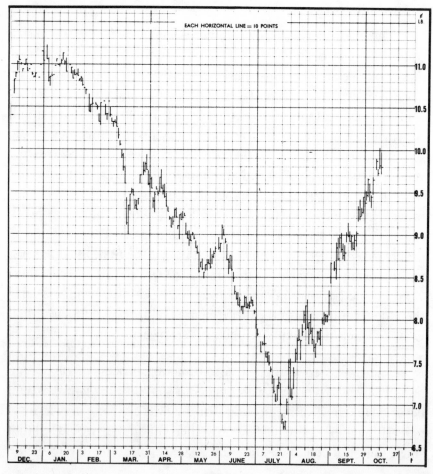

—172—

ther that Rocky and Karen **did learn** how to succeed on the tier one level. They knew the past, they bet on the future, and they were successful. Along the way they learned one thing more. Sharp "V" price patterns **do occur,** both when you are investing "on paper" and when you have "real money" on the line.

They had taken twelve steps to accumulate wealth, actually had taken eleven but considered twelve, and accumulate wealth they **did.** Price did hit 7¢, it did not reach their $2,000 risk level where their stop loss was located, (at 5.25¢), and it did rise to their $2,000 profit level where they sold out, (at 9.00¢). Wealth accumulation **is possible** in the real money world as well as the "on paper" practice world. They did buy, their stop loss was never hit, they did sell, and they made a $2,000 profit. It was not a dream. They could even go over the figures at home and compare them with their actual results as supplied by the firm at which they did business.

Purchase Price	7¢ a pound
Sales Price	9¢ pound
Profit Per Pound	2¢ per pound
Number of pounds in their single unit	112,000
Gross Profit from Investment (2¢ × 112,000)	$2,240.00
Commission to Firm	− 80.00
Net Profit	$2,160.00
Initial Investment	$2,000.00
Percentage Return	108%
Days of Ownership	52
Annual Percentage Return	758%

They had sold at 9¢ rather than 8.75¢, even though 8.75¢ was closer to their $2,000 goal than 9¢. Why? Because the 9¢ number was an even number, buy at 7¢ sell at 9¢ was easy to remember, and because 9¢ provided for the cost of doing business, the firm's commission for buying and selling, and left a little cream on the top. Their investment had been $2,000 and they had sold out for a net profit of $2,160, a return of 108% in fifty-two calendar days; an annual return of 758%, the same as you receive in a money-fund in fifty plus **years.**

It was no accident that Rocky and Karen would later look for a "bounce back" in price in home heating oil. Their first Tier One experience had been with a price bouncing back from 7¢ to 10¢, after a decline from 11¢ to 7¢. Their first real money experience with "bounce back" would be very helpful to them at a later date, when they took on home heating oil. Bounce back is like dropping a ball from a several story building, the higher up you are when you release it from the window, the higher it will respond on the upturn after it hits the ground. If you want to find lots of room for "bounce back," look for a high window that price was dropped out of. In this case, a decline from 11¢ to 7¢ was a 36% drop in price in seven months. "Bounce back" was to be expected. Had price only dropped from 11¢ to 10¢, don't look for the bouncing ball to offer much return.

Could they have done better with this, their first tier one trade? They sure could have.

They could have bought at 6.71¢ and sold at 10.01¢ for a gross return of 3.30¢ multiplied by 112,000 pounds or a return of $3,696, 185% in 52 days, 1,299% on an annual basis. They could have done this. And Richard Nixon could have burned the Watergate tapes, Jimmy Carter could have decided not to appoint his brother as a negotiator between the United States of America and Libya, and Adolph Hitler could have decided not to start the Second World War, but stay at home and collect a little bit off each postage stamp that was sold. They all could have done just that. But it is not what you could have done in life that is important, especially as far as wealth accumulation is concerned, it is what you actually do that counts.

Rocky and Karen did make $2,000 plus in profits, they did do

—174—

this in less than two months time, they did earn a return of 108% annualized to 758%, and they did succeed on the tier one level. This much they **did!** And they gained confidence and knowledge, two important factors, confidence with success and knowledge about "bounce back" of price, that "bounce back" sometimes comes in particular patterns; in particular sharp "V" patterns. This knowledge would help them throughout the rest of their business life.

They could have made over 100%, they could have gained knowledge, they could have gained confidence, they could have mastered their first try at tier one. **They could have; and they did!**

TIER TWO

T HERE WERE MANY TIER ONE TRADES BEFORE Rocky and Karen moved to two tiers in their programs. Many tier one trades, some successful, some unsuccessful, but overall a positive result. It had to be positive before they could move on, it had to and it was. Rocky and Karen had become successful tier one traders.

The tier two business they remember most was a quick and successful experience they had with units of interest rates back in 1981. You remember 1981, the year when rates were advancing, declining, advancing again, and then declining. You remember 1981 as one of the initial years in the Recession. Rocky and Karen remember it as their first successful trade on the tier two level. 1981 was one of their favorite years.

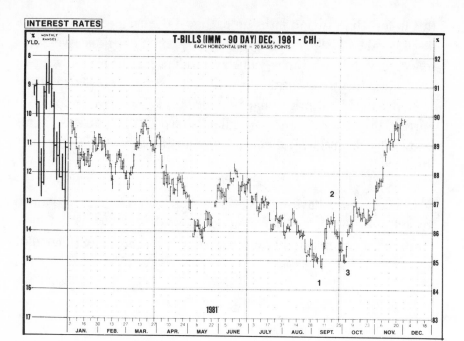

INTEREST RATES

T-BILLS (IMM - 90 DAY) DEC. 1981 - CHI.
EACH HORIZONTAL LINE = 20 BASIS POINTS

1981

    The graph that people use who buy units of interest rates is
identical to the graph above, the very same one Rocky and Karen
did use in 1981. The column to the left shows the current rate of interest, in this example from 8% to 17%. The column to the right
shows the discount that government treasury bills (90 day borrow-
ings by the United States government) are selling for. A government
treasury bill selling for 90% pays 10% interest. Treasury bills selling
for 87% pay 13% interest. The total is always 100, the discount plus
the interest rate always equals 100.

    Why is this the case? Because the United States government
doesn't pay interest in the same sense that you and I pay interest.
The government simply pays units of $10,000 each, every single
time. The discount indicates how much interest the buyer is receiving. Every government treasury bill check totals $10,000. If you
bought it for 87% of that value, you received 13% on your money
when paid your $10,000. If you bought it for 94% of that value,
you received 6% on your money when paid $10,000. The govern-

ment has designed its computer to pay all checks for the same sum, $10,000, and that is why interest is calculated in discounts from face value rather than a separate amount.

It was not the 87% or the 13%, or **any** of the percentages that interested Rocky and Karen. It was the collapse in price which occured on September 9th, 1981, and the subsequent advance which came along, a form of "bounce back", from September 9th to September 21st. **This was what really interested Rocky and Karen.** More than the current interest rates, more than the trend in prices, more than a hope or expectation of a recession or depression or good times on the horizon. It was the price pattern between September 9th and September 21st that made our couple so happy, and eventually so prosperous. **For in that price pattern, they could see the potential for a 1-2-3 price bottom.**

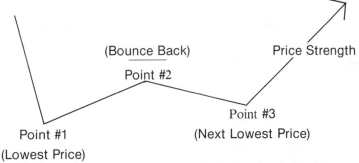

Just as there are many ways that golfers hold the club handle, so are there several distinct patterns in which prices tend to reach their peaks and valleys. One of the most distinctive and reliable is the **1-2-3 pattern.**

In this pattern, price advances to a new low (when making a bottom, to a new high if making a price top) and then rallies, the "bounce back", it then heads back down toward the new low it only recently set but fails to reach it, point #2 represents the turning point as price heads back toward point #1, and point #3 represents the level it made, never as low as the intial #1 price. **There is one rule of thumb** that Rocky and Karen knew well by this time: If the market fails to break point #1, and establishes a point #3, watch for a strong rally shortly thereafter.

It makes sense. The Dow Jones stock averages drop from 1000 to 800, rally to 900, and then drop to 825 but no lower. If 825 holds, watch for a rally above 900 and even above 1000. **The 1-2-3 points** will have been established; and they should hold.

Rocky and Karen saw the weakness of September 9th, and they saw the strength lasting until 21st. And by seeing these, they saw their **chance,** a chance for their tier two trade. How did they do it?

First Purchase	*One unit at the 85.5% level*
Second Purchase	*One unit at the 86.5% level*
Cost of the first purchase	*$2,500*
Cost of the second purchase	*0*

They bought first at the 85.5% level, right after the #3 point had been established and held firm. They didn't get the lowest purchase price, but they didn't do too badly either. In the case of treasury bills (all this will be explained in the next chapter) each 1% of discount returns $2,500 of profit or loss. If you buy a treasury bill at 85% discount and sell it at 86% discount, you make 1% or $2,500. The first unit Rocky and Karen purchased at 85.5% required a payment by them of $2,500. They then used this $2,500 equity profit to finance the purchase of the second unit at the 86.5% level. Their total out-of-pocket remained the same $2,500. But they had now advanced to tier two, and owned two units of interest rates, just as they would later advance to tier four when buying heating oil units. The first tier financed by pocket cash; the second financed by the growth in value of the first unit purchased.

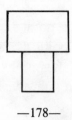

It didn't look like much, this tier two level, that is it didn't look like much to anyone except Rocky and Karen. To them, those first two tiers were higher than the Empire State Building and the Sears Tower. Their first experience with using profits from an initial purchase to finance additional units on the second tier. Their first experience and one they will always remember.

What happened to interest rates the rest of the year? Take a look back and see. Rates collapsed, the discount advanced from 85% to 90% as yields declined from a 15% rate to a 10% rate for government borrowing. How did Rocky and Karen come out **while** interest rates declined these five percentage point, a 33% decline in rates, 15% to 10%? Take a look.

One Unit purchased at	*85.5% discount*
One Unit purchased at	*86.5% discount*
All units sold at the same price	*89.0% discount*
Profit on the first unit	*3.5%*
Profit on the second unit	*2.5%*
First Unit Dollar Profit (3.5 × $2,500	*$8,750.00*
Second Unit Dollar Profit (2.5 × $2,500	*$6,250.00*
Total Gross Profit	*$15,000.00*
Initial Investment	*$2,500.00*
Additional Out-Of-Pocket Investment	*0*
Percentage Return	*600%*
Time units held	*42 days*
Annual Return	*5,214%*

It didn't look like much, tier two. Until you started to add those profits up. Then it really did end up higher then the Empire State Building, or ten Sears Towers, at least to Rocky and Karen. Their first tier two experience and a return of 600%. A world that their grandfathers never knew, their fathers wouldn't believe, and even Rocky and Karen had to work out several times before they would or could accept it.

They were learning. First, that two little tiers could work wonders. And second, that "bounce back" sometimes resulted in a **1-2-3 bottom pattern.** When you could find this, put your stop loss order under point #1 and let the market run. There might well be a great deal of profit in your future. A great deal of profit, indeed.

TIER THREE

IT WAS A LONG DRAWN OUT AFFAIR AND NOT MUCH to work with, week after week turned into month after month. There may be no never-ending events, but from July through August and all through September, the total month of October, those thirty days of November and into Christmas week, the price stayed steady. Right about 24¢ a pound, it was a long and drawn out affair.

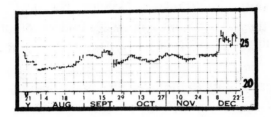

How could anyone get excited about a price of this nature, one of those major sideways price patterns.

But Rocky and Karen could hardly control themselves. They were headed toward tier three **and they knew they had a winner.** They were experienced professionals now, and they knew this one was right; they could smell victory.

It was a long drawn out affair and they took step number one, they opened the account. This was a new step number one, however, since they already had an open account with the firm they first decided to do business with. But by now they were trying out a second firm, and since it was a new firm, a fresh supply of money would be required. I forget now how much they transferred, $5,000 I think it was, perhaps $10,000. It was somewhere within those limits, I am sure of that. Step one and step two complete, open the account and transfer in the money.

Step three involved what product to buy, and they knew that immediately, it would be the product on the above graph, no hesitation here, they had their reasons. What month to buy, step number four? They selected October, the October of the following year, months away. It was already a long affair and they expected it to be even longer, so they decided, "October it shall be", about twelve months away. The price to pay was rather easy to settle upon, "about 25¢", since that seemed to be the only level price was trading at, 24¢ to 23¢ to 25¢. They were willing to pay 25¢ **and this should have been our first clue.** No one pays the highest price in five months for a product without reason. Certainly not any knowledgeable person. But they were willing to pay 25¢ and we should have been suspicious. **That was the first tip to the tier three trade.**

How many units to buy was their sixth item on the checklist and, once again, they would start with one. One unit at 25¢, it all seemed so easy. Pay the highest price in five months and buy a single unit. Ask any passing pedestrian on the street what the outcome of such a venture would be and assure yourself of a smirk and not much more. But Rocky and Karen weren't smirking, they were smiling, and about two inches of the leading edge of their chairs was being used to sustain their weight. They were, quite literally, on the edge of their seats. **Tier three.**

What did it cost them to buy at 25¢ this single unit? It was only $600, about the same price as a moderately priced television today. $600 was all they paid, although they must have had at least $6,000 in their account. This didn't mean they actually spent $600 to buy the unit; in fact the unit cost them **nothing.** But they did have to put up $600 "margin money" to show that if the buying and the selling of the unit eventually resulted in a loss, they would make good that loss. $600 was insurance money, insurance for the firm that for each unit purchased, at least $600 was set aside as a reserve for disaster. If no loss ever came, if no disaster ever hit, none of the $600 would be even touched and all would be returned, still dusty.

The actual unit order, step number eight, was again forward and simple:

"Buy one unit for us at 25¢ a pound"

If any mixup ever occurred due to this order, insanity had to be the only excuse. And no mixup ever did occur. How much risk of loss were they willing to assume on this $600 investment? They selected 19¢ as a very good level to place their "stop loss" order. 19¢ hadn't been reached for some time, at least not in the past five months, so a stop loss order resting down there should be rather safe. "Buy at 25¢ and sell if the price ever drops to 19¢." Their order, step number eight, was complete, and their stop loss, step number nine, was also entered. And how much would they lose if the price ever dropped to 19¢? Clearly they would lose 6¢ a pound, and if their unit only contained one pound, the total loss would be the same, 6¢. But their unit contained 30,000 pounds, not one. If the market ever dropped 6¢, they would lose $1,800. **Why are these people smiling?** They are buying a "dead dog" of a price, one that isn't going anywhere, or at least hadn't gone anywhere for five months, they are paying the highest price possible in those five months, and they are risking $1,800 on a $600 investment. Why are these people **smiling?**

Step number ten, deciding when all this should happen. The answer came quickly, "as soon as possible," buy at 25¢ as soon as you are able, and once the unit has been purchased, put the stop loss at 19¢. "Quickly, please", was the request, though why the big hurry one would have to wonder, especially upon examining the graph. Why the big hurry, anyway, **and** why all the smiling?

The exit order, ah yes, when to get out. They are going to buy at 25¢, each 1¢ means a profit or loss of $300 on their $600 investment (.01¢ times 30,000 pounds equals $300.00 per 1¢). If they sell at 26¢, not counting any commission they will make a $300 profit, or a 50% return on their $600 investment. If they sell at 27¢ they will make a 100% profit on the $600 investment. At 28¢ they will make $900 on their $600 capital; should they sell at 28¢?

Rocky and Karen aren't yet worried about selling. They are more concerned with **buying.** They ignore checklist item number eleven for the moment, and move to checklist item number twelve. The tier system. It is the tiers they are interested in now, really interested.

"An observation learned from successful trading on paper. The longer price stays within a sideways pattern, the greater the price advance or decline will be when it emerges from that sideways pattern. Watch this type of market. Whichever direction price emerges from its long period of inactivity will indicate the future direction of the price momentum.

The long drawn out affair was simply spring loaded and ready to explode. They had learned, these two, from that period of "on paper" watching, waiting, and succeeding. They had learned a great deal. And now, on Decmeber 11th, price gave them the **clue** they had been waiting for. Five months of sideways price pattern and then an advance on the **upside!** It meant only one thing. There would be a major price move and that move would be **upward!** Rocky and Karen were happy to pay the highest price in five months, they were thrilled, for this meant that price had broken out of its cocoon. The butterfly was about to emerge. Now it was time to plan. To plan for the tier three opportunity. This time they were moving one more step up on the ladder of success. This time, while not going for the big banana, they were sure going to take a nice bite out of a medium sized one. It would be tier three, and Rocky and Karen were on board. Meanwhile, most other market observers quietly rested and, when asked, could only comment on that "long drawn out affair." "It looks like it will never end." That is what it looked like, but not what was about to happen.

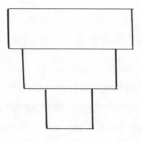

Rocky and Karen decided to buy their first unit at the five month high price of 25¢ a pound. When the price rose to 27¢, they would have a $600 profit. They would use that profit to finance a second unit. With two units now in ownership, they would realize an additional $1,200 profit with price rising another two cents (2¢ times 30,000 pounds equals $600 times two units owned equals $1,200). They would then use this additional profit to purchase two more units at the 29¢ level. By the time price reached 29¢, Rocky and Karen would have the following ownership of units.

One unit purchased with $600 at	25¢
One unit purchased with equity at	27¢
Two units purchased with equity at	29¢

The out of pocket investment would be only $600. The profits from the first unit would finance the next. The profits from the first and the next, would finance the third and fourth. No additional money would be added. By the time price reached 29¢, they would own four units, 120,000 pounds, and their total investment would be $600. Each time price rose 1¢ they would now make a profit of $1,200 (four units times $300 per unit per one cent). Each time the price rose a single penny, the return would be 200% of initial capital. The same return earned in twenty years with a bank.

And so we must return to checklist item number eleven, the price to sell. At what level did Rocky and Karen decide to sell? They never told me, they didn't have to. This was their private business now, they were learning, making decisions on their own, evaluating opportunities on their own, and whatever the results, they could keep the bottom line secret. In simple language, it was not my busines how much they profited, it was their own business. But that wouldn't keep me from *guessing*. Their average price was exactly 27.5¢ a pound. They owned four units. Each 1¢ price advance would return a profit to them of $1,200. At 30¢ they would have a profit of $15,000. At 50¢ they would have a profit of $27,000. Their investment remained the same, *$600*. Where do I think they got out? I can't say for sure, but my guess is at 52.5¢. The date of August 17th sticks in my head. Karen always called that her "third tier anniversary", and so 52.5¢ seems reasonable. A fair price for a $600 investment.

See that little line to the right, the very last line on the graph. That, I think, is Rocky and Karen getting out of their four units at 52.5¢. Their average cost had been 27.5¢, the profit had been **25¢ exactly.** A nice round number is 25¢ and when you multiply 25¢ × $300 per 1¢ × four units you end up with $30,000.00. That is how much I think Rocky and Karen made from their $600 tier three investment, $30,000.00. They held the position from the very first advance back in December until the following August, nearly nine months. It was a **long drawn out affair,** but most of the time was spent in making them money. The total return of $30,000 equalled a percentage return of 5,000% on their money. They held the position 249 days at the longest. The annual return equalled 7,330%. A very long drawn out affair on a tier three basis which they discovered by a couple of simple observations.

Nothing lasts forever, not even sideways markets.

The longer price stays within a sideways pattern, the greater the price advance or decline will be when it emerges from that sideways pattern.

Whichever direction price emerges from its long period of inactivity will indicate the future direction of the price momentum.

Rocky and Karen weren't unhappy to buy at 25¢, they were thrilled to death. Their first tier three opportunity was emerging from its cocoon. They were learning, bit by bit, how to accumulate wealth in the 1980's and 1990's, and beyond. The formula was quite simple, really.

Take a ball, Roll it across a table. Your hand has given momentum to the ball, the amount of momentum determines how far the ball will roll before stopping. This is the most simple form of momentum.

Take a ball. Roll it down a hill. Your hand begins the momentum, but an additional force, gravity, will supply additional momentum. The ball will roll faster and faster, gaining speed until a counterforce acts against it.

Rocky and Karen were learning how to roll balls down the hill. They were looking for price momentum; and they were finding it. **and,** they were doing it with no help from anyone else. For the first time ever, they were learning how to sit on top of their **own** tier structure. They even liked the view.

SUCCESS WITHOUT END?

NOTHING LASTS FOREVER, NOT EVEN SUCCESS. Rocky and Karen didn't just learn what worked in this new field of activity, they also learned what did not work. Certainly acting on hunches, or hoping for tomorrow, or crossing one's fingers, or asking a friend were not the roads to successful wealth accumulation. Each time they stumbled, they wrote that down also. Pits in the road are as important as smooth surfaces; one must be avoided if the traveler hopes to have an easy ride on the other. Most of their mistakes had been "on paper" and that is why they started learning "without money" first. New mistakes came with "real money"; for real money always causes errors of judgment. But mistakes meant knowledge and also gradual success. They were building, our pioneers, a pathway they could trust over and over again and not unlike the Burma Shave signs of the 50's, their road was marked with pieces of advice at each turn.

Watch for "bounce back" in price patterns. It happens quite often.

Sometimes "bounce back" is followed by sharp "V" patterns in price, watch for that also.

A good 1-2-3 bottom is a nice formation to work from. Put your stop loss below point #1 and let the market run in your favor.

Long drawn out bottoms often mean long sustained profits. Watch for long periods of sideways action, and the clue to future price direction by the emergence of the butterfly from its cocoon.

Absolute lows are a good price barrier. Very few prices reach zero. The closer to zero the price is, the lesser your risk of investment.

Cash prices often work as rubber bands. If the cash price for your product is above the price you pay for your unit, it will help pull the price of your unit upward. If the cash price is below your unit price, it may act as a drag on price advance.

Sometimes correlations are important. If the price of one type of product makes a sustained advance or decline, a competitive or similar product will often follow that lead. Relate products to each other and if you miss a move in one, watch for a similar move in that product's competitor.

The line was always the same, the only constant feature in their consideration. And that line had only three alternatives to pursue, advance momentum, sideways momentum, or downward momentum. There were no other alternatives.

Rocky and Karen were gradually learning to live with their new friend the line, to learn its habits and personality. To watch it grow upward, shrink downward, remain immobile. And then, with great excitement and anticipation, try to make a professional judgment which direction would be next. Of the three alternatives, certainly a person should be able to pick a winning decision now and then.

And if you could learn to do just that, pick the winning direction now and then, and use the momentum of the line to maximize your profits, the rewards were well worth the challenge. Well worth it.

Rocky and Karen told me so.

"Make a little from a lot," they said.

The secret of wealth accumulation.

There are other price formations that are useful to know about, like the 1-2-3 bottoms, the "V" patterns, the "bounce back" phenomenon, the long-drawn-out affairs. In addition, Rocky and Karen sometimes sell markets at high levels and buy back units at lower levels with the selling preceeding the buying. This technique is known as "selling short" and is as simple as buying a unit and waiting for a price to rise. With a short sale, you simply sell a unit and wait for a price decline, when you wish to complete your buy-sell transaction by buying the unit you sold at a lower level. It sounds complicated, but that does not make it so.

If you would like a **complete list** of the techniques used in this field, as well as some of the other formations you should be aware of, you can write me personally at the following address for **free information.**

Bruce Gould
Post Office Box 16
Seattle, WA 98111

Ask for Free Packet "A"

(Please enclose a self-addressed stamped envelope with your request with one current first class postage stamp and I will be happy to send you this complete list of trading techniques.)

Chapter Ten

ROCKY AND KAREN BECKET OWN **MANY** BUSI-nesses, they are the success story of their neighborhood. Businessman and business woman. Businesses that annually net the Beckets a sum equivalent to the amount they netted from their nursery in the **ten** previous years. Even in the midst of a recession. Even during double-digit inflation. Even during a period of more business failures than in any time since the Great Depression. Even during a year where Exxon recorded a 50% drop in profits; the Becket's home heating oil business recorded a 3,000% profit. They are competent business people. They have learned their businesses by experience, planning, education, study, practice, and hard work. They are getting **better** at the operation of their businesses. They are becoming more sophisticated in their use of Momentum to make their businesses grow. They are small businesspeople; they limit their businesses to the height of five tiers, one stacked atop another, each formed by the force of the one before it. They are accumulating wealth, in an era when survival and preservation are the money watch words.

Rocky and Karen Becket have worked to give themselves a future of unimaginable brilliance. This did not come about from luck or accident. One of the fringe benefits offered by these new businesses is the growth of knowledge; and how Rocky and Karen learned, and continued to learn, daily. Luck or accident played no role in their success story.

One thing Rocky and Karen learned early in their new business career was to keep an on-going journal of their investment decisions; the results, the methods, the nuggets of information that came along, the hard lessons and the milk-run trades, pieces of advice, warnings to themselves, businesses not entered and the reasons **why** they didn't enter, businesses entered and the reasons **why** they should have stayed out, successful techniques, Rules, broken-Rules; they added to the gamut of knowledge with every trade.

Let's look again at Rocky and Karen's plan for the home heating oil business:

STEP NUMBER ONE: *(Tier 1)*	*Buy 1 unit of home heating oil at 70¢ per gallon. Cost for that unit will be $1,500. Put a stop loss order at 59¢ per gallon, risk $4,620.00*
STEP NUMBER TWO: *(Tier 2)*	*If the price drops to 59¢, get out and take the $4,620.00 loss and look for another business to enter at another time, if you have some money left.*
	If the price does not drop to 59¢, but in fact rises to 74¢, use the 4¢ increase in value of the first unit to buy a second unit of home heating oil at 74¢ per gallon. Total ownership will now be two units, one purchased at 70¢ with out-of-pocket money and one purchased at 74¢ with increased value money. Average price will be 72¢ per gallon at tier 2.

STEP NUMBER THREE: (Tier 3)	If the price advance continues and prices move up another 4¢, use the increased value of the two units to buy two additional units at the price of 78¢.

To calculate the increase in equity value of the previous units consider that you owned 2 units at the 74¢ level, when prices have moved to 78¢ you have 4¢ additional profits on those two units. For the actual figures multiply 4¢ × $420 per 1¢ × the two units owned for a total of $3,360. You can use $3,000 of this $3,360 equity increase to finance the two additional units at $1,500 each at the 78¢ level.

You now own four units. One with out-of-pocket money at 70¢, one with equity value increase at 74¢, and two with equity value increase at 78¢. Your average cost has risen to 75¢. The present price is 78¢. You have an average profit of 3¢ at the 78¢ level.

STEP NUMBER FOUR: (Tier 4)	If the price continues moving upward and advances to the 82¢ level, use this additional 4¢ increase in value to finance the purchase of additional units.

An additional 4¢ price advance will yield an increase in value of $6,720.00 (To calculate this multiply a 4¢ price advance × four units owned × $420 per 1¢ price increase to get $6,720.00).

Since each unit costs $1,500, you can use

$6,000 of this $6,720 increased value to buy four additional units at the 82¢ level.

You now own eight units: One unit purchased for out-of-pocket cash at 70¢. One unit bought with value increase and no out-of-pocket cash at 74¢. Two units bought with value increase and no out-of-pocket cash at 78¢. Finally, four units bought with value increase and no out-of-pocket cash at 82¢. Your average cost is now 78.5¢ per unit. At the current level of 82¢, you have a 3.5¢ profit on the average.

STEP NUMBER FIVE: *Sit and wait and decide, plan, consider and debate when to sell your units. This is a tier 4 trade so you do not advance your tier structure beyond the 4th level.*

In addition, along the way you have raised your stop loss on the positions owned, so as you have added units you have reduced risk by moving your stop loss upward with each new unit purchased, the precise amount will vary from businessman to businessman.

Now it is time to sit and wait. To see what happens to price and decide when to sell, if your stop loss is not hit.

These are simple mechanical steps, much as outlined in the last chapter. Yet a great deal of acquired knowledge is behind these decisions, beginning, almost too obviously, with Rocky and his ice-bound football game. Rocky concluded, from watching that game, that there would be a winter in the year 1983. If you think that is an

—194—

obvious conclusion, keep in mind that many businesses, large and small, have failed for lack of even that degree of deductive reasoning. I live in Washington State, home of Mt. St. Helens. When that beautiful volcano blew in May of 1980, it blanketed much of the Western United States under several inches of ash. Some months later I visited one of the small towns near the mountain, and saw that the entrepreneurs had been hard at work: inside a general store were little canisters of volcanic ash for sale at a dollar a vial. I had read in the papers that these entrepreneurs were very bitter, because their souvenirs were selling so badly. Why, they wondered? I understood why immediately, when I parked my car in the store parking lot; it was surrounded by a six-foot high pile of shoveled volcanic ash. No one would pay $1 for an ounce when fifty pounds are free.

Always begin with simple and obvious facts. They give you something to think about, and quite often the extra edge you need in business.

Such as the price of home heating oil. Rocky and Karen didn't know much about the price of home heating oil. They knew something about the price of gasoline though, and, since both were made from the same gooey stuff out of the ground, there would probably be a correlation between the two prices. They had heard much about the "oil glut" but gasoline prices seemed to have gone about as low as the oil companies were going to allow them to go, if indeed the oil companies had anything to do with that: Rocky and Karen had a sneaking suspicion that they might.

The winter of 1983 versus fairly low prices. Two pieces of information. Enough to justify studying the business of home heating oil.

With that study came a subtle change in Rocky and Karen. They became more cosmopolitan; somewhat sophisticated and worldly. Now when they read the *Sacramento Bee* they read **all** of the long story speculating on whether the OPEC oil cartel was going to freeze, raise, or lower prices. It all started to make a difference. When they watched the CBS Evening News, a report on a war in the Middle-East and its effect on routes of distribution could launch Rocky and Karen into a discussion that could last all night. The news that Norway had drilled a new gas and oil line off their barren coastline but came up empty-handed may have been buried in a one-inch story on page 56 of the newspaper, but Karen managed to find it and think about it. They were **into** the news; they cared about events. They read more, listened better, and watched closer. And the same had happened with every business they entered. They became worldly. It was good for business, and it was good for them.

Yet with all this information, Rocky and Karen couldn't tell you exactly why they entered the home heating oil at 70¢ a gallon. They could say, "it seemed about right." A vague answer, yet accurate. By reading, listening, watching, and applying what they learned to a large picture of home heating oil, they got a sense of what would be right. It was a trapeze artist deciding the exact moment he should launch himself in order to spin three times through the air and be caught by his partner. He has no clock, no whistle; he is merely imbued with the rhythms of his craft, and can stake his life on those unvoiced and barely understood rhythms.

And Rocky and Karen could apply their unvoiced knowledge to something they were becoming very familiar with; a line. Moving across paper. Moving up, or down, or sideways, but always moving. A thousand factoids of information, but a line that could only move in one of three directions. It seemed so simple; at its essence. Rocky and Karen, in every new business, learned more about what can be done with that line. They themselves couldn't alter the direction of the line; only the world could do that; the laws of supply and demand alone could move that line. They could influence their own units by buying or selling more, but that would not affect the line. **The line is independent;** it is available to everyone; black, white, young, old, rich, poor, educated or uneducated, but it will answer to no one. **It** is the thing; **you** must adapt to its movements as it crosses the page. It will **never** adapt itself to your needs.

But learn to adapt to it and you can do things with it. Such as buy at a low point and sell at a high point. The oldest rule in the book. But it only works if the line begins at a low point and moves to a high point. You have to let the line run. Yet traditional investors often refuse to acknowledge this. They insist that there is a **right** price for everything, and that a different price is treason. And they lose, and lose badly. They study the balance sheets of corporations and determine, for themselves, what the proper stock price should be for that corporation. When the "proper" price is reached, they buy. If the price falls below that patriotic price, they sell, disgusted, and wait for the proper price to return, when the shares would be worth what they are supposed to be worth. And they never notice that they are buying a line high and selling a line low.

Rocky and Karen know that there is only one right price for anything; the price established by the line. Simply by accepting that, they can risk $4,000 in their business in exchange for riding the line to $45,000.

This meant that if Rocky and Karen were successful one time out of ten, they would at least break even. In laying out their 4 tier plan, they projected that if the line went in their favor, if everything fell into place with a resonant clink, then their reward to risk ratio was ten to one. If they succeeded they would make ten times as much as if they lost. They only needed the line to go in their favor one time out of ten. And they did not need the line to go forever in their favor, just long enough to build tiers, just as long as the line stayed true and did not dip and take them out of business. One time out of ten. Yet, if a line can only move in three directions, and if one of those directions is meaningless in regards to profit or loss (sideways), then the odds of randomly selecting the future direction of a line is 50/50. That's random; Rocky and Karen do not select the future direction of their business lines randomly. They begin their investment with an understanding that the line should move in their favor half the time, and they study to increase those odds to 55/45, 60/40, or even 75/25. 50/50 odds versus 1/10 risk-return ratio. Because Momentum makes such returns possible, Rocky and Karen had room for failure. Not many businesses would give them that room, not even their nursery. I am not familiar with many businesses that could operate their financial cash flow on a 10% profit ratio; one sale out of ten being profitable. Even the hapless New York Mets of 1962, the team on the very bottom of all league standings, won 25% of their games.

Rocky and Karen were not gamblers by nature. They did not lose 90% of the time. They did not select businesses randomly; they had no craving for action, for being in business for the sake of being in business. They wanted winners; they wanted to approach each new business with 99% certainty of the line going their way. They did not win 99% of the time, but that's the way they approached each new opportunity. They did not expect the line to adapt itself to their needs, so they adapted themselves to the opportunities of the line.

There were really only **three keys** to Rocky and Karen's approach to the independent line, to make the most of their world of potential profit.

1. Equity Financing

2. Momentum

3. MOMENTUM

One was **equity financing**. Another was **momentum**. We have dealt with these in some detail; there is no diluting their importance. Without either of these, they were dead in the water. If equity financing and momentum did not exist in this new world they were entering, they would have no new world to enter; Momentum would still be available, for those of you who wanted to open a **McDonald's** restaurant, but the dearest opportunity of passive investment in momentum would be gone. It is equity and momentum that are responsible for Rocky and Karen's success, for they not only produce massive returns, but also make possible the 10% - 90% success-failure ratio that gives the room to learn.

There is simply no other industry which allows you to use equity financing the way this new world of opportunity does. If you are making payments on a house, you've been assured that you are slowly but surely "building your equity," primarily by paying the principle. And if the value of your home was to rise from $80,000 to $92,500 — on paper only, because you haven't sold it — you would have additional equity. But if you wanted to use this additional $12,500 of increased value to buy a second home, could you do so? Yes. But you would have to visit a banker, mortgage or finance company, take out a new loan, a second mortgage, deed of trust, or note, sign some papers, and start making payments. You could not pick up the phone and say, "Mr. Harry Butcher, I saw in the paper that homes in Modesto are up 15% this year. That means my house is worth another $12,500, so please buy me another house, using this increased value as the down payment, or, better yet, send me a check for $12,500 and I will decide what to do with it myself." Impossible.

All you would hear from Mr. Harry Butcher at the other end of the line would be the stunned and uneven breathing of a banker, or perhaps disbelief. He would be unable to understand what you are saying; you might as well speak in Urdu or Aramaic.

Yet in the futures unit business this situation is not only possible, but **it is the very heart of the industry.** If the value of your units rise you may either use that value to buy more units or ask the firm you are doing business with to immediately mail you a **check** for that increase, even though you have not yet sold and realized the increase. Paper profits are buying power; or check withdrawal power;

we've seen how Rocky and Karen use this increase in value to buy a second unit, and then two more, and finally four more. We never saw them bypass additional units and ask for a check in the mail; but they did that too, many times. By using this buying power, Rocky and Karen never put up more that $1,500 out-of-pocket cash when they got into the home heating oil business, yet they eventually controlled eight units, **each** requiring $1,500 of capital, or a total investment of $12,000.

How did they do it? As we say, by a single phone call to the firm where they did business, asking them to apply the rising value of previously purchased units to purchase more units. There simply is no other business in the world where this can be accomplished so quickly and so easily. It is **true** equity financing. Realtors often talk glibly about equity financing, but they don't really know what the term means. They are talking about supplication before a banker, assumption of new mortgages, deeds of trust or notes, signing more papers, waiting for credit reports, making payments, and that whole lengthy procedure. Somewhere in the process is lost the concept of increased value, the equity. But in the world of futures units, that increase is as good as cash, and may be taken as cash, with no credit checks, new notes or payments. After all it is **your** money.

The key to equity financing is **momentum**. Simply put; there is no equity financing without momentum. **The movement of the line is the key to success. The movement of the line returns all profits, not the actual units themselves;** it was not the nature of home heating oil that produced an elegant return, it was the line. It was entering the line with one unit at a relatively low level and selling out when the line reached a higher level; within that movement of the line was the opportunity to enter with one unit and sell out with eight.

Rocky and Karen could have been content to buy at 70¢ a gallon and sell at 92¢ a gallon: a 22¢ profit or $9,240.00. It would have been a nice profit, quite respectable, but Rocky and Karen weren't so easily satisfied. Why? Because they wanted that ten-to-one risk-return ratio. If they risked $4,000 and made $9,000, they would only have a 2¼ to 1 ratio, not the edge they liked. As I've said, they wanted a 99% expectation of the price going their way, but they liked to be backed up by the ten-to-one ratio **assurance** that they could fail 90% of the time and still make a profit.

Much of success comes from an ability to fail; Rocky and Karen wanted the right to be dead wrong 90% of the time. As far as they were concerned, they wanted the odds stacked heavily in their favor. The combination of **Momentum** and equity financing were the strop for this edge. They could take the momentum of the line from 70¢ to 92¢ and turn that 22¢ price rise into $1.08 of total return, with the dynamics inherent in a line and the financing inherent in futures.

By using **Momentum,** Rocky and Karen were able to take $1.08 out of a 22¢ price move, and earn themselves a three thousand percent profit, all the while assured that they only needed to be winners in 10% of their businesses to net a profit at the end.

Equity financing, momentum, and **Momentum** are the mechanical forces of this new futures business; they enable the businessman or woman to use a methodic and scientific approach to the geometric expansion of holding upon a simple rise in price, and enable them to do so with a minimal capital base, in accordance with sound business principles and practices. When dealing with the line and the numbers, they are the whole story. But there is another key to the futures unit business, operating around the periphery, one of the variables and intangibles. **Wealth accumulation means knowledge accumulation**. Line and movement are the essentials, but the odds toward success increase with knowledge; sophistication born of study and experience. The line can be viewed as simply a line, going up, down, or sideways, and for the purposes of applying **Momentum** that is all that is necessary. But for the business of investing, a knowledge of the individual businesses and their individual characteristics can refine the application of **Momentum and vastly improve the chances of success, far above the 10% success rate needed. A knowledge of the futures unit businesses helps the trader know when, where, and why momentum may occur, helps him determine the odds for success in a field, and helps him judge to what degree he can apply this knowledge.**

There are **nine** fields of business you can enter in this new world. Of these nine, it is likely that you **already** have expertise in several, businesses in which you have knowledge now of the essentials involved in supply and demand calculations, and in price structure. Your knowledge need not be an overwhelming expertise; Rocky and Karen began their home heating oil business on an assumption that a looming winter would drive the price up. Their focused research into heating oil came with their comtemplated commitment of capital, because whatever effected the price of oil would soon effect them. Rocky and Karen have been in **all nine** of these businesses, and have become acquainted with something of the elements of each. The value of this knowledge increases with each decision they make. Momentum and equity financing are the tools of success in this new world; business knowledge is the key to the sophisticated, streamlined use of those tools. In every business, the most important thing remains the **line**. Everything else is secondary. The line leads to success or failure. It cannot be altered or influenced. But the line can be understood, and should be. The ways of the world move the line, and the ways of the world affect each business in various ways. The more you know about these effects, the more likely it is that you will get your timing right, that you will swing out on your trapeze, somersault three-fold through the air, and be caught, a success.

There are nine fields of business you can enter.

The next chapter will look at them, one by one.

Somewhere among those nine, is the right business just for **you**.

Read on, my friend, read on.

Chapter Eleven

THE NINE MAJOR FIELDS OF BUSINESS ACTIVITY you can enter as a futures unit businessman or woman are:

1. The Household, Food and Clothing Business.

2. The Petroleum Business.

3. The Lumber Business.

4. The Metal Business.

5. The Farming Business.

6. The Banking Business.

7. The International Diplomacy and Finance Business.

8. The Wall Street Barony Business.

9. The Insurance Business.

Rocky and Karen Becket had engaged in all of them at one time or another. They kept one overriding concept in mind before entering each: all nine businesses could just as easily be classified as a **single business**:

1. The Momentum Business.

What mattered in each was how the line moved. Some knowledge about the businesses prepared them to see the move and to understand **why** the move was occuring, and what could be reasonably expected within that move: how much momentum was possible. There is great pride and satisfaction involved in studying a business, discovering that the price for it goes up, say, every June by 15¢ a pound, and then seeing the price go up in June by 15¢. Momentum is an art; the knowledge of the nine features unit businesses is a science.

Every time you commit capital to one of these businesses, you pick up another shard of sophistication, a bit more wisdom to apply both to that business, the next time an opportunity arises, and to all the businesses. Every time you invest capital in a different business you change uniforms, and when the investment is over, that uniform goes into the closet for future use; you never know when you may wish to be a home heating oil dealer again. Rocky and Karen have a colorful closet, indeed. It has **more** than a heating oil jacket hanging therein.

THE HOUSEHOLD, FOOD AND CLOTHING BUSINESS

STURDY CLOTHES ARE REQUIRED FOR THE HOUSEhold, food and clothing business. Sturdy boots; the white coat of a butcher. Sometimes Karen might dress in gingham, with a clean apron, while Rocky is fond of his linen suit in which he oversees the sugar plantation. Karen once worked at a restaurant while a teenager, so flipping hamburgers is right in fashion with her. They **both** know this business well.

If you wish to get into the futures unit business in the field of food, household goods and clothing, you have **ten** specialties from which to choose:

1. Beef

2. Bacon

3. Eggs

4. Potatoes

5. Sugar

6. Cooking Oil

7. Coffee

8. Cocoa

9. Orange Juice

10. Cotton

There are **currently** thriving business opportunities in each of these ten specialties within the major Household, Food and Clothing division, and it is no more difficult to enter one than it is to enter another. Take **your** pick.

I **like** this field—it is reassuring; most of us are part of it every time we go to the grocery store. We enter these businesses with some degree of expertise from the outset. That is nice. The futures value of these consumables is our best guideline for what we will one day have to pay for them at the local merchant's store in the months ahead, and what we are willing to pay the merchant will, in turn, influence the value of future units.

Rocky and Karen especially like the household, food and clothing field because it gives them the opportunity to use rising food prices as a means of profit rather than loss. A means to actually benefit by rising prices. It was a way to make the world a little more fair. If the price of beef would double in the upcoming year, Rocky and Karen would look for a 1-2-3 or long-drawn-out bottom, or another equally valid formation and then, while having to spend an extra $200 at the grocery store, might make a "little," say 1000%, to offset the rise by buying futures units.

This **is** a familiar field. Sometimes Rocky and Karen would read in the paper that coffee supplies were jeopardized by political uncertainties in South America. **Immediately** they would consider investing capital in coffee. Or, they could watch a weather forecaster on NBC news point to shivering Chicagoans spending a winter vacation in "below zero" Florida weather and find themselves studying the price graph of the line for orange juice prices and deciding whether to profit from the cold weather down South. It was a charming sensation; to sit at the breakfast table and listen to the ever-more-expensive bacon sizzling, knowing that they held six units of bacon and each time the line rose an additional 1¢, they were making an additional 50% profit. With that in mind, they **liked** rising food prices. To them the price of bacon was simply their line, a line now advancing with time. It was more momentum.

Rocky and Karen had, through their experience, learned to trade momentum successfully and with great skill. They honed that skill by accumulating guidelines and rules, all written down in neat patterns and calculations. It was in the notebooks that they kept their unpublished thoughts about "bounce-back" and "V" bottoms, their criteria for a Tier 4 trade, where and when they would set and move their stop-losses. It was also in these rule books that they set their understanding of the strengths of each of the businesses, and the idiosyncrasies they had noticed.

Generally Rocky and Karen did not trade above 1 or 2 tiers in the household, food and clothing markets, although they had been successful there with Tier 3, and Tier 4 was not out of the question. They knew both as consumers and investors in futures units that the prices of these household goods were rising over the years, but the momentum of those prices often initiated from high levels. Special circumstances—drought, hurricanes, frost, disease—could lead, and often did lead, to spectacular momentum moves in price to even higher levels. But for the most part, at least while prices were high, Rocky and Karen invested here only in their lower tier groupings. "Gradual creepingism" was the term they coined to describe the continual upward movement in price for household and food items. Rocky and Karen preferred to trade lightly, picking up a little here and there, trying to squeeze a drop out of orange juice prices, dig a little profit from potatoes, grind coffee for what it was worth. As long as prices stayed high, they were small businessmen in this field, really small. But when price reached all the way down toward the absolute zero or relative zero levels, they started cranking up their tier graph and looking for a 3 or 4 on the horizon.

In 1980, Rocky and Karen got bruised by investing in high zones, and recorded in their rule book some cautions against this in the future. It seemed a wise investment at the outset. There had been a shortage of coffee in Brazil caused by bad weather and throughout the Western world supplies were short. You may remember this shortage from the rising price of coffee at the grocery store checkout counter. But when they checked their zones and found coffee priced at a very high level—zone 1 in fact, the highest it had ever been—Rocky and Karen decided to "take a chance" on a further rise, but they would invest at the Tier 1 level only: They would buy one unit and no more, regardless of where price went. This was not a "bounce back" opportunity, or a "sideways pattern" ready to emerge from the cocoon. It was a high risk investment at a high price zone and Rocky and Karen paid the price when the market started down.

They bought their unit of coffee at $1.90 a pound; it seemed a reasonable price. It still seemed reasonable when their stop loss was hit at $1.80, it seemed reasonable, but the line told them it was not.

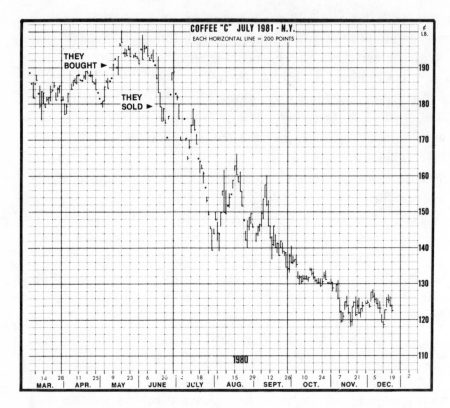

Not reasonable at all, they discovered, when price dropped to $1.20. At $1.90 they were not getting a bargain; they were buying a dog. Weather or not, coffee prices were headed down. They were glad they had only bought one unit. Quite glad.

Karen wrote it down: "When prices are at a high level, be careful. The higher a price climbs, the farther it can later fall." That was a costly lesson, the coffee investment, but worth its cost, for it has kept Rocky and Karen out of many business opportunities since then that **seemed** unstoppable. Businesses that could be entered at the very top and were expected to continue advancing "forever." That magic word which never rings true in price patterns. Every price advance comes to an end, even coffee prices; an early lesson for Rocky and Karen; the financial loss would reinforce the lesson each time they took a sip.

Household, food, and clothing businesses **can be very good for the beginning passive investor.** Momentum is clearly there and it is easy to understand "value" for these goods; we all consume them daily. Start at the one or two tier basis and, with success, consider higher levels. There is a wide range of "margin requirements," the money you will need to invest in any of these businesses, and unit sizes also fluctuate greatly. The profits or losses returned will fluctuate with the margin invested and the unit size. Margin can fluctuate from $400 to $5,000 per single unit, so the beginning businessperson can enter at whatever dollar investment is comfortable; the value of a 1¢ momentum in price can range between $375 per single unit to $1,120 per unit, depending on the unit size, allowing the investor to determine how much he would be willing to risk during his learning and growing experiences by selecting units with greater or lesser degrees of danger and profit opportunities.

How did Rocky and Karen get into this beef, bacon, eggs, potatoes, sugar, cooking oil, coffee, cocoa, orange juice, and cotton household food and clothing business? They got in precisely, and as easily, as they got into the home heating oil business. First, they learned where prices for these units could be found; in most evening newspapers across the country, in the daily *Wall Street Journal,* in every library. Then they watched prices fluctuate for a while, picked out a few favorites on the grocery and merchant store shelves and paid particular attention to them, focusing on those that seemed to be getting the most coverage on CBS news and appeared to have potential for momentum. Then they called the firm they were already doing business with and asked for some literature and information. As Rocky and Karen know, it is just as easy to be a bacon and egg man as it is to be a home heating oil wholesaler: all it takes is the single telephone call, the wherewithall to open an account, the eagerness to learn and some experience. The experience can be obtained "on paper" before any actual money is invested. In truth, it is easier to be a bacon and egg man than a home heating oil dealer. Why? Because food prices are **daily** information input into our knowledge vocabulary. Some of us never use heating oil, others only monthly, during the winter. But bacon and eggs, sugar and cooking oil, orange juice and potatoes. These we see in front of us — every single day, **especially** on Sundays.

THE PETROLEUM BUSINESS

COVERALLS, HERE. BIG BAGGY BLUE COVERALLS, with service station hash-marks on the sleeve and their names "Rocky and Karen" above the chest high pockets. These can get oily and greasy, especially for those directly involved with the business, so Karen tended to hang them away from the other work clothes in their futures unit business closet. They both loved, however, to wear the coveralls when they didn't have to worry about Mr. Dirt and Mr. Grime, especially when their business had no doors and no employees, no accounts receivable or payable. All it seemed to do, as a business, was make money. It made plenty of that.

We saw Rocky and Karen's entry into the petroleum business and the success they had with it. In two months time and a $1,500 investment, they returned with $45,000 and some sound experience. Home heating oil is one of several units of business available in the petroleum field. Another is gasoline. A third, propane.

Rocky and Karen **had** considered gasoline as a business, as an adjunct to home heating oil, but it was too explosive for them... not the gasoline, for they had no intention of opening a service station pumping gas, but the price market. Gasoline could be wild and might defy any effort they made to invest in it following the cautious business approach they think essential to success. Often gasoline prices seem to gyrate for gyrational's sake, it could make an investor uncomfortable. What looks like momentum can be momentum, but it can also be confusion. With calmness, when price settled down, they would take another look. But at the time they initially considered heating oil as an investment opportunity, gasoline was on the warpath.

Why is the price of gasoline more volatile than heating oil? They would seem to be tied hand in hand; both are refined from the same crude oil, both are fuels. The main reason, most likely, is that the price of gasoline is much more consumer sensitive than heating oil. If people need to heat their homes, they will heat them. They may be unhappy about the price, they may have to cut back on luxuries, but the house must be heated, and they must buy heating oil, at whatever price. If the price goes up or down a few cents, people won't radically alter the **way** they heat their homes or the **temperature** at which they set their thermostats. They may indeed lower the thermostate to 63° if prices for heating oil are generally high, but they won't drastically raise the overall level simply because the price drops a penny or two one week. In essence, people who must heat their homes don't care about the relatively minor fluctuations in price; it is the overall level that concerns them.

But for gasoline, motorists do watch the daily price more intently. They take it personally, quite personally. If the price of gasoline is up 5¢ a gallon, they may very well skip the trip to the country, even though they would only be paying an extra dollar per tankful. If a service station displays a price 5¢ lower than his competitors, he is likely to have land-office business, even though the 5¢ again is only one dollar savings on a twenty gallon tank. The price of gas directly influences immediate consumption. Remembering that the primary cause of price movement is the law of supply and demand, it's easy to see why the price gyrates so much. A price change of 5¢ can influence both supply and demand and can cause a decided consumer reaction. Price can go on the warpath, upward for a while, then back downward, sometimes, ever so rarely, sideways.

During these periods of time the momentum contained in the price of gasoline offers tremendous profits for units of future delivery. The difficulty involves deciding which way price momentum will go next. It can truly be a 50/50 game.

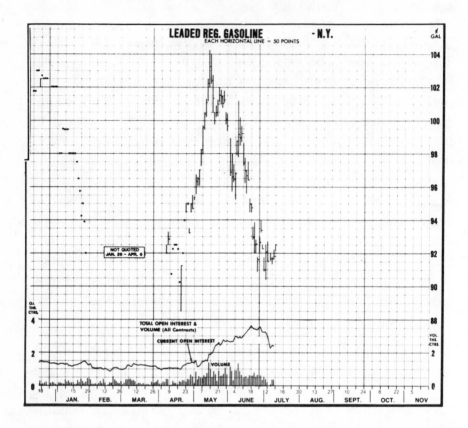

The rule that Rocky and Karen know about such wild markets is simply this: **"Avoid wild markets, or invest in them with extreme caution."** When prices settle down, establish nice zones from which to operate, then look for a reasonable investment opportunity. But when you get the sharp upward and downward moves, go back to cooking oil, or potatoes, or forward to lumber and plywood. No need to burn yourself out running on foot in the Indianapolis 500 motor car race. Look for a few slow joggers and try to give them a run for half-a-mile, let the wild markets carry on alone or with others more brave and foolish, and less knowledgeable and experienced than yourself.

—214—

Home heating oil prices and gasoline prices would seem to be twins, but twins they are not, though affected by many of the same factors. In practice, they are dissimilar. Each a separate business, and each must be judged on the nature of its own line and price momentum. The line is paramount. You may indeed own a service station; you may know the business of pumping gas inside and out. But if you can't work with a line moving across a piece of paper, that knowledge may be of more harm than good. Expertise in the units of the future is listed in terms of lines, not gallons pumped.

Should Rocky and Karen (or yourself) ever decide to get into the gasoline business, all they will have to do is pick up their phone and make the request. Each unit consists of 42,000 gallons of gas, enough to take a Volvo around the world 52 times. "Buy one unit for me at 90¢ a gallon," would be all that it takes to get into the petroleum business specializing in gasoline. But before you make that one phone call, wait for price to settle down a bit. **Wild markets are hard to trade, slow smooth movers are very easy.** Look for an easier target, especially if you are a beginner.

THE LUMBER BUSINESS

A H, THE GREAT OUTDOORS. THE SMELL OF PINE and pitch filled the closet. Karen especially liked these uniforms of business; the warm flannel plaid shirts, the worn, soft jeans, the woolen stocking caps. It was Rocky who liked the lumber boots; he was forever stomping around and seemed to be having a great time as a lumberjack. As long as he stayed outside, he and Karen made great partners in their one of many businesses, the lumber business.

Good times, bad times. This is what the price of lumber — 2 inch by 4 inch boards used for framing and wall support — looks like when the building business is thriving and housing construction high. The price of lumber and plywood advance appreciably when coupled with low interest rates for home mortgages and buyers standing in line to buy or build their first home. It is the year 1979, a year when lotteries were held simply for the right to buy a house, when condominiums were selling for $750,000 with more than one buyer bidding, and when price momentum for 2 × 4 lumber started at $180 and climbed to over $260 for one thousand board feet.

1979, remember that year, the year "BC"—before the collapse in housing starts and sales. There is a lot of history in that line you are looking at, a history of happiness—for buyers and sellers—a history that would turn to gloom when some balloon payments came due on the $750,000 condominiums, but history nonetheless.

But what happens when interest rates are at the 15-20% level, when buyers disappear like volunteers as cleanup time arrives, when

a seller is defined as someone who took a 20% cut in price and carried the contract of sale himself with no down payment? What happens to the line of price when unemployment keeps mounting as
new car sales collapse, you can have "BC" in other fields than
housing, when the lottery tickets are not for the right to buy but for
the chance to own at only $100 a ticket, when houses go on sale in
pointless parade? This is what happens to the line of price:

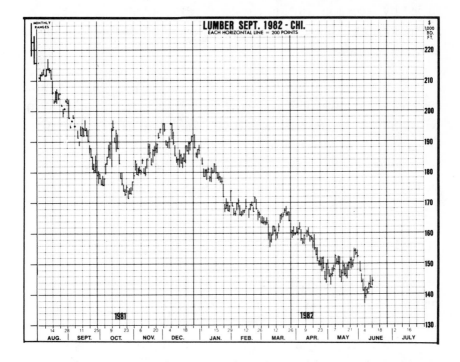

Does one look bright and cheerful and the other look dire and
forlorn? One prosperity, the other doom? Sure. But these two
charts have very much in common, despite the profiles you immediately detect. If you asked Rocky or Karen what these two
charts show, they would answer that **they are both the same thing:** a
picture of lines. One simply shows a line moving from the top of a
sheet of graph paper to the bottom; the other shows a line moving
from the bottom of a sheet of graph paper to the top. If you had a
third graph showing a line moving from side to side, you would

have completed the gamut of what line on graph paper can do. The charts are identical, not only to each other, but to **all** the charts you have seen in this book.

You may apply meaning to them. You can look at the top of the charts and see the word "lumber" and the years "1979" and "1982" and believe you are looking at the housing boom of the late 70's, pressured by inflation, and the housing bust of the early 80's, fueled by recession. But, in truth, you are looking at neither. You are looking at two lines and nothing more. The reality of the line is always paramount.

Take the name "lumber" off the top of the page and substitute "coffee" and few would know the difference. Many great words of wisdom could be spoken about the coffee collapse of 1982, until the speaker realized he was looking at a doctored graph. Coffee actually went up in 1982. Start with the line, then work forward to the business. In this case, the lumber business, Rocky in his boots and Karen with her woolen stocking cap.

There are two fields in the lumber industry you can consider for investment opportunity: raw 2×4 lumber and sheets of plywood. When considering the investment of your capital, you may wish to dwell on whether boom times for building are around the corner, or whether a slump, continued or greater, is on the horizon. Interest rates, housing starts, unemployment, tight credit all affect the price of timber. Start with the zones. Are prices **currently** high or low, based on the past few years of history? The higher the price, the less the risk you may wish to take; while the lower the price, the more eager you may be to take a 2 or 3 or even 4 tier trade.

There is one special consideration worth thought when you debate entering the lumber business for investment purposes: the laws of supply and demand can be bent a little by the laws known as the closing of plants and lumber mills. The supply could be ample:

Whole forests uncut, lots of trees, willing lumbermen and chain saws. But if the owners of the mills shut them down and no trees are being sawed, you can have rising prices even with an abundant supply. The mill owners, with their ability to close plants, can directly influence price. Not in an evil fashion — no mill owner makes much with his mill closed — but in an economic fashion. It makes no sense to cut lumber if there are no buyers, and mill owners reached that title by having good economic sense.

You can get into the lumber and plywood unit business for about $1,500 (it may vary, firm to firm). A unit of lumber consists of 130,000 board feet, each $1 price rise per 1,000 board feet returns $130 in profit to the owner of a unit. The unit of plywood could be 76,032 square feet or 150,000 square feet, depending on which exchange you do business. The return per $1 of price change would vary accordingly. To get into the lumber or plywood business as an investment, take the twelve steps that **Rocky and Karen took** and which should be pretty familiar to you by now.

One of the main reasons for starting your futures unit experience in this field may be your own specialized knowledge. You may know something about housing starts, or about the price of lumber and plywood, or about interest rates and home mortgages. You may be personally interested in lumber prices because you are building or plan to build a new home and fear rising lumber prices. You may wish to offset rising costs by owning one or two units of lumber for future delivery. A skillful investor, one who spent the time "on paper" at the tier 1 and 2 and 3 levels, might not only offset the cost of buying lumber through his futures units, but also make enough to build the **whole** house — carpets, bathtub and kitchen sink thrown in.

Lumber may be **your** starting point, **but always remember that it is the line you are investing your money on.** Watch that line closely, and make your decisions accordingly. Lumber will **never** make you a profit by itself unless the line moves from the bottom of the page to the top of the page, and you bought near the bottom. If you are a buyer, it is the line that must go up. If it doesn't, lumber won't make you a penny. A nice business to begin "on paper" experience with. Give it a try for a few weeks, months, years. Learn to profit by trading the lumber line "on paper" with no actual money invested. If you can successfully handle that, one day the momentum of that lumber line may build your house for you, your new eight bedroom home. All it will take is for the line to move upward, and for you to have a few tiers of units under ownership. Not much, really, and a nice place for you to begin; "on paper."

THE METALS BUSINESS

K AREN LIKED THE PANNING FOR GOLD MOST; Rocky was into spelunking and looking for precious metals. During the hottest days of the summer it was cool in those mines. Rocky loved them. Wherever they found it was unimportant. They both liked the metals business, the lure of gold would drive them on. And platinum, silver or other metals would make the search interesting along the way. They never stopped looking.

This chapter cannot bypass one of the saddest stories of mining history; Boyd Hawley and his two and a half million dollar loss in the rich metals. We might like to skip past that part, but fairness drives us on. The story must be told, of the investor and his 2.5 million dollar loss. **It is a story of tragedy.**

Boyd Hawley was a classmate of mine and today he is a practicing optometrist in a small Arizona town. In the late 1970's he made one of the most brilliant business decisions of his or anyone else's lifetime, yet his decision would cost him millions. Not many optometrists can afford to lose millions, and Boyd counted himself among that fraternity. He couldn't afford the loss either.

How had it all begun? The decision itself was not an average, dull, run-of-the-mill business decision. It was an outstanding decision. I mean a star, a supernova, a grand slam home run. Brilliant, well thought out, well executed, a business decision in which everything was done right, and in which only tiny flaws could be found. But a very sad story.

In January Boyd opened his metals business. He opened it with tier 1, the purchase of a unit of silver, a very small step. Why did he take the first step? There were many factors which entered into his decision to buy: the high price of gold, and when silver idled as gold soared, watch for silver to soon follow. The economy was starting to show renewed strength. Inflation was high, which meant normal price barriers were becoming ineffective. The photographic industry had a desperate and continual need for scarce silver. With such pressures soaring against supply, with demand now at record levels, Boyd believed (correctly it turned out) that the price of silver at $6.50 an ounce seemed reasonable, even absurdly low. Silver seemed like the perfect unit to buy. It seemed too good an opportunity to pass by. "No way to lose," situation.

When one examines zones, however, $6.50 an ounce was a very high price for silver in January of that year. The previous price history of silver had been a range from $1.25 to $6.40. The price of $6.50 was so high, in fact, that they hadn't yet had time to graph it on the monthly price charts.

And yet, I will repeat that even buying a unit at the $6.50 level, a new high price, was a brilliant decision, one without question that would be so considered at the Harvard School of Business. Our small town optometrist from Arizona was deciding something that would place him in the history books of successful and unsuccessful ventures. He had a tiger by the tail, but didn't quite realize it. He had merely reached his hand around the wall and grabbed the furry ball; never knowing that a 400 pound body was hooked to that fluff at the other end.

Did Boyd realize that silver was at the zone 1 level, its highest price ever? **He sure did**, you couldn't make a brilliant decision if you didn't know that fact. It is no accomplishment to run through a field of war mines without hitting a single one if you think you are running through a pasture of daisies. The skill is in knowing the mines are there, and still having the guts to traverse the field, and then miss. Boyd **knew** silver at $6.50 was a record high price, he missed **most** of the mines on his journey.

Rocky and Karen would never consider buying a unit in a market such as this. They might also realize that demand was high, which is what had forced price so high, but they had some strict rules against investing capital at the zone 1 high price level. Their rules said that if price was at its highest level ever, stay out, or trade in a very small unit, perhaps one divided equally among your family and 49 other friends and relatives. That way a $1,000 price move would only affect you $20, should your one-fiftieth interest ever result in a loss. Rocky and Karen began their learning process with "bounce back" markets. With price at its very peak, there was no such opportunity. Silver might one day develop such a pattern, but it had not yet done so. So they stood off, which was in its way as good a business decision as Boyd Hawley's. Knowing when not to dive into the pool of alligators is often as good a business decision as diving in and coming out whole. Rocky and Karen watched silver that year; they watched it closely, fascinated, and they traded it "on paper," learning all the while. They knew that one day they too might have enough professional experience to invest in such a market; one day they might be able to master the alligator swamp; and that thought alone was one of the rewarding facts about the business they were learning. There was a great deal of opportunity for the successful entrepreneur.

Rocky and Karen invested "on paper" and lost nothing. We know how Boyd looked when he came out of the "live swamp".

Boyd was a seasoned Momentum investor. He had bought units of silver before, many times in fact, and had done quite nicely with his silver, learning as he went. He seemed to watch the world with a silver tinge, much as Rocky and Karen would tend to see things with an oily sheen after their successful experience with the heating oil business. For Boyd old zones meant nothing. The world was changing, new zones were being formed daily in silver. The price of $6.50 was not a zone 1 level to him, it was the beginning of a major price advance. His experience told him that he could ignore many of the normal rules of Momentum investing and take a reasonable risk by buying units of silver at this level. Historically true, $6.50 was the very top of zone 1 for silver. Boyd felt that was not reflective of true value. If new zones were in the process of formation, $6.50 could be a zone 2 price, or even a zone 3, perhaps a zone 4 one day. That he couldn't and wouldn't guess. The price **was** rising, no doubt about that. Rocky and Karen had to stand off in the face of such strength. They were looking for dropping prices that might "bounce back" after a 1-2-3 bottom, or other formation. But Boyd considered the rise in silver price to be the **beginning** of the momentum, not the end. He wanted on and he wanted on quickly. And so, into the swamp of alligators he jumped. He didn't even wait until after feeding time. If there was one thing that could be said about Boyd, it was that he was eager. All his friends would remember him for his enthusiasm.

The rules said, when faced with a rising Zone 1 market, proceed with caution. Buy just one unit and wait it out. Trade prudently and with care. Go quietly, the rules said, for there may be danger ahead at these high price levels. Boyd's acumen said **Charge!** Price was not at its all-time-high level; it was at Zone ?, the bottom of a new level of zones. This price advance had simply been silver's method of opening a new door and walking into the business world in style, no longer the second cousin to gold. Boyd would trade, and he would trade **with panache.**

He told his friend Barney that he was going to trade on a tier 3 level. Barney didn't know what he was talking about, but we sure do. Most likely that is why he told Barney and not us; he didn't want any reasoned opposition. Boyd would buy one unit at tier 1, another unit at tier 2, and double that at tier 3. But he would not start with a single unit at the first tier. Silver had been very kind to him in the past. He had some money in the bank, and so, in recompense, he would increase his risk at the outset. He would buy five units to begin; doubling that to ten units at tier 2, and doubling that again to twenty units, if the price and the momentum allowed. Look out alligator swamp, here comes Boyd Hawley cannonballing off the high diving board. There is going to be a splash.

He was ever so calm when he entered his intentions in his log of activity he regularly kept. The entry for his metals business would look like this:

Tier 1 — At $6.50 an ounce buy five units of silver.

Tier 2 — At $7.50, should price ever rise to that level, use the increased value of the previous five units to *buy an additional five units. If price rises to $7.50, ten units will be owned.*

Tier 3 — *At $8.50, should price ever rise to that level, use the increased value of the previous ten units to buy an additional ten units. If price rises to $8.50, twenty units will be owned.*

Tier 4 — *Go no higher than tier 3. (Even Boyd avoided suicide).*

Each unit of silver for future delivery consists of 5,000 ounces on the exchange where Boyd transacted his business. He bought his first five units totalling 25,000 ounces late in January. They cost him $7,500, and this was the first and last out-of-pocket payment. Every 1¢ rise in price was now worth $250.00 to him, .01¢ multiplied by 25,000 ounces. Boyd saw price, however, in $1.00 increments. When the price moved $1.00, he would have an equity profit of $25,000. His first units were purchased in January. By early February, the price had advanced the one dollar, and he bought another five units using only part of his ever-increasing profit. The price then lingered briefly, bounced and sputtered, then finally moved up to the $8.50 level. He now had a profit of $75,000.00, $50,000 from the first five units and $25,000 from the second five. By calculating how much increased equity value he had to spare, Boyd was able to finance an additional ten units at the $8.50 level. Now he had his total of twenty units, each unit consisting of 5,000 ounces of silver, 100,000 ounces in total. Each subsequent one dollar rise in price would make Boyd, our optometrist from Arizona, $100,000 richer, all done in three steps, three tiers. If he sold out at $9.50, his total net would be $175,000 profit. At $10.50, the total profit would be $275,000. By holding his twenty units — not an overwhelming quantity — at the final accumulaton level of $8.50, Boyd stood poised to become a very wealthy man in the metals business, that is, **if** price continued to rise. His judgment up to this point had been absolutely flawless, if one ignored all the rules

Rocky and Karen followed. **And then it came to him,** like a flash from the sky, **ELEVEN-FIFTY-SELL.** And sell he did.

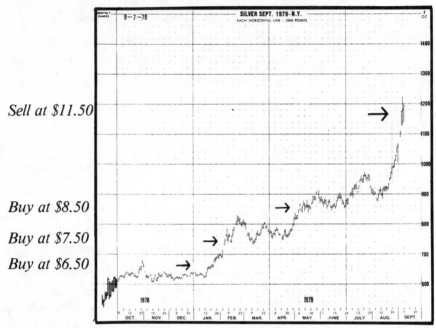

He had found that $6.50 was really not the zone 1 level, but, in fact, a low price level from which the market was working upward. The investment was very similar to the long-drawn-out affair that Rocky and Karen had invested in, and made so much money. $6.50 represented an advance out of a sideways pattern of price and the talent of Boyd was to see it as this advance rather than as a ceiling limitation. He was 100% correct, $6.50 for silver was a very low price and the market would soon soar to $7.50 and to $8.50 and finally to his selling price of $11.50.

By breaking the very rules which drove Rocky and Karen on, the optometrist from Arizona made himself a wealthy man. On September 7th, almost exactly eight months after the time he had first taken a position in silver and metals, he sold out at the $11.50 level. He had started buying in January, added more in February, and finished off his units in May. Here is the profit he made:

The units purchased at $6.50 were sold for $11.50.

The units purchased at $7.50 were sold for $11.50.

The units purchased at $8.50 were sold for $11.50.

He made $5.00 an ounce on the first five units.

He made $4.00 an ounce on the second five units.

He made $3.00 an ounce on the third ten units.

The first units purchased totalled 25,000 ounces (five units of 5,000 ounces each). He made $5.00 per ounce on that group for a total profit of $125,000.00.

The second units purchased totalled 25,000 ounces (five units of 5,000 ounces each). He made $4.00 per ounce on that group for a total profit of $100,000.00.

The third units purchased totalled 50,000 ounces (ten units of 5,000 ounces each). He made $3.00 per ounce on that group for a total profit of $150,000.00.

His total profit was $375,000.00.
He had invested $7,500.00 out-of-pocket.
All additional units were purchased by the increased value.
His return was 5,000%.
The longest he held any units was eight months.

It was a brilliant investment, a daring trade. Boyd had taken the largest risk of his investment life and had turned his $7,500 into $375,000.00 within an eight month period by advancing from tier 1 to tier 2 to tier 3. Momentum coupled with an uncanny analysis of price had returned to him pure, elegant, solid sterling silver profit.

He had read the market beautifully; $11.50 an ounce was far and away the highest silver price in history. Boyd was not one to test fate. He had been dealing with intangibles; what was the true zone of silver prices, $6.50 or $11.50? It had only fairly recently been $1.25. How much momentum could be generated out of the price of the metal silver? How long could this market be ridden? At

$11.50, his "voice from the sky" price, the optometrist netted a third of a million dollars. **Now** he had wealth to preserve, he had to be cautious. He had just made the most brilliant business decision of his life while Rocky and Karen sat on the sidelines and watched, "on paper." But I promised you a sad story. I promised you pathos. For that, we have to look further, at a couple more charts. It will break your heart. It broke mine, and it made Boyd Hawley cry.

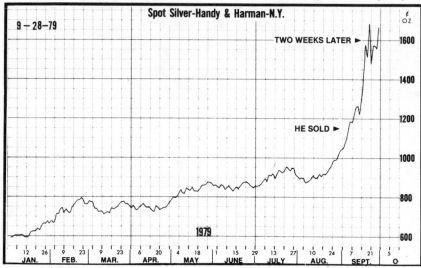

Within **two weeks** the price of silver had risen to $16.00 an ounce. Boyd's twenty units could have been sold for an additional $4.50 per ounce; an additional $450,000.00 — within **two weeks!** Within **five months** additional strength would be manifest. The price of silver units would **not** stop at $11.50. It wouldn't even stop at $16.00. It would only stop when it reached $41.00 an ounce, the highest dot you can see on the next graph.

$41.00 an ounce.

At $11.50 the twenty units owned by the Arizons optometrist were worth $375,000.00 of accumulated profit. At the price of $41.00 an ounce, they were worth $2,850,000.00 pure profit. Boyd settled for $375,000.00. Within five months he could have settled for $2,850,000.00. The "voice from the sky" was ministerpreted when it said "$11.50"; $11.50 was the price at which to **buy**, Boyd Hawley had though it meant **sell**.

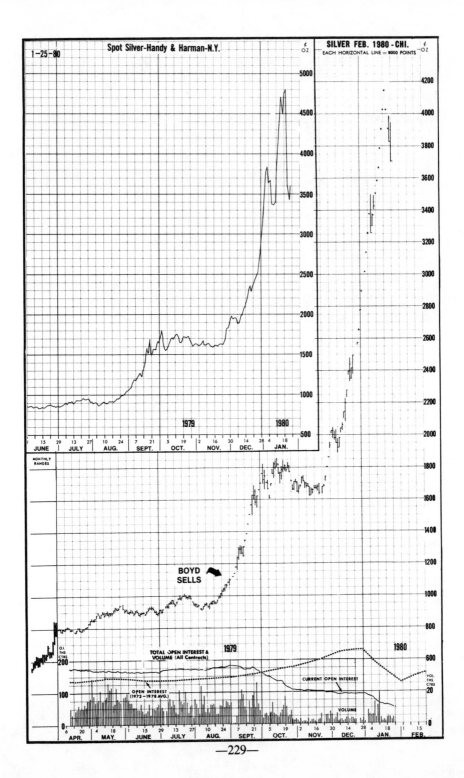

Spot Silver-Handy & Harman-N.Y.

1-25-80

SILVER FEB. 1980 - CHI.
EACH HORIZONTAL LINE = 9000 POINTS

1979   1980

BOYD
SELLS

TOTAL OPEN INTEREST &
VOLUME (All Contracts)   1979   1980

OPEN INTEREST
(1973-1978 AVG.)

CURRENT OPEN INTEREST

VOLUME

—229—

The difference was $2,475,000.00, or $20,625.00 **per day** during the next five months. Had he remained with his original twenty units, and had he sold out at $41.00 an ounce (two big "if's") the **daily return** would have been 275%, the annual return would have been 38,000%. Thirty-eight thousand percent on his initial $7,500.00 out-of-pocket capital.

Meanwhile, Rocky and Karen could only sit and watch. They were thunderstruck. The nursery business had never been anything like this. They were pioneers in a new generation, a new age, and a new tradition. They hardly dared to believe what they were now seeing. 38,000% within a twelve month period of time, from three tiers of investment. Boyd had emerged from the swamp with no parts missing, but he had crawled up on the bank much too soon. About 2.5 million too soon, in fact, just about 2.5 million dollars too soon. It was 1979, and they all watched in amazement.

The metals business is an exciting business.
It even surpasses heating oil, from time to time.

Dare we dream if for just a moment. What if Boyd had advanced to tier 4, if he had purchased another twenty units at $9.50 and held them until the end? Or, just suppose in our few moments of fantasy that he had moved on to tier 5, another forty units for a total of eighty, and then, as long as we are playing games, had held these eighty units to even the $30.00 level. What **if**; dare we dream such dreams?

A new world in which a ball of fluff around the corner really can be attached to a price tiger. Boyd used the same rules as Rocky and Karen. He simply saw $6.50 as the beginning while they saw it as the end. But the rules were the same. He traded silver in much the same fashion as they had traded their tier 3 investment. The similarities between the tier 3 trade of Rocky and Karen and the tier 3 trade of Boyd Hawley are remarkable. They started with $600, he started with $7,500; both made astronomical profits.

How does an investor avoid the problem that Boyd faced of selling out at $11.50 and watching price advance to $41.00? There is no easy answer. **One answer, however, can be given: "Let the market price run."** When you have a winner in hand, let price take you where it is taking you without trying to prejudge where the trip will end. One method is to take your stop loss order and trail it below current prices, say 5% or so, and let your stop loss eventually take you out of your investment when prices reverse that 5%. If they never do, if they keep going in your direction, then you will stay on board and watch the profits endlessly accumulate. That is nearly endlessly; even silver eventually declined 5%. All price advances one day do end. But if they can make you 2.5 million along the way, you won't mind the pause; the chance to reflect, and perhaps spend a little of your newly accumulated wealth.

There are other opportunities in the metals business besides silver. In total you can make passive investments in several precious and non-precious metals.

1. Copper

2. Gold

3. Palladium

4. Platinum

5. Silver

They all have one thing in common; they are **lines** moving across a piece of graph paper, and each line is no more difficult than another to master, once you learn the rules. New businesses in a new world, and new methods of running those businesses to accumulate wealth. You may **never** be in a position to earn a 38,000% return;

but just to know it is there is something to drive you on. Boyd sold at the beginning, not the end, of this price move. He sold at the very beginning, and he still made 5,000%. You can't make 5,000% in the nursery business, nor in the insurance business, or even in the real estate business. But buy units of silver at $6.50 and $7.50 and $8.50 and sell them at $11.50 months before the price comes to a halt, and you **will** make 5,000% profit. It is permissible. It is being done. And it is being done on a United States government regulated business exchange each and every year — sometimes every month. To enter this business **learn to master the line;** the line of whatever price you are following.

THE FARMING BUSINESS

BEFORE THEY ENTERED THE BUSINESS, ROCKY AND Karen had romanticized notions about farming. They imagined it a business of the independent farmer, with a broken down tractor, the little loyal wife raising vegetables, of husky sons doing the chores: something like the "Real McCoys" television show. They couldn't shake this notion, even though they lived in the heart of the San Joaquin Valley, the agricultural center of California, the birthplace of "Agribusiness." They couldn't shake the John Steinbeck/Willa Cather portraits of the lone, hardbitten farmer in his quaint house and his "lower 40." They thought the farming business was a matter of chores, 18 hour days of work, and little or no money. It was romantic, it was American: but it didn't sound like a lot of fun.

Especially, they had no idea as to how grain was sold; how it was merchandized. Their image of the farmer's product on the international markets was radically altered when they read Dan Morgan's book, *Merchants of Grain,* and learned the full scope of the grain business, at home and abroad.

"The five enormous companies that controlled the global grain trade. . .all had their origins in that period a century ago when the cities of Europe, and England in particular, needed foreign wheat. By 1975, the founding families of those companies had meandered about and maneuvered all over three continents, surviving wars, famines, economic crashes, and revolutions, always moving, changing countries, trading their nationalities as well as grain, forming alliances with kings, queens and communist rulers, and disengaging when historical developments required it.

Yet the companies managed to stay in the shadows most of the time. Perhaps it was the ancient nightmare of the middleman-merchant that made them all so aloof and secretive — the old fear that in moments of scarcity or famine, the people would blame them for all misfortunes, march upon their granaries, drag them into the town square, and confiscate their stocks. And they had grounds for concern. The Fribourgs of Continental were twice uprooted from their home base by German armies, in 1914 and again in 1940. The Louis-Dreyfuses saw their Black Sea assets seized in 1917. The Cargills and MacMillans, heirs of the Cargill grain dynasty, were twice at the brink of losing everything. Whatever the source of their anxiety, their secrecy was part of their means to alleviate it, part of their knack for survival. Throughout most of this century the fact of the matter has been that most Americans have never heard of the companies that distribute and sell American grain all over the world. . . . There is Cargill, Inc. of Minneapolis; the Continental Grain Company of New York City; Andre of Lausanne, Switzerland; the Louis Dreyfus Company of Paris; and the Bunge Corporation — companies that all can boast, with Cargill, that 'some of our best customers have never heard of us.'

These five companies have grown, diversified, spread their operations to almost every continent and country so successfully that by the time most Americans heard of them for the first time, during the grain sales to Russia in 1972, the firms were among the world's largest multinational corporations. Cargill and Continental probably rank as the two largest privately held companies in the United States, and Bunge may be one of the largest in the world. Cargill's annual net profits from its worldwide operations exceed those of Goodyear Tire and Rubber and its annual sales are greater than those of Sears, Roebuck. The companies have interests in banking, shipping, real estate, hotels, paint and glass manufacturing, mining, steel plants, cattle ranches, flour milling, animal feed processing, and commodity brokerage. Bunge has an estimated 50,000 employees, mainly centered in its paint, textile, food-processing, and milling plants in Argentina and Brazil, but scattered around the world too. And the companies run their own intelligence services all over the planet—private news agencies that never print a word.

Whatever romance Rocky and Karen lost when learning of the scope of Agribusiness on an international scale was regained when they considered the new romance of buying a unit of farm products and profiting from price momentum along with the farmer, the Cargills and the Continentals. With their knowledge journey farmers Walter Brennan and "Luke" became replaced by a sleek, Lord and Taylor clad, Brooks Brothers man, continental in manners; working and selling at the international level. It was not so much a matter of getting up at three A.M. to milk cows, but a matter of getting to JFK airport in time for the noon Concorde flight to Paris. They were learning.

Once they entered the world of investment tiers, Rocky and Karen discovered that there were two possible ways to accumulate wealth in the farming business. One was to be atop the corporate structure of Andre of Lausanne, the Dreyfus Company or the Bunge Corporation of Argentina. **The other was to be atop the tiers in their own unit structure, the Rocky and Karen Grain and Export Business.** Sad as their conclusion was to draw, they saw little chance for wealth accumulation for the small farmer himself, not in the face of agribusiness, not with only so many acres to work with. The average farmer was trying to make a lot from a single piece of land; and that is not how wealth builds up. The agribusiness firm made a little from huge portions of land, the little from the lot. The international exporter did the same, billions of bushels shipped abroad and each bushel putting a penny in their pockets; much like a Big Mac for Ray Kroc. Rocky and Karen decided to follow the proven route to success, momentum and the tier structure.

They had several businesses open to them. They could be wheat, corn or oat farmers with approximately $500 to $1500 in margin money. They could select rye or barley and have price moves in those farm products offer the momentum that would yield the profit. Rapeseed, a small reddish brown grain the size of a BB pellet, and grown primarily in Canada for use in oil based paints and plastics, was open to new businessmen and women. The flax-seed market was readily available, also grown primarily in Canada.

Incidentally, I once had a personal experience with flaxseed that was rather interesting. I was working in Minneapolis at the time, for the Pillsbury Flour Corporation, a huge exporter of grains and the largest buyer of wheat in the world. One one occasion, I happened to be having lunch with a banker, a black man who had grown up in the South and whose education, abilities and training had taken him to success in the land of 10,000 lakes. All of a sudden something flew into my eye, or was rubbed in, or simply myster-iously appeared. It hurt, it really did, and I was unable to rid myself of the immediate problem. This friend of mine then told me of a home remedy he had been raised with which worked quite well. Whenever he, or his brothers or sisters, would get something in their eye, their mother would ever-so-gently open the corner of the eye a bit and put a small single grain of flaxseed into it. The flaxseed would slip around within the eye socket like an eel in fresh water, it was impossible to feel or pin it down. Finally, within a moment or two, the flaxseed would have traversed a large portion of the eye and attached itself to whatever it was that caused the problem. By then removing the flax from the eye corner, both the flaxseed and the problem would be gone. My own and only experience with the grain flaxseed; a technique I tried, with success.

And then there is the unassuming miracle crop: soybeans, the high-protein legume that may eventually feed an over-populated world, available as a business in three closely related markets; for the passive investor building his tier structure within the farming sector: Soybeans, soybean meal (the ground-up end product, heavily used as livestock feed) and soybean oil (the cooking oil that was listed under the household and food section earlier). Take your pick of any of these farm products and start considering your investments. It is as easy for you to enter any of these farm businesses as it is for you to pick up your telephone. Good farm land is disappearing, but telephones are on the increase, getting into farm units won't require you to even move out of your living room chair.

Tier units of grain even offer a cheaper, easier, and often more profitable business than farming itself. By owning units, tier 1, 2, 3 or whatever, you can have the advantages of rising prices, without the drain facing the modern farmer, nor the problems: hired help, feeding livestock, drought, storms, equipment breakdowns, rising cost of farm machinery. There are historic seasonal rises and falls in price for farm products, particularly around harvest time. The farmer must live with falling prices, but you don't have to be in the unit business when prices are falling, if you learn the seasonal nature of the prices of these farm products, and learn to watch the line closely, you can simply stay out during periods of downturn. The farmer has no such luxury; he can't close down his farm for two weeks and wait for prices to rise again, the hay must be cut at haying time. You can even get into units for farm products on a tier structure for less than $5,000, often quite a bit less. Try to start operating a farm for that today: try to buy ten good acres of farm-land and discover the cost. Then discover that to make a living for your family you don't need ten acres, you need one thousand. Your $5,000 wouldn't even buy the seed, fertilizer, insecticides, equip-ment and help you would need to make a living in farming. In essence, there is no comparison. If you want to make money in farming, start with units and a tier structure. If you want to live dreams, start with a farm. But be careful about your dreams; there is not much difference between a dream and a nightmare, and many persons who returned to the land during the 70's and 80's, are giving up today. It is nearly impossible to make an honest living as a farmer, no matter how hard you try, in today's economic farm world unless you have 500+ acres, and no debt.

Back in 1972, way back then, Rocky and Karen were just be-ginning Becket's Nursery, struggling to keep their heads above water, working 16 to 18 hour days. They had never heard of units for future delivery or the tier structure at all, let alone did they know that such units were a business accessible to them. Rocky and Karen's entire idea of investment and finance was centered around faceless, amorphous shapes, clad in business suits, who they called either "Big Boys" or "Fat Cats." In 1972, Rocky and Karen had reason to be angry at the Big Boys. The price of bread was going right through the roof. Rocky and Karen were helpless against the price rises. And **why** were prices going up? Because Cargill, and Continental Grain, Andre of Lausanne, the Dreyfus Company and Bunge Corporation were selling American wheat to the Soviet Union. It was 1972, the year of the Great Grain Robbery; the year the Russians bought our wheat, and price soared.

The Soviet Union has always had a problem meeting the food requirements for their 270 million people; if they did not hold the Ukraine by force, they would have no chance for domestic food production to equal needs. The Soviets have two main problems with food supplies; the first is weather. Take a look at a map some time, the Soviet Union, a nation **larger** than the United States, China, and all of Western Europe combined, is located on this globe called earth too far North. They do not have a long enough growing season for food to emerge in quantities necessary for 270 million people to survive. The second problem is their economic system. They are racing a Mercedes Benz in a Honda Civic, or a broken down Model T, depending on how you view their economic structure. No way will they ever win the race. Real food is produced by farmers who love the land, who **do** rise at three o' clock A.M. to milk the cows, but who expect to be minimally rewarded for all their hard work. In America there is a **chance** for the farmer to make a living; at least he is his own boss, he is a free man. In the Soviet system the farmer is much like a member of the armed forces, he does what he is told and doesn't get paid much more if the crops are good. Some would say, and I would agree with them, that the Soviet system is based on slave labor, not free labor, since in the Soviet system the government is the only employer, there are no unions with bargaining power, and you work for your slave master, or you don't eat. So, the people work, but not very hard. It was once written that in the Soviet system the people pretend to work and the government pretends to pay them; and so not much ends up being accomplished by either side. That is the second reason why the Soviets don't grow enough food to feed their people. People in prison simply do not work as hard as free men with their own land; economics at kindergarten level.

To make up this shortfall of production, the Soviet Union has to buy grain abroad, normally from the United States, Australia, or Argentina. In 1972, as in each year since, they were looking and looking hard, and they were looking for a **bargain price**. And they were looking in the months of June and July.

Why these two months as the best time to buy grain at a bargain price? One word: **harvest.** Do strawberries normally sell at a lower price during summer harvest or during the winter when they have to be flown in from New Zealand or Mexico? We all know that strawberries are cheaper during harvest, and the Soviets know that grain prices are also cheaper during summer harvest; especially wheat, and the months of June and July are the cheapest months of all, in each normal year. The patterns have been well established with history.

Normal Seasonal Price Pattern	Odds of Price Being Higher or Lower than the preceeding month's price.		
WHEAT PRICES	**WHEAT PRICES**	**Higher**	**Lower**
	January	66%	29%
	February	37%	55%
	March	50%	42%
	April	39%	53%
	May	32%	61%
	June	18%	74%
	July	42%	55%
	August	45%	42%
	September	66%	26%
	October	74%	21%
	November	76%	11%
	December	84%	11%

Simply observed, through history, wheat prices normally reach their lowest level during July harvest, and start to move higher thereafter. The mathematical odds of wheat prices being higher in August than July are only 45%, nearly 50/50. But the chance of them being still higher in September than August is 66%, and the chance of wheat being higher in October than in September (which was higher than August) is 74%. Still higher yet in November is 76% and there is an 84% likelihood that price will go still higher in December, and even a 66% chance the uptrend will last until January. It is only in February that prices start working their way back down, in anticipation of a new year's July low. The moral can't be missed by even the Soviets: If you want to buy American wheat, buy it in **July!** Or better yet, buy it in **June**, when the odds are 74% that it will be lower than the previous month, the greatest percentage odds for the entire crop year.

Firsthand Report

For Russia: Stunted Crops, Stunted Hopes

Wind, drought and official bungling in a lonely corner of the Soviet Union are forcing Moscow to turn to Western countries for food.

ALMA-ATA, U.S.S.R.

All the hopes and frustrations of a grain-hungry Soviet Union are evident this summer amid the parched farmlands of remote Kazakhstan.

It is areas like this that are supposed to liberate the Communist nation from an embarrassing dependence on the United States and other nations of the West for food. But that day still is far in the future, and many formidable obstacles remain.

Russia's continued inability to produce enough grain to feed itself has become a humiliating symbol of a failed Soviet economy incapable of providing enough food for its 270 million people.

Weather woes. While Kazakhstan slowly is helping the Soviet Union turn the corner, there have been many setbacks along the way. For every good harvest, the region's extreme weather brings about several disastrous ones. Another skimpy yield, perhaps one of the poorest in years, seems to be in prospect for this year.

Forgelike heat and constant winds have dried out a broad swath of prime grain-growing territory from the Ural Mountains across the Kazakhstan steppes to Western Siberia. Torrential rains at planting time are believed to have washed out part of the spring wheat crop.

The U.S. Department of Agriculture, which monitors Soviet fields by satellite, has cut its estimate of total yield in 1982 from 185 million tons to 170 million tons. That would be 65 million tons less than the crop of 1978, the Soviet Union's biggest ever.

For their part, Soviet authorities predict normal yields. Yet they have taken the precaution of placing the headquarters of the major grain-growing area at Tselinograd off limits to foreign correspondents. And Soviet travelers in the region report a continuing lack of rain and field upon field of stunted crops, especially in the southern part of Kazakhstan.

Even the Soviet Union's national television-news program *Vremya* seems to be hinting at trouble ahead. Usually upbeat, it lately has stressed this year's unusually hot weather, as if to prepare the Soviet people for the fourth bad grain harvest in a row.

The weather is not the only problem worrying Moscow. Some of Kazakhstan's best farmers—descendants of the Germans and German-Swiss lured to Russia in the 18th century by Catherine the Great—want to pull up stakes and leave. Their departure would be a crippling blow to an agricultural system that remains short of farming know-how.

Today, these people number about 900,000 out of the Kazakh Republic's 15.3 million population. No one here can say for sure how many would depart if given the choice, but the West German Red Cross believes up to 100,000 want to leave for West Germany or Canada, where many have relatives who left in the 1920s. In addition, many Mennonites—perhaps as many as 60,000—would quit the country in the unlikely event that the emigration doors ever were opened.

There is some basis for that optimism. From a region that once produced almost nothing but dust and despair, the Soviets now get up to 20 percent of their grain, 24 percent of their wool and about 5 percent of the nation's meat, milk and eggs. It is the U.S.S.R.'s third-largest producer of coal and electricity.

Just 30 years ago, Kazakhstan was mostly desert, a vast and lonely place written off by the Moscow government as a worthless liability. Before the Russian Revolution, the region was aptly called "the land of a thousand ills," and its capital consisted of little more than an Army garrison.

And so, in June of 1972, with help from the Big Boys and the Fat Cats, the Soviets bought American wheat. They started in June and they finished in July. By the end of July, all their buying was done, and the **line** was starting up.

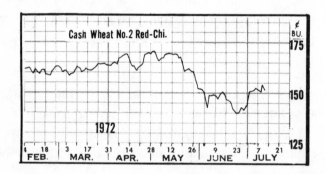

They started buying at $1.40 per bushel, during the month of June, the historical low period of the year, and they continued to buy into July, another historical low period, paying up to $1.50 a bushel. Did they get a bargain? Can a bird fly?

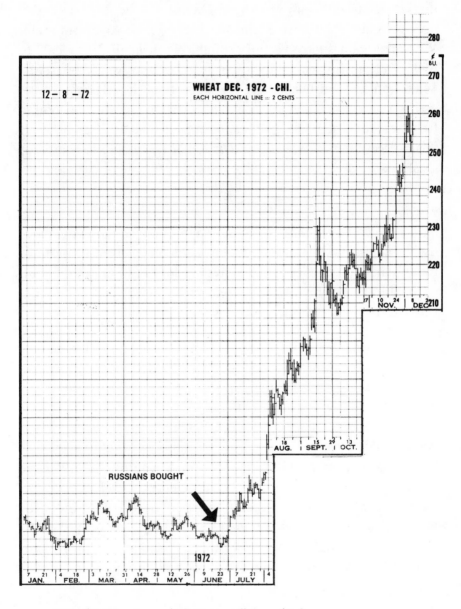

WHEAT DEC. 1972 - CHI.
EACH HORIZONTAL LINE = 2 CENTS

12-8-72

RUSSIANS BOUGHT

1972

Was $1.50 a bargain? Can a fish swim?

If you think $1.50 was a bargain in 1972, keep this in mind. Within twelve months the price would rise to $5.00 a bushel. The $2.75 peak you see on the graph paper was not the top of the market, it was only **half** way there. On average the Russians ended up paying less than 40% of the eventual price of American grain. When companies like Pillsbury sought wheat in 1972 and 1973 to mill into flour for the baking of your bread, they would be paying $4.00 and $5.00 a bushel. **At the same time**, in American ports across this country, wheat was being loaded on Russian bound freighters for which the price had been $1.40 and $1.50 a bushel. If this subject interests you, read *The Great Grain Robbery* at your local book store, the fascinating story of this very transaction.

Who were the winners besides the Soviets?

The people of the Soviet Union were winners, they were able to use the capitalist system to feed themselves for a few more months, though their government would have to return to capitalism for additional food on a regular basis thereafter. The Soviets hate capitalism, except when it comes to eating.

The farmers of America were winners. The price of farm products started an upward momentum that would return greater rewards for the farm life for many years into the future. Most farmers were winners. Those who used the high price levels to finance new machinery and new land purchases would suffer when prices started downward in the early 80's and the payments on the equipment and land could not be met. But the owe-no-debt farmer clearly came out a winner. The United States government was even a winner. It did not have to buy low priced grain from farmers and store it for sale at higher prices at a later date, or give it to a friendly third world nation. The free market was now buying the grain that our government always stood by as the buyer of last resort to purchase, and so we, as taxpayers, benefited.

There were the losers too, however, and the biggest loser of all was the United States economy. 200 million people depend on a viable economy and the double digit inflation of the 70's and 80's really began with the Soviet wheat purchases of 1972. The effect of this sale was immediate. Consumers had to pay higher prices for bread, cake, flour and all other prepared foods in their groceries. As the price of grain soared, so did the price of meat, potatoes, sugar, vegetable oil, even hot dogs. 1972 was only the first waters flooding over the dam, by the mid and late 70's, the dam was broken and disaster had struck. The inflation rush was on; and in order for our government to meet its needs and the needs of its people, more money had to be in circulation, so the printing presses started printing money like wallpaper to finance the goods and services now available only at these higher levels. The printing of money only aggravated the problem; it was the snowball rolling down the hill, each new inch increased momentum and size. There was no way the recession of the early 80's could now be avoided. One day the bottom of the valley would have to be reached, and the depression in the midwest indicated just that. The Soviet wheat sale inflation of the 70's was coming to an end, ten years later. The losers were the American people.

"We are mad as hell, and we're not going to take it anymore!" consumers shouted, without realized that their fate had already been decided, in June and July of 1972, at $1.40 and $1.50 a bushel.

There was one small group of winners I forgot to mention but you know who they were. They all wore a small patch on their sleeves and that emblem looked like this: the sign of success in a new world.

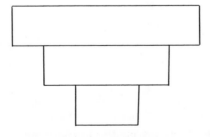

Dare to dream just a little longer. Suppose **you** had bought one unit of wheat for future delivery in 1972 for the very same reason that the Soviets did. Not because you were hungry, but simply because it was June. A period of normal seasonal low price. The Soviets didn't buy in June because their people were hungrier during that month, their people are hungry all year round. They bought in June because that is when the prices are normally the lowest, and they bought in July because prices are still low then. That is why they bought. Like Willie Sutton who robbed banks because that is where the money was located, the Soviets bought because they like bargains, and June-July offers the most of that commodity.

So dream on for a minute. You bought too, because the price was low, and you bought only two units of wheat at the $1.50 level. At the $1.60 level you used your accumulated tier profits to add two additional units, and at $1.70 you added an additional four units. At $1.70 you would have owned eight units of wheat for future delivery, exactly 40,000 bushels of wheat. Not a huge quantity by any means. But when price rose to $2.70, within a few weeks, that single dollar bill on 40,000 bushels would return you enough profit to offset all the loaves of bread you will ever buy throughout your buying lifetime. There were winners besides the Soviets, the farmers, and the United States government. You could have been one of them; that is, had you known back in 1972 what you know today.

Units of farming can be very profitable.

Very profitable.

After all, the price of every farm product is identical, absolutely identical.

The price is simply a **line** which moves up and down the sheet of graph paper. You may not know much about farming, but you are learning a great deal about the **line** business.

Take the ball, and give it a shove. . . .

THE BANKING BUSINESS

A BANKER IS A MERCHANT, JUST LIKE EVERY other merchant. His product is money and his profit is calculated in interest rates. He buys money from you or me in the form of deposits into our bank accounts. The price he pays us varies, like all prices; at 10%, he is giving us $100 for every $1,000 we give him, at greater or lesser rates, he will give us more or less for our $1,000. He is simply paying us for our money, the same money he later hopes to sell at a profit.

How does he sell our money? He sells it in the form of loans, first mortgages, second mortgages, deeds of trust, demand notes or chattel paper. For the banker, the only thing that is important is that he is able to buy and sell money and that the **spread**, the difference between the interest rates he has to pay to buy money and the interest rates he will receive when he sells the money, is sufficient to provide him a profit from his merchandising. He is just like Cargill or Continental Grain Company; they buy and sell bushels of grain, he buys and sells dollar bills. The principle of success for each is identical: make a little off a lot.

Rocky and Karen buy and sell money also. They buy money at one interest rate and they sell it at a different interest rate, and if their **spread** is great enough to provide a profit, they profit. If it is not, they break even or suffer a loss. Rocky and Karen are in the banking business, just like the man in the suit at the corner location. The main difference is that they have no overhead, no building, no employees, no heating bills to pay, and no window tellers. They are in the identical business with your friendly neighborhood banker, but they have a hundred advantages over the actual banking world as most people know it.

They did not enter the business of buying and selling money without first hand experience. Remember that Rocky and Karen are small-business people, the owners of the modest nursery and flower shop in Modesto, California. That business is their first love. But it is a business that needs money to survive, just as their trees need water. If they want inventory, they have to borrow money to pay for it, and pay the going interest rate for that money. If their customers are slow in paying, they may need to help their cash flow with a short term loan using the accounts receivable as collateral for the debt. Money is absolutely essential to them and their business, without it they would simply be working for someone else, ownership would be out of the question.

How do they do with interest rates in their nursery business? They felt they were always on the losing side; no matter what they are paid in interest for their bankbook, 90 day, 1 year, tax free or other accounts, they always had to pay a little more for their loans. That little more was the spread on which their banker made his living, it had to be there, for, like the potato bug, the banker only appears when opportunity presents itself. All Rocky and Karen could do was live on hope, a hope that rates would decline. But if this were to happen, then the rates of interest they were paid on their savings would also decline. The spread would never disappear. If rates went down, they suffered on the return of their investments, but if rates went up, they really suffered. In a world of two negative alternatives, declining rates seemed to offer the better hope.

REGULAR SAVINGS ACCOUNTS: The familiar accounts, no restrictions on deposits or withdrawals; federally insured to $100,000; interest 5¼ percent at commercial banks, 5½ percent at savings banks. Ridiculously low rates in today's market.

NOW (NEGOTIABLE ORDER OF WITHDRAWAL) ACCOUNTS: Interest-bearing checking accounts; 5¼ percent interest, minimum required. Insured.

TIME DEPOSITS: Deposits that can be withdrawn only on notice, usually at least 14 days, otherwise a penalty. Since May 1, banks can offer time deposits with no interest rate ceiling but with initial minimum term of 3½ years, reduced annually until 1986, when minimum term becomes 14 days. Penalty for early withdrawal. Insured.

Also since May 1, banks can offer short-term time deposits, $7,500 minimum 91-day maturity, interest ceiling tied to three-month Treasury bill rate. Early withdrawal penalties. No compound interest. Insured.

Starting Sept. 1, banks can offer seven-to-31-day time deposit accounts, interest rate tied to three-month Treasury bills. Minimum $20,000. No check-writing. Insured.

MONEY MARKET CERTIFICATES: Six-month certificates of deposit, interest indexed to the 26-week rate on T-bills, new rates set each Tuesday, after T-bill auction. Minimum $10,000. Some banks arrange pools of small savers to hit $10,000 minimum and extend loans for part of purchase. Insured.

VARIABLE CEILING CERTIFICATES OF DEPOSIT: Terms 2½ to 3½ years. Rate ceiling based on yield of 2½-year T-notes. After next April 1, maturity range will drop to 1½ to 2½ years, and maximum rate will be tied to yield on 1½-year T-notes. Early withdrawal penalty. Insured.

REPURCHASE AGREEMENTS (also called "repos," or various bank trade names such as "Liquid Investment Certificates"): These have terms of eight to 89 days, pay money market interest rates comparable to a money market fund. Not federally insured.

ALL SAVERS CERTIFICATES: Unsuccessful effort by Treasury to lure more savings into thrift institutions. One-year certificates with interest exempt from taxes up to $1,000 per person, $2,000 on a joint return. Yield is 70 percent of the average yield on 52-week T-bill, at time certificate is bought. No compound interest. All Savers sales to end Dec. 31, 1982.

SWEEP ACCOUNTS: These combine features of an interest-bearing NOW account at a bank with the higher interest yield of a money fund. Banks require minimum be kept in the NOW account, at 5¼ percent, usually around $2,000. Anything over that automatically swept into the money fund for higher return. Checks can be written on entire account, but only the NOW account portion is federally insured.

MONEY MARKET FUNDS: Two types are generally offered. One invests in short-term debt of large banks and corporations, as well as U.S. Treasury issues, and thus is able to earn interest rates that usually are somewhat higher than the average of Treasury bills. Another type, for maximum safety but yielding lower income, invests only in securities issued or guaranteed by U.S. Treasury. Funds are not insured by federal government but minimum purchase is usually lower than that required to buy a bank C.D. Interest can always be compounded and there is no withdrawal penalty.

An excellent free leaflet "Options for Savers," is available from Department of Consumer Affairs, Federal Reserve Bank of Philadelphia, P.O. Box 66, Philadelphia, PA 19105.

Once, when the nursery was thriving, Rocky had wrestled with City Savings and Loan and emerged with a "victory," for once. He had secured a large loan at "one-quarter point above the prime interest rate." This was the mark of his success as a small businessman; the Savings and Loan would loan him money at only ¼ of a single percentage above the best credit risks in America. This left our nursery owners with that warm glow which comes from being treated really decently, and from success achieved by hard work. They were proud, real proud, deep down inside content. Until the prime rate rose to 20%, and they had to pay 20.25% for the money they needed to purchase their plants from the wholesaler. Only a few years earlier, a loan shark would go to prison for charging more than 12%—limited by law—interest on a small loan. Now their well respected Savings and Loan was charging 20.25% and instead of going to prison, it was going broke. The spread had simply disappeared for the banker who found himself, crazy as it is to believe, unable to buy money at a lower rate than he could loan it out for. No one was winning in the interest rate surge to 20% prime. That is, almost no one. **Remember that "no one" is a bit like "never ending." There always is a winner somewhere,** it is just a question of finding behind which corner he is hiding.

Think of it as being done with **windows** as the dividing barrier. On one side of the window you have Walter Persnall, Jr., and on the other side you have the Rocky and Karens of the tier world. The window separates them by more than distance.

Walter Persnall, Jr., president, keeps his bank open every day of the week and until noon on Saturday. He even takes deposits after 5:00 P.M., when the blue collar workers return from a day on the job and the secretaries start to head home. Walter drives a crew of loyal but rather badly paid employees, in fact employees in the banking world are among the lowest paid white collar workers in the world; they have to be low paid, that keeps the **spread** nice and wide. Persnall worries about his employees, but only part of his worries are spent on their health. He also worries about theft, known as embezzlement, or their inability to size up a credit risk, or the granting of a loan to a cousin whose last name happened to be totally different from the employees'. Yes, Persnall worries about his employees a lot. He doesn't like worry, no banker does, he prefers counting and sleeping—in that precise order.

On the other side of the window are the **new** Rocky and Karen Becket. They have learned how to use units of interest rates as a means of being in the banking business with no traditional banking worries. It is not they on the outside looking in at Mr. Persnall. It is Mr. Persnall who is looking out through the window and wondering what it is that he is missing. For once, the banker is on the losing half of the transaction, that thought alone kind of made Rocky and Karen's day.

Rocky and Karen are in the banking business, but they have no staff, no employees, no offices, no overhead, no debts to collect, no borrowers like themselves to complain, no mortgages to foreclose, no embezzlement, no toasters, no advertising. They have none of these, it is like home heating oil business, they are in the business and yet they are not in it. All they have is a **structure**. The structure of their banking business looks like this:

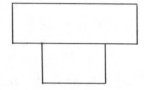

Karen understood interest as the payment for a piece of goods, a concept that Rocky understood intellectually, but was uncomfortable working with. She had more of a math bent, and she was much better than Rocky in an essential skill of Momentum—**line examination.** She saw the line of the sheet of paper as just that, a line going up and down and sometimes sideways; and she saw the movement **before** she saw the name. Sugar, silver, plywood or interest rates, she would only check the name out after she had first looked at the line. As she always said, "if the color is no good, I don't want the dress no matter how great the cut," and if the line didn't look worth pursuing, then **why** care about the name at the top of the page.

Rocky had difficulty with this. For him interest rates seemed solid, somehow sacred, not subject to fluctuation like potatoes or peanut butter. He realized that interest rates went up and down, he had paid the painful price of that knowledge when the prime moved from 8% to 20%, and his cost of staying in business advanced from 8.25% to 20.25%, but he simply could not initially approach interest rates the same way as he might look at corn syrup. So he would learn from Karen, that a line is just a line much as a road is simply a road, some are paved, some are twisted, a few are overgrown with bushes, but in the final analysis all roads are the same, they all begin somewhere and they all end elsewhere and you can follow that distance from start to finish. Rocky liked this analogy; he would view interest rates as simply price, the price of buying money or of selling money, and he would view the line of that price as a **road**, a road to wealth accumulation. One he was already started down and on which he greatly enjoyed traveling.

Walter Persnall contemplated interested rates as they related to his business, his county, his city, even his own block on Main Street. Karen contemplated interest rates as they pertained to life. She saw interest rates as basically a conflict between accumulated wealth and wealth being accumulated, between the old and the young, between those who already have it and those who are starting to get it. One aspect of social reform that the reformers so often forget is that in general wealth is found with age; the two go hand in hand. When we talk about passing laws in Congress to take money away from the people who have it and give it to those who do not have it, **we are basically talking about taking it away from older people and giving it to younger people.** 95% of all wealth is found in the hands of older people; the people with really nothing, nothing at all, are those just out of high school. No one mentions that if you pass a law to take from those who have to give to those who do not, the effect of your law will be to strip the wealth from the older generation and give it to those just beginning to experience the wonders of life. Those in Congress may not so see it, but Karen did. Rocky and Karen were in both worlds. Young people have to borrow money. Older people essentially live on savings, interest paid on their accumulated life's work. The young need low interest rates so that they can accumulate wealth anew, so that they can enter their fields of endeavor, so that they can put themselves through dental school. Older people need high rates of interest so that they can live on their life's summary. The interest rate battle is in many ways a struggle between the established and the intrepid. Karen saw it clearly, though she never so read about it in her local evening newspaper.

Karen and Rocky had another feature of their tier business that looked pretty attractive to Walter Persnall as he peered through the glass window. When rates were very high, when the cost of money was up, Walter **had** to pay it, he had to meet the competition otherwise the money would flow out of his bank like a running stream and head toward another firm or toward the ever expanding money funds in New York and Boston. Walter had to pay the price for money, no matter what it was. And the high interest rates that should have worked to his advantage were ruining his business. As the cost of money rose with the rising line of interest rate prices, the **spread** between price of goods sold and cost of goods acquired narrowed and narrowed. In addition, the value of all old loans on the books started to shrink, a mortgage on the books providing a 20 year payment at 6% mortgage rates was not worth 100% of its value. Would you buy a 20 year piece of paper paying you 6% interest, taxable, for 100% of its list price? Not today you wouldn't, and neither would any one else; and so the value of reserves in Walter Persnall and all other banks shrunk as fast as their spread was shrinking. Before their very eyes the spread and the retained wealth were shrinking and there was absolutely nothing that the banker on the corner could do about it, but sit and watch. He was a captive as well as an owner of the cornerstone business that financed America's growth.

Every time interest rates advanced, Walter Persnall, Jr. winced. Every time interest rates went up, Karen Becket contemplated filling her second tier.

On his side of the window, Walter read the *Wall Street Journal's* comments on money supply and the Federal Reserve

Board with mixed feelings of hope and despair. On her side, Karen read to refine her knowledge of the line. One, a passive act; Persnall could not change the prime rate on his own, he could do nothing but wait. One, an active viewpoint; how could Karen take advantage of interest rate momentum, and what might the line do next.

Where would rates be next week, next month, next year, even in five years? Walter would give you a complex, sadly sadistic, sodden answer which really meant that nobody knows. Karen would tell you she had narrowed the possibilities down to three. The cost of money will be higher within those time periods than it is today, or it will be lower, or it will be exactly the same. An impertinent answer? Absolutely not; Karen's banking business is thriving on the basis of just such a simple conclusion, while Persnall's banking business is collapsing in complexity. He's helpless; Karen has the line, she really doesn't care about the money supply. Persnall moans and blames outside forces, Karen quietly watches and plans. Persnall watches money figures with fear and dread; Karen has already left town for the weekend by the time they are released.

Pick your choice, randomly if you wish, or use your gut feeling or personal knowledge. You select rates as advancing over the next thirty days? You have a 50% chance of being right. Rates are to fall by next winter? You have a 50% chance of 100% accuracy. The trick is to have a slight edge beyond the 50% working for you, to increase your odds to 51% working upward to a level where you feel comfortable. It is all a matter of degree. Suppose I ask you, will rates be higher or lower in 90 days, and you reply "higher," 50/50 odds. Suppose I ask you, "are rates more likely to move to 5% within the next year or advance to double digit?" Now the odds are no longer 50/50. 5% rates are **very unlikely,** and so your opinion may well say, "double digits." **Suppose I then said, "okay, expect a rise in rates and put your stop loss order at 4.9% interest."** You see, trading the **line** can be fun, and unless rates fall to 4.9%, and stop you out of your position, you may well be on board a very profitable tier position. It is learning **how** to trade the line that will make you money; not watching the money supply figures released by the Federal Reserve Board. Economics may be an inexact science, but trading the line is 95% common sense. Karen isn't an economist, but she doesn't have to be, she has plenty of common sense and that will be more important to her than a degree from NYU without such common sense judgment. Focus your attention on the line and then learn to sharpen that focus. That is the simple mathematics of Momentum and wealth accumulation.

When the government of the United States borrows money, and it is the largest borrow of money in the world being over $1 trillion in debt, it does so in three principal ways: **Treasury Bills,** short term loans to the government from its citizens, **Treasury Notes,** intermediate term borrowing by the government from its citizens, and **Treasury Bonds,** long term borrowing, long term debt. In each case the government has no money, it has to borrow from its own citizens. The only other choice would be to have a balanced budget and need no money from the citizens, but that seems to be out of the question. Spend all you take in and borrow as much as

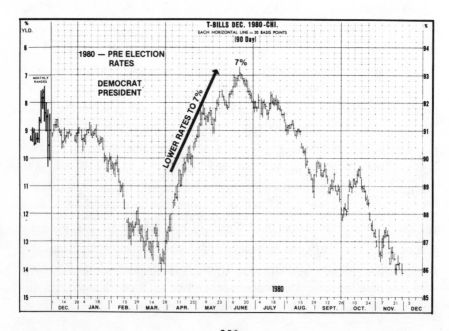

you possibly can is the modus operandi for today's politician, and let the next generation stay awake at night worrying about how to pay off $1 **trillion** in debt, the interest on which is over $100 **billion** a year.

The graph of short term debt, Treasury Bills, illustrates a couple of interesting points. The first thing it illustrates is the cost of borrowed money to the United States government during the period from December of 1979 to December of 1980. The column to the left reflects the interest rate, the column to the right reflects the discount. As you can see the rate of interest for the United States government, the best credit risk in the world—even better than the prime bank borrower—fluctuated between 7% to 14% during this single calendar year. Our own government was able to borrow money for as low as 7% interest and had to pay as much as 14% interest, all within a single twelve month period of time. That is one thing the **line** shows.

It also shows political history. Real world stuff.

Take the price in March of 1980 and the price in November of 1980 and you will see that it is about the same. The rate of interest in both these months is about 14% and the discount shows an 86. **Stop and think** for a minute about this graph. In March the rate is 14% and in November the rate is 14%. What is the big hump in June? Why in the world would rates drop from 14% to 7% within a three month period of time, and then move back up to the initial starting level? What could possibly have caused that? You won't like the answer.

Jimmy Carter wanted to be re-elected in 1980 and the huge drop in interest rates reflected a pumping of new money into the economy by the Federal Reserve Board at such a rate that interest rates collapsed. You are looking at political history in this hump; it is the desperation of one man, one party, the Democratic Party, trying to be re-elected in the elections of 1980. Did it work? Not for

Jimmy Carter. It did not work not because he did not try, he tried with all his might to reduce rates, reduce the rate of inflation and thereby be re-elected. **That whole hump on the graph is his trying.**

Why didn't the plan work? Most likely Jimmy Carter would not have been re-elected if rates had fallen to 1%; but the interest rate fiasco did not work because once rates fell to 7% the demand was so huge by borrowers that not even the United States government could hold the rates there forever. They could push the rates that low for a while, but when the line outside the borrower's window was 45 miles long, they could not hold them there. And so, the snowball edged over the top and right back down to the level from which it started, a lesson in political history, a lesson of the Democratic Party seeking to hold the controlling reins of government for another four more years.

Ronald Reagan was charging from the West and even 7% rates would not stop him. He was a man of destiny, a man of principle, a man whose time had come. No controlling of interest rates right before the election would ever work to unseat him from his stallion. This drop in rates from 14% to 7% was the single greatest decline in interest rates in the history of the United States of America. No decline has ever been greater, at least not during a three month period of time. Even during the Great Depression interest rates did not drop seven percentage points within twelve weeks of time. Jimmy Carter had learned the peanut business well, and he knew when there was a lot of goober peas around, price was on the defensive. If the Federal Reserve Board would only print a lot of money, the principle should work again and prices, or rates, should drop.

There is only one thing wrong in using the economics of peanuts to establish the money supply volume of the United States of America. During a period of inflation, which was what we experienced during the years Mr. Carter was in office, money was a hot item. If you had money you could buy goods, if you had goods you could re-sell them for a profit as inflation forced prices higher.

Now lower the cost of money from 14% to 7% and watch what happens.

What would happen if you lowered the price of steak to 15¢ a pound. Would it ever stay at that level? At 15¢ a pound you would be eating steak, your dog would be eating steak, your cat would be eating steak, even your goldfish would get steak crumbs. You would use steak for frisbees, you would freeze 85 years of supply in the largest freezer you could buy, you would drive Arthur Treacher's Fish and Chips out of business within hours. There is **no** way steak could remain at 15¢ a pound, not top quality steak. The demand would simply be too great, it would absorb all supply no matter how much supply was available.

The increase in money supply did not keep interest rates down because money at 7% seemed a steal, and many people were lining up to do just that—borrow all they could, for as long as they could, as close to the 7% prevailing rate as they possibly could. A political quick fix by the Democratic Party in its efforts to retain poltical power. Thank goodness for the White Knight on the White Horse. Remember, interest rates and money supply affect every living human being in our country in one fashion or another. They are not something you tamper with for short term political purposes. You are affecting lives, jobs, futures, values. If you print so much money that it is freely available you make it not more valuable but worthless. **Why is a Mexican peso worth so little? Because there are so many of them,** and every time the Mexican government needs a hundred million or more, it prints them and spends them and bit by bit makes them more worthless.

No political party should ever use money supply and interest rates for short-term political ends.

None should, but they all do.

Richard Russell once wrote that **every** politician will do whatever he has to to stay in office regardless of the consequences. Politicians will retain their jobs **first**, they will worry about the consequences, hopefully never. Let Joe worry about that. Read it and weep, it is August 2nd, 1982, two years later and the Republicans are now in control of the Senate and Ronald Reagan has tied his White Horse up to the hitching post on the front lawn of the White House. Quick fixes are not his style. So read it, my friend, and weep a little as you do. Mr. White Knight was not quite as white as everyone had hoped. He, too, will do whatever is necessary to retain political office.

> *US NEWS & WORLD REPORT MAGAZINE, August 2nd, 1982. "Before the Federal Reserve Board reduced its discount rate, at least two top White House aides bluntly told Chairman Paul Volcker that President Reagan wanted to see faster expansion of the money supply to cut interest rates and boost economic recovery before Election Day."*

Where are interest rates headed this time? Back toward 7%. Who is pushing them there now? Ronald Reagan and the Republicans. They too want to hold office.

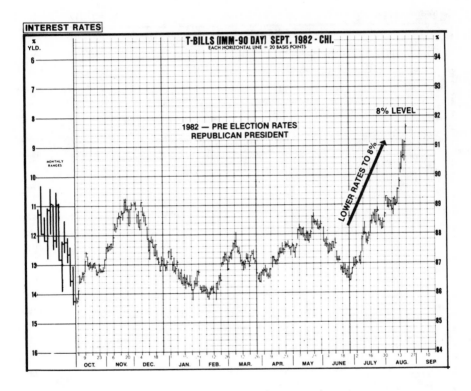

T-BILLS (IMM-90 DAY) SEPT. 1982 - CHI.
EACH HORIZONTAL LINE = 20 BASIS POINTS

1982 — PRE ELECTION RATES
REPUBLICAN PRESIDENT

8% LEVEL

LOWER RATES TO 8%

T-BILLS (IMM-90 DAY) DEC. 1984 - CHI.
EACH HORIZONTAL LINE = 10 BASIS POINTS

1984 — PRE ELECTION RATES
REPUBLICAN PRESIDENT

PRE ELECTION

1984 Pre-Election with a Republican President. Rates drop from a 12.25% high to the 8% level right before election day.

And again, in 1984, it was low interest rates right before election time.

Should **you**, like Walter Persnall, Jr., Karen and Rocky and all the politicians want to get in the banking business, the steps are relatively simple.

There are many fields open in the banking and interest rate business and more are opening each year. You can buy units of interest rates in Treasury Bills, and actually **profit** when rates are shoved from high rates to low rates for politican purposes, Treasury Notes, Treasury Bonds, Certificants of Deposit, Government National Mortgage Association contracts (known as "Ginnie Mae's"), or even Eurodollars. The interest rate markets are one of the fastest growing in America simply because so much depends on how high or how low rates are, and because so many people like Rocky and Karen and bankers and insurance men and builders need to participate in units of interest rates to protect their actual business from the high cost of operation.

Walter Persnall would much prefer that Rocky and Karen and you and me knew nothing about units of interest rates and how to invest in them on a tier progression. He would be much happier if we would deposit our money in his bank in a passbook savings account and earn 5.5% interest while he loaned it out for 15.5% interest. It is that kind of spread, not our advancing knowledge, that a banker dreams about. But there are too many Rocky and Karens out there today who are learning, and who are seeking to survive in a new world. There are too many people who believe opportunities to profit from the momentum of the line of interest rates should be available to all, and not just to bankers and savings and loan institutions. By waiting and watching and investing on a tier basis **after a 1-2-3 bottom,** Rocky and Karen were able to take $2,500 out-of-pocket cash and make a profit of $15,000 in a forty-two day period. The return on their money for those forty-two days was 600%; on an annual basis it was 5,214%. With that kind of opportunity in the banking business now open to us **all**, it is no wonder that the Persnalls of the world are on the inside looking out. We are the ones with success on our doorsteps. It is the people in the traditional fields of banking that are suffering. It is true that it is **safer** for you to accept 5.5% on a passbook account at the corner bank, it is safer. But if you only made a profit of 600% once every twenty years, you would be paying a high premium for that safety. For the first time in their adult lives interest rates of 10, 12, even 20 percent don't seem high to Rocky and Karen any more. In fact, they seem low. After all, it only took them forty-two days to make that 600% return, an average of 14.28% **per day**. 20% annual interest doesn't seem high to them any more, it seems downright puny.

Karen leads the way, and Rocky closely follows.

They like being bankers and they like the **spread**. Their money costs them 20%. They expect to earn 600% on it. The spread is only 580%. Enough for a little leeway for an error now and then.

Does the party in power really use interest rates to gain votes in election years? *U.S. NEWS & WORLD REPORT* magazine and numerous other publications think so.

"Many suspicious Democrats in Congress openly predict that the drop in interest rates won't last. Their scenario: The Federal Reserve Board will permit borrowing costs to decline only until after the November 2nd election—to take Reagan and the Republicans off the hook."
(US NEWS, August/1982)

Both parties do whatever they can to lower rates in the months prior to an election. Want some proof of recent history? You saw rates drop to 7% with the Democrats facing re-election in 1980, and the rates drop when the Republicans were starting to worry in 1982 and 1984. **What about the year 1981, when neither party was up for re-election?** What did rates do that year? They didn't drop to 7 or

8%. They stayed at 15%. Not absolute proof; but a pretty good piece of evidence.

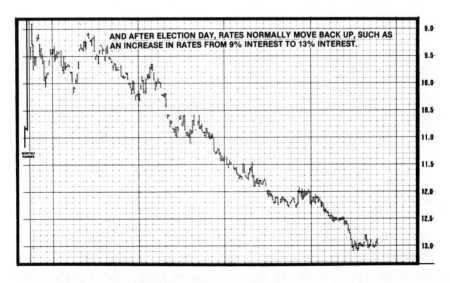

THE INTERNATIONAL DIPLOMACY
AND FINANCE BUSINESS

HEADLINE: FRENCH TO SELL NUCLEAR FUEL
IN MIDEAST
HEADLINE: JAPAN DEVALUES YEN: EXPORT
WAR BLAMED
HEADLINE: MEXICO FACES NEAR COLLAPSE,
SEEKS INTERNATIONAL HELP
HEADLINE: GERMANY: ECONOMIC MIRACLE,
THEN AND NOW
HEADLINE: BRITISH ARMADA NEARS
FALKLAND ISLANDS, IT IS WAR!

T HERE ARE TWELVE-YEAR-OLD CHILDREN IN
France who have been taught, and can tell you, the names of
all cabinet officials in the United States government. They know the
names of many senators and congressmen. The affairs of America
and Americans are very important to Europeans; their newspapers
often are as full of U.S. news as domestic news. They have a vora-
cious appetite for our doings. So they were understandably dismayed when they read that the nominee for American Undersecre-
tary of State—our nation's second top diplomat—did not even
know who the Prime Minister of a major world nation was. They
were even more dismayed when this candidate was confirmed.
When he later moved into the White House, there was disbelief.

International news is not front page news in our daily papers
unless it is news of war, or has an immediate and direct effect on
American policy. This is a reflection of America's confidence in its
world position. It's the same attitude that results in many French
schoolchildren knowing more about U.S. history than their American counterparts know about U.S. history, let alone French history.
We do not apply the same importance to Internationalism and

history as other nations. Our experience as a nation is shorter, and our outlook on international politics is often on the edge of isolationism. It may be a flaw. It may be an asset.

But I know two people to whom the five headlines above would be of compelling interest, headlines that could break them away from their television set for an immediate conversation about the importance of the latest bulletin. I'm talking about that cosmopolitan couple, Rocky and Karen Becket, of course.

HEADLINE: FRENCH TO SELL NUCLEAR FUEL IN MIDEAST

The rumor that the French government would sell nuclear materials to a Mid-Eastern country, with payment in French francs, francs accumulated through years of petroleum business transactions caught Rocky's eye. Years before, Rocky would not have even paused at such a story. He would flip forward to the sports pages, and read about the San Francisco Giants languishing in fifth place. But now Rocky read every word of the story and speculated about the result. The payment would involve a huge quantity of currency. It couldn't help but hurt the world demand for the French franc. It looked like a sharp downturn should be anticipated. What could ambassador-without-portfolio Rocky Becket do, if not to help the French government then certain to help himself in the unit market for french currency?

HEADLINE: JAPAN DEVALUES YEN: EXPORT WAR BLAMED

Japan, incorporated. Say the word "export" and you've said Japan, to the advantage of the Japanese and the rancor of importing countries, whose exports Japan will not accept. The Japanese economy was planned around exports, and when exports drop off, they must be perked up. What better way to increase exports than by devaluation of the yen. With a decreased value for the yen, foreign currency will be worth more in Japan. If it is worth more, it can buy more Japanese goods. Exports will rise. The Japanese economic system would return to its accustomed prosperous level, and Sony and Honda can again flood America, selling and unemploying workers at the same time.

This move, the devaluation, looked smart to Rocky. But the second Ambassador-at-large Karen Becket thought that it would not work. She felt that the yen would continue to slide and she was prepared to act on that diminished value, and act soon. She looked for her graph paper and the line.

HEADLINE: MEXICO FACES NEAR COLLAPSE, SEEKS INTERNATIONAL HELP

This is real world stuff. Ian Brodie of the London Daily Telegraph reported it this way: "Rush to exploit oil wealth drags Mexico to the brink of bankruptcy." "Mexico City—Many Mexicans watching their country go hat in hand to world money sources yesterday were beginning to regard their great oil wealth as the godsend that failed. Without oil we would have never got into this mess, said one disillusioned businessman in Mexico City, where the economic crises has cast a pall over everybody except tourists awash in devalued pesos. While oil should still ultimately benefit Mexico, the decision to exploit it so vigorously as a means of industrial expansion has certainly dragged the nation down for the time being. Buffetted by rising interest rates and an oil glut, the policy is the direct cause of Mexico's near-bankruptcy with a world record foreign debt of $80 billion."

Real world material and both our Ambassadors watched the news closely. They were ready to buy on the basis of "bounce-back," but not quite ready yet.

HEADLINE: GERMANY: ECONOMIC MIRACLE, THEN AND NOW

—268—

A thought piece in a well respected newspaper: an essay contemplating divided Germany's place in the world since the two great wars. Germany could and never would shake the idea that it was their destiny to be the major power in Europe, and in forty years of post-war rebuilding, they were once again in a position to challenge the Soviet Union for that title. For good or ill, Germany was the greatest retooler of all time. With the rebuilding and accumulation had come strength to the German Deutsche Mark, their national currency, and to their strong economy, partially preserved through the heroic efforts of Albert Speer, Hitler's Minister of Armaments. The line for the German Mark was moving up; Rocky and Karen watched it closely. It reminded them of heating oil.

HEADLINE: BRITISH ARMADA NEARS FALKLAND ISLANDS, IT IS WAR!

This time international news made the front page of the *Sacramento Bee,* a rarity. For the sake of national pride and international law (much easier to enforce against a weaker party), Britain was pouring millions upon millions of pounds into war, and, once the islands were retaken (no question of if, but simply when), would pour more and more millions of pounds into holding them and maintaining a force, 9,000 miles from the beautiful British Isles. An enormous, but I won't say unending, drain. Rocky admired the British for their stand on behalf of international law, never asking himself if they would have been as eager to enforce international law had the Soviet Union decided it needed those islands instead of ill prepared Argentina. He admired them, but he regretted the war and the suffering. And as a diplomat in the international diplomacy and international finance business, he understood, sadly, that the drain of British pounds would sorely try the embattled British economy, and that the pound itself would lose value. A sorry fact, but one that the financial diplomats of the world had to weigh and consider. It was their business to do so, their unit and tier business.

Diplomacy is not so much a matter of courtesy and protocol, or the fair and the reasonable, as it is an exchange of weakness and strength, of problems and solutions, of action and consequence, of trump cards, of towels thrown into rings. The diplomat is he who can best weigh and consider the strengths and weaknesses found in the international arena, and strike the most advantageous bargain in light of these.

Rocky and Karen Becket are consummate diplomats in these terms. They run a business in international currencies. They look for units of currency to buy and select the time they think is best for selling, depending on where the winds of world economy seem to be heading. For this, they need information, and they dug for every word they could find about nations in international transactions. That simple line we are all so familiar with was now making new horizons meaningful to them. Rocky and Karen were international currency buyers who specialized in European and Japanese and sometimes Mexican currency units, but their business was born at the same birth that produced a home heating oil business, a lumber and plywood business, a copper business and a 7% interest rate business. Their new international diplomacy and world financial outlook suddenly made the world totally fascinating.

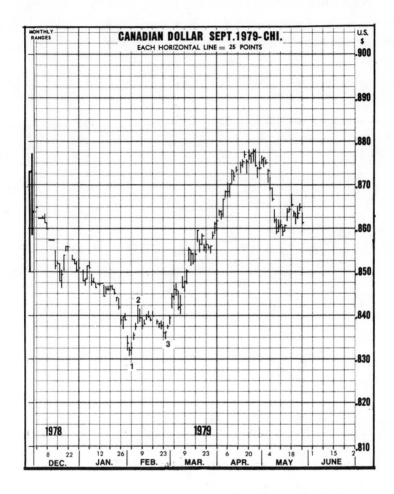

MONTHLY
RANGES
CANADIAN DOLLAR SEPT.1979- CHI.
EACH HORIZONTAL LINE = 25 POINTS
U.S.
$
.900
.890
.880
.870
.860
.850
.840
.830
.820
1978   1979
.810

8   22   12   26   9   23   9   23   6   20   4   18   1   15   2
DEC.   JAN.   FEB.   MAR.   APR.   MAY   JUNE

Strength in the Canadian dollar had made believers out of Rocky and Karen. Why the Canadian dollar? It wasn't the Canadian currency that was so important to them, **it was the fact that Rocky had spotted the 1-2-3 bottom in March** and they had bought a unit at 84¢. It wasn't the Canadian dollar that focused their attention on international news, and especially Canadian news. It was all the U.S. dollars they were making from their two tier investment. It was the profit which grasped and held their attention.

And when the Swiss Franc struggled to form its 1-2-3 bottom price pattern, Karen saw it first. She always had liked Switzerland, investing in Swiss francs she loved.

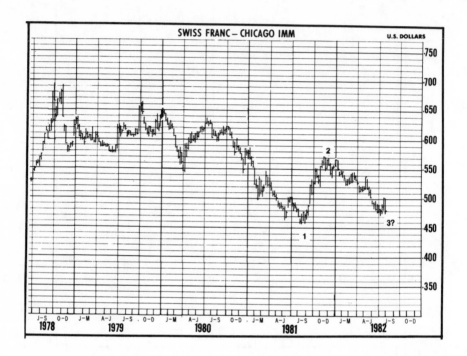

It was the Mexican peso that made the evening news really fascinating. This time they both watched in amazement.

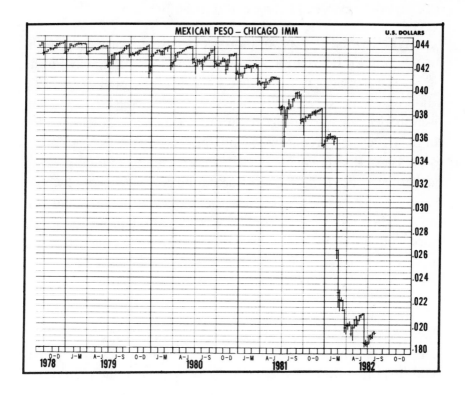

I am sure there were many people who had confidence in the currency of Mexico in 1982, but not one of that many was a member of the international diplomacy and world finance club. The peso was on its way to a penny, one hundred to the dollar, and Rocky and Karen watched with fascination. They would **never** have believed their ever expanding world of knowledge.

When Mobil Oil Corporation decided to buy Norwegian drilling rigs for North Sea drilling operations, they agreed to pay for the rigs in the Norwegian krona. It took two years for the rigs to be built. Within those two years the cost of the Norwegian krona had risen sufficiently to cost Mobil Oil Corporation an additional 50% for the goods delivered. Many companies, in fact, have been forced to set aside departments within their corporations that do nothing but protect those firms against fluctuating currency values by buying and selling currencies for forward delivery. If a sale is made today based on today's price of the German mark, and if a rise in the mark would destroy part of the profit from that sale, then an astute businessman has to consider buying units of Deutsche Marks for future delivery to protect against such a rise in value.

Bank of America, Bankers Trust Company, Chase Manhattan Bank, Chemical Bank of New York, Citicorp, Continental Bank of Illinois, First Chicago Bank, First National Bank of Boston, Harris Bankcorporation, Irving Bankcorporation, Manufacturers Hanover Trust Bank, Marine Midland Bank, J.P. Morgan Bank, Security Pacific Bank and many others have full time extensively staffed departments which do nothing but buy and sell units of foreign currencies. Is it difficult, beyond average comprehension, way past the heads of Rocky and Karen Becket? If Russia has to sell gold to enable Poland to prop up the Polish Zoylot, while South Africa is pushing Kruggerrands and France trades francs for British pounds, has this complicated world of international diplomacy and finance passed Rocky and Karen by? **Not at all, not for a second. They are absolutely fascinated by it,** it even makes their nursery business more interesting for nations, like nurseries have ups and downs with the passing of time. Afterall, international finance in-volves **one single line**, and sometimes that line **goes up**, and some-times it **goes down**; it very rarely **sits still**. Diplomacy is a business they truly love.

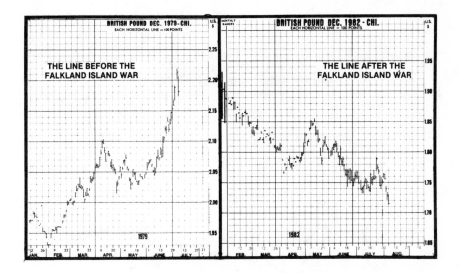

THE WALL STREET BARONY BUSINESS

BRUCE RAMSEY, A SYNDICATED NEWSPAPER COL-
umnist, says that predicting stock market prices is risky, and he
is right; it is a very risky profession. During the week ending August
20th, Wall Street experienced history—the biggest single weekly advance in history and the largest advance in the Dow Jones Averages
ever. Stocks were soaring and boom times appeared peeking over
the horizon.

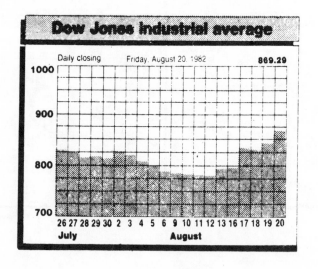

You could see the strength from the box graphs printed in most newspapers around the country; from an August low of about 788 the Dow Jones Industrial average moved to its highest levels in months, nearly 870, an 80 point advance from the bottom. It was a week of historic proportions. The start of the historic bull market of 1980-1983.

Bruce Ramsey says that Robert Nurock, a regular member panelist on Wall Street Week, told him in a telephone interview that much of the forecasting success of Mr. Nurock is based on contrary opinion—whatever most investors think will happen, won't. "Don't follow the crowd" is his principle which he says works especially well at market extremes, like the month of August, 1982.

Did this weekly jump in the stock market signal an end to the recession, Bruce asked himself. Perhaps, responded Nurock. A similar frenzied jump on Wall Street in January of 1975 signaled an economic turnaround later that year. History repeats itself—sometimes. There were now several good signs besides the stock and bond markets for the optimists to chew on. Real consumer income was rising despite layoffs and despite consumer reluctance to spend extra cash. The Wall Street investment firm Bear, Stearns & Co., said that the rebound would come and it would be self-financed, an "income-based recovery" rather than a "credit-based recovery." Meaning that as incomes rose the economy would rebound and people would spend real net income increases rather than borrowed money. The upshot, said Bear Stearns, was that the recovery will last longer but it would be slower. The recession was over, but hard times have awhile to go yet.

Were Rocky and Karen watching and listening to all this talk about Wall Street and the stock market? Why should they be listening; they did **not own a single share of stock** in any corporation traded on the New York, the American or the Over-the-Counter stock exchanges. Rocky and Karen owned absolute zero shares of stock; and yet they read and listened intently. They were one of the most fervent watchers of PBS-TV's *Wall Street Week*. They even took notes and discussed the program when it was all over. **Why were the nursery owners so vitally interested if they did not own a single share of stock? Why?**

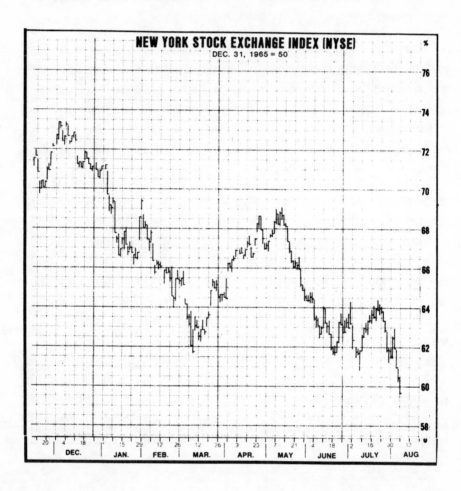

Because the New York Stock Exchange index is just a **line**. And sometimes that line goes up, and sometimes it goes down, and ever so rarely it sits quietly. And not only is the average of stocks traded on the New York Stock Exchange a **line**, so is the index composed by the Value Line corporation. And sometimes that line goes up, and sometimes it goes down. It virtually never sits still.

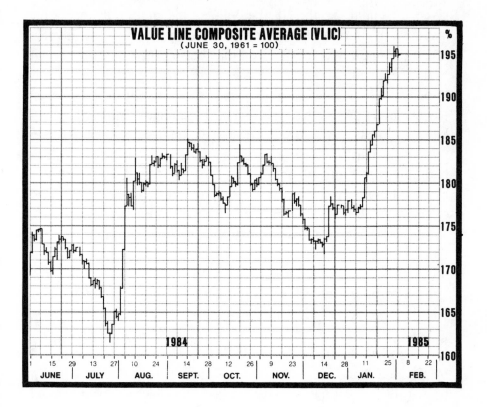

This is **why** Rocky and Karen watch the news on Wall Street so intently. They are not into stocks, they own not a single one, but they are sure into **lines**, and with lines, they can do a great deal.

The Value Line index above is the index of the average price of 1,683 stocks selected purposely by the Value Line firm as indicative of how stock market prices "in general" are doing. Each stock is given an equal weight. If the Value Line index advances, the chances are good that **most** stocks owned by investors are advancing, if the **one** you own isn't, you may be an expert in picking what Wall Street calls "dogs." The New York Stock Exchange index is known as a "weighted average," because greater influence is given to certain key stocks than to others. The change of price of a well-known and large firm such as IBM or Exxon has a greater effect on this index than the change in price of a smaller firm. The index naturally represents **all** stocks traded on the New York Stock Exchange, but different firms are "weighed" differently. Is this good or bad? Value Line says treat all stocks the same; the New York Stock Exchange says just as it would make a difference to the United States if Iceland or China declared war against us, so too does it make a difference in economics if IBM falls by 50%, or little-known-corporation declines from $1.00 to 50¢ a share. Both maintain their opinions with firm conviction.

Another alternative **line** of Wall Street is the average compiled by the Standard and Poors Corporation. This index was begun back in 1917 and it has been the standard by which the professional stock portfolio manager measures his performance and abilities. If the Standard and Poor average advances 25 points and the manager of J.C. PENNEY PENSION FUNDS sees his portfolio drop an equal amount, there is a means for judgment. Originally the Standard and Poors index consisted of only 200 major stocks traded on major stock exchanges, but in 1957 this list was expanded to 500 corporations and that is where it remains today. The Standard and Poors 500 includes 400 industrial corporations, 20 transportation businesses, 40 financial institutions, and 40 public utilities representing about 80% of the value of all stocks traded on the New York Stock Exchange. The United States Department of Commerce uses this Standard and Poors average as one of its twelve leading economic indicators to judge the strength or weakness of the American economy.

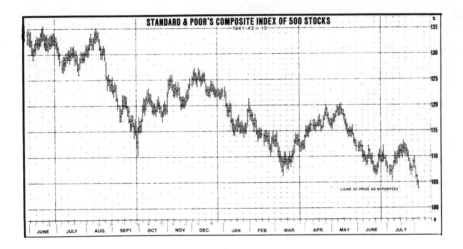

They are all different indices but to Rocky and Karen they are all **identical**; just graphs of lines moving ever so gradually across a piece of paper.

Think back for a few minutes to the beginning chapters in this book, to the discussion of how Wall Street really has **not** been the route to wealth accumulation for very many investors. As the road to wealth, even as a means of keeping ahead of inflation, Wall Street has been one of the biggest losers around. It is tradition, sure, and we all understand tradition, a means of getting us to sit on the bottom step of someone else's tier structure, but it is definitely **not** the road to wealth accumulation for most young and middle aged persons today. Why then are Rocky and Karen suddenly finding their interest aroused by these lines of the various indices moving

—281—

across a piece of paper, why do they care about this traditional business at all? Money, my friend, money. Our favorite five letter word. It is the line and the potential profit that interests Rocky and Karen; without owning a single share of stock, they have become one of the most observant spectator couples in America, and their attention is focused sharply on these indices. The reason is **money!**

Simply put: One of the nine fields of opportunity you now have in the **new** world of tradition is the ability to invest in the index of various stock market averages. You can buy the index when you think it may advance, you can sell it when you think it has reached its peak, or you can stay on the sidelines altogether. You need not own a single share of stock in order to buy a stock market index; just as you did not need to own a silver mine to buy a unit of silver for future delivery. From your viewpoint, there is not one whit of difference between buying a unit of silver, or a unit of bacon, or a unit of interest rates from buying a unit of a stock market average; not one whit of difference.

Buy one unit of the Standard and Poors Averages for me at 100 with a stop loss at 95.

If you believe the line of the index is about to advance, you may wish to consider buying that line. If you feel otherwise, you may plan to sell or stand aside. If the name on the top of the graph paper confuses you, simply cross it off and change it to potatoes. It won't make any difference to the line; **the line just moves**, we are the ones that give it all these familiar titles.

How do you profit from the momentum of the line? The same way you profit from the momentum of the price of any of the other items covered so far in this book. Each index has a specific size. For example, the Value Line Average Stock Index consists of multiplying the index by 500. If the index advances one percent and you purchased the line at the lower level and sold it at the higher level, say

115 and 116, you made **one times** $500 or $500.00. If you bought that line at 120 in March and sold it at 133 in May, you made thirteen percentage points, or **thirteen times** $500: $6,500.00. To calculate your profit or loss from any index for Wall Street simply find out the size of the unit, multiply that size by the advance or decline in price, and then multiply again by the number of units you own. Three simple steps to **money!**

The real key to this profit opportunity is leverage, the ability to deposit only a small portion of "margin" with the firm you do business with to control a substantial amount of value. Take the New York Stock Exchange Index for example. What would it cost you to buy **one hundred** shares of every stock listed on the New York Stock Exchange? Chances are you don't have that much money, **yet!** Even if you were to buy one share of each stock listed on that exchange, there are something like 1,500 + stocks so listed, at an average price of even $10 a share, the total would be $15,000, and **many** stocks on the New York Stock Exchange sell for above $10 a share. The cost, paper work, and time required to buy each share of stock in any of these averages would be prohibitive. So, like Rocky and Karen, you can keep your ownership of America's tradition at absolute zero while you profit from the ups and downs of the index average of that very same tradition. It is a strange new world. Own all stocks on the New York Stock Exchange and watch prices rise an average of 10% and you will net 10% on your capital. But own the New York Stock Exchange average **index**, and watch that index move from 62 to 68, as it did in the same March to May period, for a 10% advance and you will net $3,000 per unit profit. As each unit normally requires about that amount in "margin" deposit, a 10% advance in the index can return a 100% profit to the owner of the index unit. That is on the **one** tier level. On the five tier level, the return would be many fold.

Tradition says "buy and hold" and Rocky and Karen were holding Ford Motor Company years after it should have been sold. "Buy and Hold" simply will **not** work if you need to accumulate real wealth today, it is a dead end road. But buy a single unit, if the market moves in your favor add another tier with equity value, and when the advance sustains itself move to an additional tier, now you are talking real money. Tradition can still work, you just have to redefine your terms.

Most actives

Sears Roeb	1,793,800	22	$+1\frac{1}{2}$
Cities Serv	1,650,200	$45\frac{1}{4}$	$+2\frac{5}{8}$
Pac Gas&El	1,612,700	$26\frac{7}{8}$	$+1\frac{1}{4}$
IBM	1,355,900	$68\frac{1}{4}$	$+2\frac{1}{4}$
Am Tel Tel	1,303,000	$56\frac{1}{2}$	$+1\frac{1}{2}$
Exxon	1,198,700	$27\frac{1}{2}$	$+\frac{3}{8}$
Citicorp	1,139,800	$24\frac{3}{8}$	$+\frac{3}{8}$
Gen Motors	1,079,100	$47\frac{3}{8}$	$+2\frac{1}{4}$
Champ Int	1,011,200	$14\frac{5}{8}$	$+\frac{7}{8}$

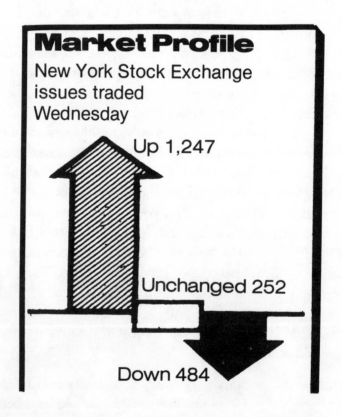

Market Profile
New York Stock Exchange issues traded Wednesday

Up 1,247

Unchanged 252

Down 484

If you already own a portfolio of stocks, you can use these units of the averages as a means of protecting yourself against price declines, or as a means of selling at a high level without having to sell your portfolio. To accomplish this you simply decide if price has gone high enough, or is low enough to justify more buying, and then you consider what you already own in your portfolio and take the appropriate action with respect to the unit for future delivery. For example, if the averages soar, you may not wish to sell your portfolio which you are holding for long term capital gain. But you could sell a unit of the index. Then if the price collapsed, your portfolio would be worth less by the decline, but you could buy the future unit back at a lower level for a profit to offset that reduced value.

Or, if the market moves sharply downward offering you a key opportunity to buy, rather than buying one hundred more shares of a stock selling at $50 a share, for a cost of $5,000, you could buy the unit for the index on the exchange where that stock is traded. Chances are, if the index rises your stock would have risen also and you can profit from your unit, but the profit may be entirely different. For your stock to return you 100% profit, it will have to rise from $50 to $100 a share; for the index to return you 100% profit on your $5,000 margin money, it may only have to rise the equivalent of from $50 to $55. The leverage allowed permits the opportunity to profit from a rising line of price to a greater degree by buying the index unit than by buying the actual stock itself.

Heady Days for Index Futures

Profits Soar With Volume

By WINSTON WILLIAMS
Special to The New York Times

CHICAGO, Aug. 22—The record volume and record price advances on Wall Street last week have created a booming market in the financial community's newest trading instrument, stock index futures.

Three exchanges—the Chicago Mercantile Exchange, the Kansas City Board of Trade and the New York Futures Exchange— have for the last few months offered investors, through futures contracts, the chance to bet on the direction of various stock exchange averages. Partly because of the intense competition among the exchanges, trading had been sluggish and erratic on all the markets until stock prices became volatile.

Near the end of July, volume improved perceptibly, and it exploded last week, ignited by the surging stock market and sharp drops in interest rates. Now traders are heartened by large profits and the prospect of growing commissions and the exchanges are predicting that all the contracts will survive and flourish.

At the Chicago Mercantile Exchange, where more than 50 percent of stock index contracts are traded, stock index trading volume set back-to-back records on Tuesday, with 20,687 contracts, and Wednesday, with 23,458. Volume continued strong Thursday, when 22.470 contracts were traded.

"This is off to the hottest start of any new futures contracts," said Charles Epstein, a spokesman for the Chicago Mercantile Exchange. "Its growth potential is just beginning to be realized."

Mr. Epstein said the reception of the financial futures contract by the investing public has surpassed the reaction to the futures contracts on certificates of deposit, which had been considered the pace-setter for new contracts.

In the last two weeks, traders from the other pits have crowded into the stock index ring to take advantage of the action in the Standard & Poor's contracts. More than 80 Merc members traded stock index futures last week, compared with about 40 two weeks ago.

The frenzy has been repeated across the country. On the New York Futures Exchange, where the contract is based on the New York Stock Exchange Index, officials reported record volume for Wednesday of 11,103 contracts, almost double the volume of recent weeks.

In Kansas City the Board of Trade saw trade in its Value Line contracts soar to a record of 4,858 contracts on Wednesday.

Remember the problem that Rocky and Karen faced when dealing in the world of international diplomacy and high finance: the lack of worldly news. You won't find this problem when investing in units for future delivery of the stock market indices. Most daily newspapers carry domestic economic news religiously, and Wall Street news almost sadistically. Most people simply do not care what Wall Street did on Tuesday, yet the news is front page stuff if it rose so much as ten points. Rocky and Karen never used to care at all, in fact they even said they had the reverse feelings; they flatly did not like to see so much news about Wall Street on TV and in the papers. That is how they **used** to feel; now their favorite paper is the *Wall Street Journal* and their favorite TV show is *Wall Street Week*. If total and daily information is your pabulum you have found your sweet pasture of plenty. Become a Wall Street Baron by buying, selling, or simply watching and investing "on paper" in units of the stock market indices and there will be enough news in your daily papers to keep you happily content.

Did Rocky and Karen profit from the greatest week ever on Wall Street? Were they on board this racing line in time to pinch out a few dollars for the kid's education? You bet they were, they profited and they profited handsomely. **How?** By their keen economic insight and judgment? By taking a "contrary opinion" to everyone else and buying when all the experts said prices were about to collapse? By simply "guessing" that the end was near, like the man on the sidewalk with his message to humanity? By blind luck? What was responsible for their success?

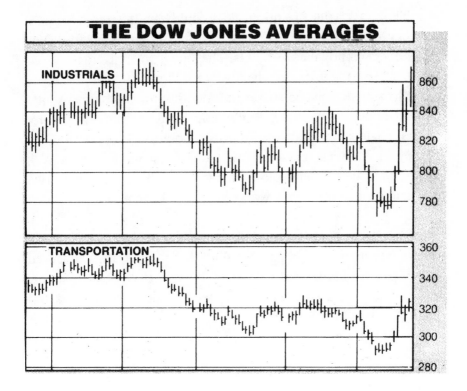

THE DOW JONES AVERAGES

INDUSTRIALS

TRANSPORTATION

It was none of those methods. They were consistently success-ful and consistency can never be based on luck. **First,** they saw the obvious: The averages had declined to the zone 4 level, a nice time to buy. **Second,** they expected "bounce-back," which their own ex-perience had told them was quite common. **Next,** they saw the mini-1-2-3 formation, not enough to act on by itself but certainly enough to strengthen their zone 4 conclusion and their "bounce-back" ex-pectation.

They took a tier 3 position. They could have advanced to tier 4, but they stayed with tier 3. The week on Wall Street saw the Dow Jones averages advance 81 points. The Down Jones average moved from 788.05 to 869.29, an advance of 81.24 points or 10.3%. People who actually owned shares of stock saw those shares rise approximately 10% in value. Rocky and Karen admittedly did not own a single share of stock in any corporation listed on any exchange in America; not one. Yet the greatest week ever in Wall Street made them enough money for several college educations, two new automobiles and four weeks in Miami Beach.

Our Wall Street Barons pulled this coup off by first being successful buying units "on paper." With that success, they advanced to buying units at the "one tier" level. When they could consistently buy and sell and profit at one tier, they advanced to two tiers and finally, by Wall Street's greatest week, they were experienced at tier three and tier four.

Wall Street soared and Rocky and Karen profited.

It wasn't until it was all over that Karen changed the name. Neither of them really felt too comfortable with stocks, they didn't really understand price-earning ratios, dividends on preferred stock, "contrary opinion" or convertible debentures. They didn't truly have a feel for Wall Street, they didn't even have an instinct for the index they had just made so much money on. And that was probably why they did it. When it was all over, she took it down and put the original name back on top. You see the little graph they had been keeping on the index which had been so kind to them, the graph which had shown the zone 4 opportunity, "bounce-back," and the 1-2-3 was covered over by a tab of paper. It didn't say anything about a stock index at the top, there was nothing to indicate that Wall Street was even involved. To everyone else that line may have looked like a stock market index, but to Rocky and Karen it looked like good old **Home Heating Oil.**

So they taped that name to the top and pretended they were back in the heating oil business. And it wasn't until it was all over; when Wall Street had made them so much money, that our Barons took the tab off. **After all, it was just a line.** And that line can only move in three directions. It was the line which returned the huge profit; in truth, it wasn't either home heating oil or a stock market index. **It was simply a line!**

THE INSURANCE BUSINESS

T HE LAST OF THE NINE NEW FIELDS OF OPPORTUN- ity isn't really a separate business like each of the previous eight have been. Rather, it is a new means for entering other businesses; it is not a **house**, it is not the **down payment on a house,** but it is **an insurance policy** to protect you against rising house prices should you ever decided to buy one.

Here is how the insurance business in which you can buy units for future delivery works:

You invest $1000 for the right to buy coffee at $1.00 a pound. Your right is good for three months.

*If the price of coffee stays at 90¢ a pound for those three months, you will **never** exercise your right to pay $1.00 a pound for it.*

*But if the price of coffee should rise to $1.50 a pound during that same time period, you **will** exercise your right to purchase it for $1.00.*

*Once purchased, you **won't** use it, you will simply sell it at the new price of $1.50. You will have made 50¢ a pound. 50¢ **times** the unit size of your insurance policy.*

Then you will sit back and start all over.

The insurance business protects you against price momentum passing you by. If the momentum comes, you can cash your insurance policy in. If it never comes, you will have paid the premium for an opportunity which never came.

In each of the previous eight fields we have examined you enter the business by actually buying the unit for future delivery and profiting if the momentum of the line moves in your favor. But in the insurance business you do not actually buy the unit. You purchase the **right** to buy the unit, an insurance policy that if the momentum comes you will be able to cash your policy in and own the unit at an agreed upon price. But if the momentum never comes, you simply see the insurance premium as a cost of doing business and you look for another alternative. Entering the insurance business commences in the identical fashion as all the eight previous businesses began; you make that single telephone call and tell your friend at the other end that you want to buy (or sell). Everything is identical except instead of buying (or selling) the actual unit, you are buying insurance against price momentum in that unit which might pass you by. The **name** at the top of your graph this time is "option." In the world of units for future delivery, **insurance** is known by the title of **"option"**; but it is an insurance policy nonetheless.

Why would you wish to buy an "option" for a unit of future delivery rather than buy the actual unit itself? The primary reason is to limit your risk of loss. Remember that a line moves in both directions and if you buy the actual unit, and prices advance $3000 in your favor, you will have profited by $3000. But if the line moves $3000 against your position, you will have suffered a $3000 loss. From the very day you buy a unit and the line starts to move it will be providing either a profit or a loss to you, minute by minute. **When it moves in your favor, it is providing profits; when it moves against your position, it is resulting in losses.** One thing is always certain, the line will be moving, and as it does your cash register is both adding and subtracting. The "option" business starts out with a big loss right off the bat—the cost of the insurance policy—but from that day forward your loss will never increase. Why not? Because you have paid the policy or "option" cost and now you simply sit back and wait to see if the momentum you are insuring yourself against ever occurs. If it does, then you exercise your option and take your profit. If it does not, the option cost was your cost of being in the game.

Isn't this identical to a "stop loss" order when one owns the actual unit? It is similar, but it is not identical. There are a couple of distinctions. The first is obvious; when you pay the "option cost" or "premium" you are out that money for good, just as you are when you pay your insurance company a premium for insurance on your house for a year. If you have a stop loss, you do not suffer that loss unless the stop loss price is reached. An "option" results in immediate loss, a "stop loss" is a loss only if the stop loss price is ever hit.

In addition, you may have a "stop loss" at a fixed price but due to market momentum your specific unit may not be purchased or sold at that price. Suppose your stop loss order was at $1.00 a pound and if that price was ever reached you would lose $1,800. It might well happen that when price declined from $1.05 to $1.00 there were no ready buyers, and so the selling of your unit for future delivery was accomplished at 98¢ instead of $1.00, and your total loss advanced from $1,800 to $2,000. **A stop loss order does not guarantee a buyer, it merely defines the area where you start looking for one.** Quite often stop loss orders are executed at prices different from the precise specified price. That is one of the risks of the new world of finance, but a risk Rocky and Karen and hundreds of thousands of other people just like them are more than willing to assume, because of the rewards for success.

If the concept of an "option" on a unit for future delivery causes you a momentary problem, drift back a minute to your knowledge of real estate. Think of it this way:

THE OPTION	THE UNIT OF FUTURE DELIVERY
Your right to pay $80,000.00 good	The house across the street
for three months	YOUR COST FOR THAT OPTION
to purchase a unit	
for future delivery	$500.00

Assume that you wish to purchase the house directly across the street from your own. That house is for sale for $80,000.00 on a depressed market. Since you are perfectly content with your own home, which you have worked hard to fix up, you have no interest in buying this neighborhood house for the sake of your own personal residence. Rather, you wish to buy the house across the street because you think it is worth $100,000.00 and you want to make a $20,000.00 profit from it. You believe it is worth that amount because you feel your own house in identical condition and built the same year by the same builder is worth that sum. You are interested, but purely as an investment.

Now you could buy that house outright, assuming a lot of **ifs** fell into place, in the time-honored way, making a down-payment, having your credit okayed, finding the seller willing to sell to you on your terms, and negotiating an agreement. Once agreed upon, you would be the new owner, you would start making your monthly payments and start looking for that buyer willing to pay $100,000 for the property. He's out there somewhere. But it is not always easy or necessary to make such an expensive commitment in order to profit from real estate. There is another approach. You could call the listed real estate broker at his office and offer him $500 option money for a three month right to buy that same house for $80,000.00 on terms agreed upon. Since business is slow in your neighborhood, real estate wise that is, the seller and the broker might just be interested. You could propose that you would pay $80,000.00 cash for the house should you decide to buy it within those three months. If, however, at the end of the 90-day period you decide that you do not wish ownership of the house after all, the realtor and the owner can keep your $500 "option" money, and your business relationship will end.

Why would you risk $500 for this kind of a business transaction? **The reason why you would pay $500 for an option is not to buy the house but to buy yourself time,** the three months of time, during which you hope to locate another buyer who will pay $100,000 for the property with at least $80,000 down. I am not saying that you will succeed; I am telling you why you would pay $500 for the **chance** to succeed.

If success does come your way, and you find a buyer who is willing to pay the total sum you require and the down payment you need, you can then "exercise; your option" to buy the house-across-the-street for $80,000.00 while at the same time negotiate the sale for $100,000.00 and transfer the down payment money given to you to the original seller in one clean-quick-smooth handslide. If you are successful, and assuming for the sake of analysis that there was no real estate commission involved, you would have made a $20,000 profit. Your total out-of-pocket investment was $500. $500 invested turned into $20,000 is a return of 4,000% — right up there in the Rocky and Karen category. Even if the real estate commission took $10,000 of the transaction, you would still have netted $10,000 from your $500 investment and hard work, a return of 2,000%.

If you fail, what is your loss? The $500 "option" money and nothing else except personal effort. An **option** is the risk money or insurance policy you pay to have the right to buy something at a fixed price for a fixed period of time. That is how options work in real estate and they work in the identical fashion when related to units of the eight previous businesses described so far. An option is an option regardless of whether it is the right to buy a house for

$80,000.00 or coffee for $1.00 a pound. The principle is identical.

The **advantage** of an option for a unit of future delivery of the businesses we have examined versus an option for a piece of real estate is that the eight fields of business we have covered in this book all have active markets of buyers and sellers, hundreds of thousands of buyers and sellers. You don't have to go out looking for a buyer like you do in real estate; if the price rises, the buyers are there and your single phone call can both exercise your option for the unit of future delivery and sell it at the same time. It would go like this:

Exercise my option to buy silver at $8.00 an ounce immediately.

At the same time sell that unit of silver at the current market price which is $10.00 an ounce.

You don't have to look for anybody. If price has risen sufficiently to make the exercising of your option profitable, that means there is a ready buyer available—it is the buyers who have forced the price line up. You simply exercise your right to buy at your agreed upon price and then immediately sell at the current market price. No looking for **anyone** to buy the house across the street. You need not even leave your office. An option is simply insurance. For the cost of the premium at $8.00 an ounce you are protecting yourself against a price momentum advance to the $10.00 level without your being on board the rising line of silver prices. On paper, it looks like this:

THE OPTION

THE UNIT OF FUTURE DELIVERY

Your right to buy
a unit of silver
good for a speci-
fied time period at
the fixed price of
$8.00 an ounce.

One unit of silver

YOUR COST FOR THAT OPTION

Market price at the time you agree
to buy it.

Real estate has been replaced by silver, but other than that everything else remains the same. Silver could just as easily be replaced with any other unit for future delivery that you wished to buy an option for and which was available for purchase. Whatever price you pay for your option is your insurance premium cost, an insurance that if the momentum comes, you can profit from it.

What are the attractive features of options on units for future delivery? As outlined, there are a couple. The first is absolute dollar risk. If you have a $300 insurance policy against fire to your $400,000 home, you have $300 of absolute risk, the insurance company has $400,000. If you pay $2,000 for an option on silver, your absolute risk is that $2,000, you will never lose more. If the price of silver rises to the level where it will return you an $8,000 profit, you can exercise your $2,000 option and realize that profit. $8,000 minus your $2,000 option cost will leave you $6,000 net from the transaction. Since you initially invested $2,000, your $6,000 profit will return 300% on your capital. The period of time will depend on how long your option was for and the day you decided to exercise it.

This answer in itself illustrates the advantage of being able to take a profit from momentum if it comes, but not risking anything beyond the option cost if it does not. You are not sitting and waiting with ownership of a unit for future delivery for momentum. By paying the premium price you have done all that is required. Now you simply watch. If it ever becomes profitable to exercise the option, you will do so, if it does not, you won't. **You don't own anything except a right, and that right will either vanish with time, when your time period expires, or it will be exercised for a profit.** Those are the only two alternatives. If the momentum comes you can take advantage of it; if it does not, it is like your house that did not burn to the ground, the protection was worth the premium cost.

What are the drawbacks to options, for if there were none no one would buy units for future delivery, but would concentrate solely on options for those units. One drawback can be illustrated by the price of silver again. If you buy the actual unit of silver at $8.00 an ounce and you sell that same unit three months later for exactly $8.00 an ounce you will have lost **nothing** except perhaps a $90 commission. But if you buy an option for silver good for three months and pay $2,000 for it, you have already lost $2,000 right off the bat. Without price momentum you will never get that $2,000 back. For you to break even, the market must advance sufficiently to return at least $2,000 above your cost. For the purchaser of the unit of silver for future delivery, to break even the market does not have to move at all. **You now require momentum to break even; he requires none.** If the market returns an $8,000 profit, the buyer of the unit will make $8,000; you will make $6,000, the profit minus your cost of the option. That is one of the major drawbacks, the purchasers of options start out with a loss at day number one.

Another advantage of the units is the ability to more easily work with tiers. If you own the units you can use the accumulated profits from price momentum to finance additional units with the advance. You may well start with one unit of silver for future delivery and end up with twenty units, or start with five units and end up with twenty as Boyd did. It is a great deal more difficult to use your option as a means of financing additional tiers and few investors use the tier technique when working with options. You may make $6,000 from your silver option while, at the same time, the investor who bought actual units of silver for future delivery was able to tier his return into $60,000.00, from the **identical** movement of price. That is why many people like Rocky and Karen prefer the units themselves to the options on units and why the unit businesses are so much larger than the options business.

One distinct benefit from options that has found a wide following is the ability to use the option as an insurance policy against interest rate fluctuations, and for this purpose you may wish to pursue the field even further. By buying an option on advancing interest rates you may protect your very business from an adverse effect should rates once again rise to astronomical or even unbelievable levels. The option will insure you that if rates do skyrocket, you can exercise the option, take your profit from so acting, and use that profit to help offset your loss of business in your day-to-day life. Rocky and Karen sometimes use options in this fashion. They seek to protect their nursery and flower shop against rising interest rates; against the experience of seeing the prime rate rise from 8% to 20% and their cost of borrowing money rise from 8.25% to 20.25%. They feel the cost of the option is worth the benefits it offers if they hope to remain in a competitive business or to have a small "edge" up on their competitors. They base their decisions primarily on how high or low rates currently are, whether the trend in interest rates is upward or downward, and what they anticipate for the future. In many ways they feel that an "option insurance policy" against interest rates is more valuable to them than a "fire insurance policy" on their nursery out-buildings. Those could always be replaced at minimal costs, but a prime interest rate at above 20% could cost them their very business.

If they are seeking insurance, they normally trade the options market. If they are seeking profit, they invest on the tier program in the actual unit market. Sometimes they do both, insurance and profit; nothing wrong with that. Options offer insurance protection without actuary tables, the knocking on your door of an agent or official risks to be judged and forms to be accepted. No one asks your driving record when you take out an options insurance policy.

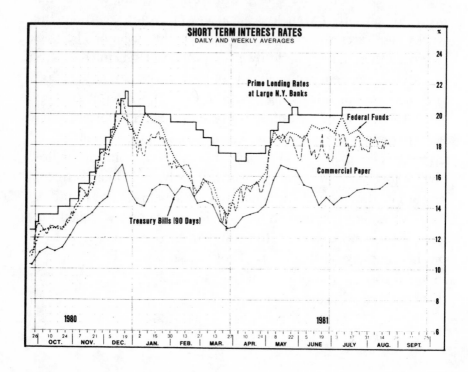

Which option is best for you? Sit down quietly and make a decision. A decision on an insurance policy known as an option. A **new tradition** being formed, tradition based not on seniority, or passed down generation to generation, or even based on the traditional knock on your front door by a salesman in training. Tradition based on risk, new risks in a new age, and most of all tradition based on momentum, momentum for you and momentum against you, momentum that comes when whatever line you are watching starts its move, from the bottom of the page toward the top, or from the top slipping back down. **We are the founding fathers of the tradition to be passed to our sons and daughters, and to their children also.**

It all began with a rolling ball.

Take it and give it a shove.

You are creating momentum.

And from momentum, all profits are born.

Chapter 12

THE SUPER ACCUMULATION OF WEALTH

HOW DO YOU ACCUMULATE WEALTH IN TODAY'S world? There are only **three** steps between starting with a small sum and ending up with a fortune.

1. *Step #1: You have to start looking for it.*

2. *Step #2: When you find a potential source of real wealth you have to stop looking and start thinking.*

3. *Step #3: Once you start thinking, you must plan to use the momentum of your opportunity to make a little from a lot.*

Someone once asked a famous writer what it took to be a successful writer. He responded, "first you have to have something to say." When asked what was next, he replied, "I can't think of anything else." Well, that is the same situation with respect to the accumulation of super quantities of wealth; you have to take the three steps above and "I can't think of anything else."

Once you realize this, you narrow your walking or running path to two broad choices: **active** real wealth accumulation and **passive** real wealth accumulation. The active real wealth accumulation route involves being in thriving, pulsating, down-to-earth businesses; you recognize the names by now: Avon, McDonald's, Chain Letters, Books for Sale, House of Pizza, Louie's Shoe Store Chain, Century 21 Real Estate, Holiday Inns and Diner's Club. These are active businesses that have one purpose, to accumulate wealth for the people at the top of their tier structure through the principle of **"making a little from a lot."**

All these businesses have identical operations even though they are in separate fields and operate totally independently. If you would diagram them on a piece of paper, their essential corporate structure looks the same. They are businesses that are expanding horizontally with vertical growth and profiting from their momentum. They all have different names, but they have identical corporate skeletons. McDonald's, Avon Products, Century 21 Real Estate and all the rest look exactly like this:

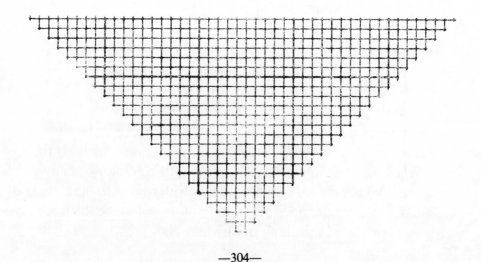

They are clones, each identical with the other, all making a little from a lot and, in the process, accumulating huge sums of real wealth for the people at the top of their tier structures. You, too, can make a great deal of money by repeating the steps that the founding father of these firms took: start looking for a business, when you find it stop looking and start working, and as you *work* expand upward and outward at the same time. These are the three steps they took and you can take the same route with the same amount of effort these pioneers exerted. Take a close look at the grey hair on some of the men who sit on top of these business tiers; that came from hard work and worry, not from idly sitting by and watching their fortunes grow. Active wealth accumulation on the tier structure basis in a real world business involves a lot of very hard work.

The other alternative to active participation in an expanding tier structure of wealth accumulation involves **passive** investment. **In the passive field, there is really only one alternative open to you, like it or not, and that alternative is the nine fields of business outlined in the previous chapter.** You may prefer to get rich in real estate, or you may like insurance adjusting for a profession, or perhaps being a buyer or seller of bonds is more your style. If those are your choices, you should pursue them to the maximum but realize when you do that unless you start out with a lot of money, the chances are they will not accumulate super sums of wealth for you during your lifetime. If you enter them for the challenge and the lifestyle, that is one thing. If you enter them in an effort to **passively** take a small amount of money and make a huge sum with it, there is small chance of success. **Sure,** you may still make yourself a millionaire in real estate, even starting from a small base. But you will not make it as a passive investor. If you hope to have any chance of succeeding in real estate today you will require a lot of luck and have to engage in hard, demanding work. Real estate may make you wealthy, but not passively. Not in a million years, not starting with only a small sum of capital.

Do I recommend that **you** personally commit capital to each and all, or to only part of the nine businesses discussed in chapter 11. That is a decision you will have to make. I will tell you this, if you have a small sum of capital to start with and you hope to accumulate a substantial sum of wealth during your lifetime, you have **no choice** but to consider these nine fields of business. If you want to make some money, in a **passive** investment, you need to find a field with three main characterisics:

1. *You must be able to passively enter that field with only a small amount of capital.*
2. *As the value of your initial investment grows, you must be able to use that growth to finance the purchase of new investment.*
3. *The field must have price momentum. The line must move.*

Insurance allows no equity financing, real estate does not have the necessary momentum, bonds require huge sums of capital to make modest returns, and the stock market is a "sit and wait" game which probably won't make you rich. I would be more than willing to add any other fields to the nine outlined if any reader can send me some additional names, the names of businesses where you can passively invest a small sum of capital, increase your ownership with internal financing and no additional out-of-pocket cash, and then have the necessary momentum required to "make a little from a lot." I will be happy to add any names to this list of nine such qualifying businesses; but I know of no additional names to add. If you want to accumulate a substantial sum of wealth within your lifetime by passive investment, you will enter these fields perhaps not from choice, but because you have **no choice at all**: There simply is no alternative available to the super accumulation of wealth passively.

1. *The Household, Food and Clothing Businesses*
   Available units of beef, bacon, eggs, potatoes, sugar, cooking oil, coffee, cocoa, orange juice and cotton.

2. *The Petroleum Businesses*
   Available units of crude oil, gasoline (leaded and unleaded), home heating oil and propane.

3. *The Lumber Businesses*
   Available units of lumber and plywood.

4. *The Metals Businesses*
   Available units of silver, gold, copper, platinum and palladium.

5. *The Farming Businesses*
   Available units of wheat, corn, oats, barley, rye, rapeseed, flaxseed, soybeans, soybean meal and soybean oil.

6. *The Banking Businesses*
   Available units of interest in the form of treasury bills, treasury notes, treasury bonds, eurodollars, certificates of deposits and "ginnie mae" insured mortgages.

7. *The International Diplomacy and Financial Businesses*
   Available units of world currencies including the German deutsche mark, the Canadian dollar, the Swiss franc, the French franc, the Italian lira, the Japanese yen, the Mexican peso, the British pound.

8. *The Wall Street Barony Businesses*
   Available units of stock market indices, including the Value Line index, the New York Stock Exchange index, the Standard and Poors 500 stock index and the Dow Jones Industrial averages index.

9. *The Insurance Businesses*
   Available "options" for units of the previous eight businesses with selection on a selective basis for key opportunities.

With Time

There will be more names to add to this list. It is an expanding compilation and, as you learn of new names that fit within the nine major categories, or even of entirely new categories, simply add them to your ongoing list of business opportunities for the new generation of investors.

Can you do it?

Can you decide to start, traverse horizontally until you find an appropriate "start-up" point, and then start up in a tier expanding fashion? There is only one way to find out and that is to begin. And as you begin, you should keep these words of advice in mind; words of advice which come from personal experience as I have invested 70% of my adult life in these various forms of business.

Traditional fields of passive investment will not make you wealthy. This is not an indictment, it is a fact. No longer will you be able to start out with a small sum of capital in the normal fields of traditional investment and accumulate real wealth. The traditional fields simply shuffle the players around and allow a few people at the top to make a bundle. But the traditional fields your grandfather and father knew so well will not be kind to you.

No one will ever make you successful except yourself. If you wish to achieve fame, personal wealth, recognition and success you may well so achieve it, but if you do there will be two main propellers: your drive and your inner strength. No one ever makes anyone else wealthy or successful, with very few rare exceptions which you had better not plan on. Every successful person is a self-made person, and you are patterned in the identical mold. Remember that life is a process of getting weak hands to part with the single dollar and every person who offers you advice, free or paid for, is simply trying to get that single dollar bill to slip through your fingers. If you wish to succeed, then take the steps necessary and depend on no one but yourself. That is the only sure route. View all others as simply players in the game who are inviting you, in one form or another, to join their tier structure on a bottom rung.

Succeeding is challenging. If you hope to reach a pleateau that others do not commonly reach, you will have to meet and overcome the challenge. Why is success defined as levels of non-common achievement? Because if it was common, there would be no challenge. Tell your spouse that you drove your car from town to home safely tonight, and the response you will elicit can be predicted. But tell your spouse that you drove in the Indianapolis 500 race and passed 80% of the other cars by finish line time, and you **have** achieved a measure of success. Success spelled backwards is challenge. If you like a challenge, then you may wish to chase after success. That does not mean the challenge is the end-all, for it is not. Many people are very successful who appear as calm, collected, accountant-type businesspeople. You need not drive race cars to like a challenge; a college degree and showing up each day for work can mean you are meeting life's challenges with forward progress. In the nine businesses previously described there will be stimulation sufficient to drive you forward. You will be up against some of the brightest and the best, in intellectual talent and in achievement records. But let that not get you down. The line can still only move upward, sideways, or come cascading down, no matter how many Ph.D.s are watching its progress. It is the **line** that you will always be pitted against, and nothing else.

Look for business familiarity. If you decide to pursue one of these nine fields of business, the best approach is to start in an area where you already have some knowledge. Don't start with the French franc if you have never been out of your home town and believe France is the smallest country in Africa. If you are familiar with the stock market, start with the stock indices. If you buy oranges each week at the supermarket, give a glance now and then to units of orange juice for future delivery. You might be surprised at what you see, both in terms of immediate price and expected price over the long haul. If there is a freeze, the first skyrocketing of the line will be on the unit price for future delivery, it will not be at your grocery store counter. That will come later, about a month or two later, and you may be the only one on your block who **knew** it was coming. Why? You were tier 3 up on orange juice in units for future delivery.

If you know something about farming, maybe stick to the various farm businesses; there are plenty of those to select from. Your knowledge need not be of great detail; Rocky and Karen entered the home heating oil market with little real knowledge about that product of petroleum, but they did have some knowledge of it. They knew more about heating oil than they did about rapeseed or palladium. And most of all, they knew that price was simply a line anyway. One field that is especially appealing is interest rate units. Everyone complains about interest rates, but no one does anything about them. Now is your opportunity to accept the challenge; you **can** do something about interest rates, you can buy a unit and **profit** from an advancing prime, perhaps for the first time in your entire life.

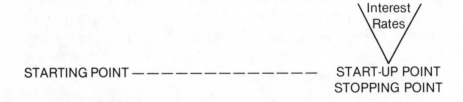

STARTING POINT — — — — — — — — — — — START-UP POINT
STOPPING POINT

Learn every day, it is fun. This is a business of knowledge growth as well as financial return. It is a simple truth that life will be more interesting to you, events will have more meaning and your company will be worth more once you take an active interest in these new fields of investment. The very fact that you know prices will advance at the supermarket will distinguish you from your neighbors. If the Swiss franc is collapsing, no one in town may be aware of it but you, and that can be important. Think of Mexico, you read all the news, now you know how to interpret it, in terms of a line moving across a piece of graph paper. This knowledge will not come like the evening paper, simply deposited on your doorstep, but it will come **with** the evening paper; you will read and you will learn, there is no way to avoid it. Study, expand your horizons of interest, make a few notes here and there, and **think**. With time you will enjoy the entire process.

As you progress, keep a **Rule Book**. It doesn't have to be anything more extensive than a lined school traditional collection of blank pages we are all familiar with. When you find a new technique that works, add it to the section of your book on "things that work." When you find something that is lousy, add it to the "lousy" section. You may wish to have a separate part for your goals, the criteria you use when establishing tiers, the dollar amounts you are willing to risk on any venture and the type of opportunities that justify greater dollar risks. Keep a record. Judge your performance. Update, modify, rework your papers continually. Remember even Albert Einstein was working until the very end with new thoughts. With time your book of rules will mean more to you than any other non-human item in your house. That little notebook will become your diary, a diary of experience and a roadmap to the watering holes of life.

Remember always that the risks are real. Can you name any field of passive investment which offers returns in the hundreds or thousands of percent that does not carry risk? **No, there is none.** You can partially reduce that risk by buying "options" instead of buying units, but you are paying a premium for this insurance which you may or may not be willing to spare. **The steps I recommend are simple:**

Do not advance to investing real money until you have achieved continual success "on paper" with paper money. If you cannot win at poker playing for toothpicks, you will not be able to win playing for hundred dollar bills; the pressure will be worse, not less. Succeed first consistently on paper. If you can, and many people cannot, then proceed to a single unit of investment. Buy at one level and sell at another, and do this over and over again until you can do it over and over again **successfully**. The prerequisite for success on the two tier level is historic success on the first rung up. If you cannot succeed at level one, you will have difficulty succeeding with two tiers and the cost may be very expensive. **The risks are real,** do not increase them with lack of experience or knowledge. I have been at this game in excess of eighteen years and yet I still trade "on paper" numerous markets. Why? Because I am always learning, and by being in positions at least "on paper," I can always benefit from watching the price line move. Einstein still did experiments "on paper" while in his eighties. Don't rush in to tier 4 just because you have two weeks of successful experience on tier 1 behind you.

In other words, go slow. Money is very hard to accumulate in this world of ours, and it is very easy to part with. We are all weak hands each and every day. Keep that in mind as you proceed, whatever you lose will be hard to get back, so lose it slowly. Remember, too, that no one on the face of the earth will ever care about your money like you do. When you get a call in the middle of the night from a person asking you to invest in condominiums in Hawaii, he cares only about getting you on his tier. You care about your money. The difference is the distinction between being dead or alive, **a great deal**. Since no one will ever care about your money like you do, and since the financial and business world consists of strong hands seeking out the weak members of society to part with the single dollar, adopt the go slow approach. These nine businesses have been around for many years, some over a hundred years, so there is no need to rush in tomorrow without preparation.

Trust nothing except yourself. Systems, sure-fire-never-losers, "the price can't go lower," chance-of-a-lifetime approaches are normally another means for getting you on the bottom tier. Resist temptation. Trust yourself, your own experience, your own knowledge, talent and abilities, but trust nothing else. Each new idea, each new method offered, each proposal add to a list of things you do **not** trust. Only after you have real life experience with that item for a considerable period of time will you consider transferring it to your "trust through thick and thin" column. I have a column like that in my rule book, also; it is very **short**. The things I don't trust take up almost an entire notebook by themselves. People may hope you do well, but no one will ever care about your money like you do. Never forget that, and trust nothing until time and your own experience justifies such trust.

Even with success proceed slowly. If you are able to succeed on the various tiers and advance to consistent success at the tier 4 level, do not invest each and every time at that height. Evel Knievel was very successful at jumping over 23 automobiles parked side by side with his high powered motorcycle. But that did not mean every time he saw a car parked sideways on the street he put a ramp in front of it and flew through the air with his bike conquering another challenge. You may be successful at tier 4, but that does not mean you should abandon the lower levels. All success at tier 4 means is that if such an opportunity ever presents itself you are qualified to handle the situation. It does not mean every opportunity is a fresh ride. If you believe it is, go back to "on paper" investing for another six months, there is much still left to learn.

This is a field of emotions, you are about to learn your inner self. Personality, the stuff you are made of, will be important in this journey of yours. When Rocky and Karen think about their nursery business, they dwell on $15.80 tickets for new shrubs, or $110.00 electric light bills. When they got into heating oil, they were involved with taking $1,500 and making $45,000 in a period of weeks. You cannot operate in the world of successful high finance without drawing from deep inside yourself emotions you may not even know are there. We are all barrels full of many diverse elements, the pursuit of money will tell you about some of the gunk that lies at the bottom of yours. One way to help yourself deal with emotions is to define your goals and steps-along-the-way in advance. If you have it all pretty much laid out on paper, there will be less decisions to make and less turmoil to suffer through. If you have a $3,000 profit from a $1,500 investment, should you take it or stand aside and wait for more? Whatever you decide, the line will quickly tell you the results of your decision. Some people cannot deal with immediate answers to important questions, but the line acts without knowledge that it is being followed by a crowd living on rollaides. Set your stop loss in advance and you have eliminated one problem. Move your stop loss up closer to current prices as the market moves in your favor and you have reduced that same problem. Start slow and take a small profit first, and be happy with it. Even if your quick decision resulted in missing a large profit. Agree in advance; no complaints. And with time work forward to more success and to larger profits, for they will surely come to those who persevere in this field

Spend those earnings along the way, at least a portion. If the line is so generous to offer you its rewards and favors, don't be afraid to accept the benefits and spend a little of the cash along the way. I wear a solid gold Cartier wristwatch that cost me nine thousand dollars. Why? Because I like the flash, the glamor, the sign of success. Yes, partially, that is one reason I wear the watch. But another reason is simply to remind me that this is not a game of numbers, of tiers or of units, it is a game of financial success which means financial rewards. If you benefit naught from any of the rewards, then you are missing the essential part of the game. Take a vacation. Be the first at work to own 500 shares of IBM for the "long-haul." Treat your sister to a new car, even pay off the debts your father accumulated raising you to be a man or woman. Don't fall into the trap of taking $5,000 and making $100,000 and not using some of that profit to maximize your life style. You may not like gold watches, but each of us knows a little widow down the block who could make loving use of a hundred dollar bill. Profits are to be enjoyed, not lost. If your run is from $5,000 to $100,000, pay your taxes and pocket your benefits and then use the same skills that made success possible in the first place to repeat that success, starting again with only $5,000. **Even the greatest track star begins each new race fresh at the starting line.** He counts on his talents, experience and hard work to project him forward to the finish line. It is nice to start over with money set aside in the bank. When you are successful, don't work with $100,000 in your account, start again with $5,000 and build it up.

Remember, this is a field of wealth accumulation but without fun the goals may not be worth the effort. Don't make yourself and family or friends miserable by your constant anxiety. Start slow, start small, and always keep relatively small and on a slow pace. Wealth accumulation is not the **only** measure of success; enjoyment of life rates up there somewhere near the top also. Aim for an increase in your finances, but aim for a good and happy life. Help a few people along the way, don't deliberately harm anyone, march to the tune of your own drummer and do your very best. A good and happy life is your focal point, it is not the accumulation of wealth. To keep your experiences fun, spend a little from time to time and don't invest more than you can afford to work with. The results will be better and you will appreciate them much more. If you are truly successful you will be known by your smile and not a worried brow or frown. Anyone who implies they are a great success, but is afraid to smile is no success at all. Smiling isn't a sign of weakness, it is a sure indication that you are repaying God for the life He gave you.

If you need a little help to get started, I will be happy to offer a gentle nudge. The best step to put your first foot on is to gather in a set of price charts so you can see where prices currently are and whether there are any 1-2-3, bounce back, long drawn out affairs or absolute zero opportunities open for you today.

To receive information on how to start in this game feel free to write me personally. I will always be happy to help you. Write me at:

Bruce Gould
Post Office Box 16
Seattle, WA 98111

There is something you should know as you decide whether to take your first step and venture into business in one of these nine areas: The field is **exploding** with growth! The reason for that explosion has nothing to do with gasoline, or with cocoa, or interest rates, copper or the Soviet wheat purchases of 1972. Growth is on an aggressive upward curve because the generation of today realizes that yesterday's news will not work for them. Wealth is there to be accumulated, in fact there is more money available for accumulation today than ever before in the history of the world. **Think of this single fact for thirty seconds:** More money has been printed since 1967 than had been printed in the entire time from the Continental Congress and the Declaration of Independence up to 1967. Since 1967, the Federal Reserve Board of the United States printed more money for distribution than was printed in the 191 years from 1776 until 1967. **Wealth is not harder to accumulate today because there is no money out there, there has never been so much money available.** Wealth is harder to accumulate because most people spend their time sitting on the bottom tier of someone else's structure passing along their single dollar bills. **Then take a look at this growth curve of the nine business you have been studying.**

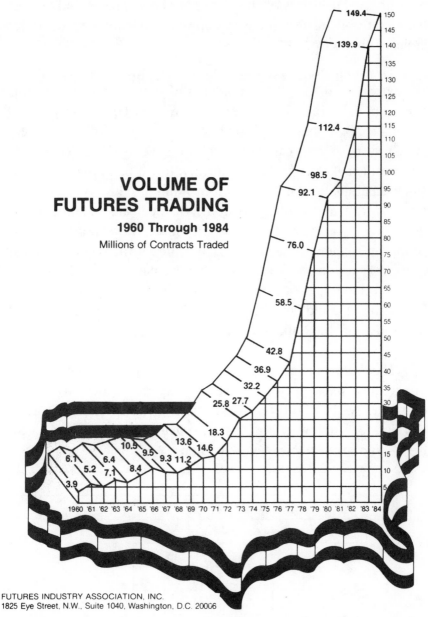

VOLUME OF FUTURES TRADING

1960 Through 1984

Millions of Contracts Traded

149.4 — 150
139.9 — 140
112.4
98.5
92.1
76.0
58.5
42.8
36.9
32.2
25.8 27.7
18.3
13.6 14.6
10.5
9.5 9.3 11.2
6.1 6.4
5.2 7.1 8.4
3.9

1960 '61 '62 '63 '64 '65 '66 '67 '68 '69 '70 '71 '72 '73 '74 '75 '76 '77 '78 '79 '80 '81 '82 '83 '84

FUTURES INDUSTRY ASSOCIATION, INC.
1825 Eye Street, N.W., Suite 1040, Washington, D.C. 20006

The reason for this explosive growth can be summed up brief-ly: **the opportunity for wealth accumulation through the momentum of the line.** There is no other reason. A great many people have searched their horizontal lines of life and found their "start-up" point in the businesses of this book. Nothing is never-ending, but the growth of this new industry appears to be attacking the outer limits of that term.

The momentum is found in the line, but the use of Momentum is what offers the explosive potential of such tremendous profits from that line's movement. You can buy at $1.00 and sell at $1.50 and make 50¢ a unit, and if you have one unit you will make a very large return on your capital. But if you have used the tier system, you won't make a very large return; you will be in the process of super accumulation of wealth. Momentum has this essential factor working for it and working for you: When you are on board a winner — man, you are really on board a winner. Momentum takes the simple movement of a line and maximizes the return through horizontal expansion with vertical movement. And Momentum allows you to fail 90% of the time and still end up a winner; Argentina wishes it could have had such odds in its favor when it kicked the British off the Falkland islands.

The vertical line will carry you profitably upward. The horizontal expansion along the vertical axis can sufficiently rid you of money worries forever. Momentum has this essential factor working for it and working for you: **When you are on board a winner — you are really on board a winner.**

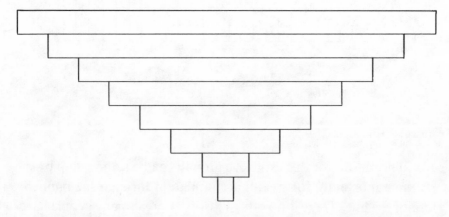

Read on, my friend, read on. **The best is yet to come.**

Chapter 13

TAKE A BALL. ROLL IT ACROSS A TABLE. YOUR HAND has given momentum to that ball; the amount of momentum determines how far the ball will roll before stopping. That is the simplest form of momentum.

Take a ball. Roll it down a hill. Your hand begins the momentum, but an additional force, gravity, will supply additional momentum. The ball will roll faster and faster, gaining speed until a counterforce acts against it. The same flick of your wrist that rolled the ball across the table has started the ball down the hill, yet momentum has sent the ball rolling at 5, 10, 25 miles per hour: Other forces can act on momentum.

* * * * *

You can know something of Irene's mettle by the manner in which she conducts her days.

On the winter solstice, the shortest day, the sun rises heavily and hangs in the sky with scarcely enough room to slip a knife between sun and earth. For a few hours it gives a light of little use or substance. Inturak is ninety miles south of the Arctic Circle, and so no day is completely without sun. That is small comfort: for the entire winter the village will be long shadows, dusk, and darkness.

In winter, Irene's days begin in darkness. Her first act every morning is to check the oversized thermometer mounted a few feet outside her kitchen window. She wipes a circle in the frosted glass; thirty degrees below zero, Fahrenheit. An average winter morning in Inturak. She'll be teaching that day. She cannot open school when the temperature dips to forty below. Too dangerous, read the regulations. There are many days in winter when school does not open.

Irene dresses before the stove while listening to the morning news from Edmonton on the radio. The dressing is an ornate and clumsy ceremony—fishnet thermal underwear, whipcord woolen trousers, blouse, fur trousers, leggings, parka, shell parka, underboots, overboots, gloves, mitts—a bloody nuisance for a hundred yard walk to the school building. But she never argued with the Northwest Territories and its winters. She had taught through three of them, and had argued with winter only once, her first winter in Inturak. She had dropped the school key while fumbling to open the door with her heavy gloves. Stripping off the gloves, she picked up the key, turned the lock, grabbed the doorknob with her bare hand, and stuck fast. The moisture on her hand had frozen instantly to the steel. She whooped for help for a couple of minutes, until a villager happened by, impassively judged the situation, and resorted to the Indian's solution for that common problem: he fumbled for a moment and urinated her hand free. From that day on, Irene touched nothing with her bare hand when outdoors at forty below.

Walking to the school she marveled, as always, how dry and mild below zero temperature could feel on the clear gray days of the North. A dusting of old snow swirled around her books; she passed rough planked houses on stilts above the permafrost, kerosene lamps glowing yellow through the windows. The village had electricity; the Indians preferred the softer kerosene light.

From the classroom window she could see her students winding their way to the school, furry lumps skittering over snow. Twenty-one students made up her class, drawn from two hundred miles around, boarding with families in Inturak, children from six to thirteen.

Her work was extremely satisfying. The children were shy, respectful, curious. She was the sole white person in 400 square miles, but she had been accepted fully by the villagers: she was their pet, and they teased her unmercifully about her naivete about something so simple and basic as winter. They were warm people, social people.

She was well paid by the Canadian government for her work: it was acknowledged to be a difficult life, an isolated life, and pains were taken to reduce the isolation. The government had recently installed a satellite dish-antenna, and had provided the school building and Irene with television and telephone. She used the telephone rarely, but welcomed the television: she could plant the youngest children in front of *Sesame Street*. She didn't mind the isolation: she enjoyed the solitude. In the winter she could read for hours, listening to the immaculate cold, or pursue her business. The work of teaching and the nourishing life of the village were comfortable: she thought her life ideal.

It was the winter when she wrote me.

*   *   *   *   *

Where do old friends come from? I met Irene during a late night poker game as a student in Washington, D.C. She was murderous; I remember she always dealt Stud, and would raise you to an inch of your life. Political Science was my study, her minor to a major of English. She covered a lot of ground on a tennis court, even though she would have had to levitate to make five feet tall. A friendship: we went our ways, occasionally wrote. Over the years we independently came to learn about buying units for future de-livery, and in our letters we compared notes occasionally, but of-fered each other no advice, no congratulations, no condolences. She did well. I did well.

Irene's letters from the Northwest Territories dealt with the teaching of native Canadian children, who absorbed their educa-tion as if it were something rare and precious. She wrote about the silence and the hard beauty of tundra and thin forests, her excite-ment over the land and the life. ("Temperature this morning is –58°. You can hear trees exploding when their sap freezes. Having a great time. Wish you were here?") It was unusual, then, for her to write and detail her plan for me.

Nothing much was said about the plan, just a few short words, a couple of prices; no questions, just a few sentences in a postscript. But it floored me.

To teach in a native reserve in Canada's Northwest Territories, Irene was paid $40,000 a year. This was in 1973, before the super-inflated dollar days of the late 70's and early 80's, when $50,000 **bought** a beautiful home instead of making a down payment, when interest rates stood at eight percent, not eighteen. $40,000 was a stellar salary, but it was coals to Newcastle for Irene. There was very little Irene could do with money in Inturak; her provisions were supplied by the government; her house was supplied by the govern-ment; her transportation was supplied by the government; she had little need or taste for luxuries. For three years her only interest in money was to see what could be done with it, to see what sort of future could be built from it.

The letter had been written on December 21; I received it in the middle of January, but her mail was dependent on bush, which was dependent on the weather. The weather had clearly been forbid-ding. Irene wrote about her day, the shortest day of the year, and added:

Have you been watching sugar? Isn't the price ridiculous? Do you know what I'm going to do this winter? I'm going to stare at sugar until my eyes glaze. (Sugar glaze?) I'm in for the long haul this time. I got in last October at 8¢ a pound, which I find unbelievable, and, at 8¢, I may put my stop-loss at 0¢. There is going to be some momentum, Bruce.

I had been watching sugar, as she figured. In the fall the price of sugar—the cash price on the day-to-day market—had risen above 10¢ a pound from a low of 5½¢ a pound and had then retreated back toward the 8¢ level.

In October, when Irene was entering the sugar business, a division of the Household, Food and Clothing Businesses, a unit required about $1,500 in margin money, about the same amount it would require ten years later.

I know sugar. I know it from every excess pound on this compact little body that helps to keep me warm up here. And 8¢ a pound is cheap for 1973. I think it's going to be absurd for 1975. I bought 2 units of sugar for March, 1975, delivery, and I think I can stick it out for all that time. So if I don't write, you'll know how I am doing by the price of March '75 sugar. If I don't get the momentum, the next sound you'll hear is me, licking my wounds and looking for something else.

Irene was **really** in for the long haul. March of 1975 was seventeen months away, a long time to stick it out. She was going to take a chance, go for the long haul, ride the line from beginning to end.

Is it possible to enter the sugar unit business and wait out a move for as long as seventeen months? Rocky and Karen Becket never considered spending more than a year in any one business. Most unit businessmen are involved in transactions that last less than a year, but about 10% of the various units do have lives up to two years; sugar is one, copper another, opportunities for the businessperson, like Irene, who chose a long ride.

Seventeen months of being on board the line express.

I thought, reading the letter, that it was an intelligent, well reasoned decision. Her logic seemed sound. If the "cash" price of sugar, the nearest price, was able to rise from 5½¢ a pound level to above 10¢ a pound, all within a thirteen month period, then within the next seventeen months—before March, 1975—any sugar purchased around 8¢ a pound should rise to at least 16¢ a pound, perhaps higher. If nothing else, sugar bought around the 8¢ level should at least return to 10¢, with only minimal risk of it dropping much below 8¢ a pound. I'm certain Irene spent her spring and summer watching the current price of sugar rise and fall which she determined the shape of her trade.

The full dimensions of the trade were offered at the bottom of the letter, in a few words. At first, I discounted it as a typographical error. Then I re-read the note, and remembered our poker games, and realized she was dead-serious. I knew that she was going to go for it, and it scared me to death.

In any case, wish me luck. I'm in with two units at 8¢, so I can build a tier at each 1½¢ move. I think I'm going to get a little momentum, so watch sugar. I'm going for Tier 8.

I read that letter from the Northwest Territories, and have never felt colder since. Tier 8: Irene was going for a lifetime's momentum.

        *   *   *   *   *   *

A neatly typed letter accompanied a check for $5000. A precisely worded list of instructions to her broker in Vancouver, British Columbia, Canada, detailed every step he should take concerning her units in sugar, in case she would be unable to telephone from Inturak, a frequent occurrence. $5000 to reopen her trading account with the firm. Each unit of sugar cost $1500; her two units would cost $3000, and she would give herself a cushion of $2000 to protect her against a decline.

Mr. Mathiesson:

*As we discussed, if the price of March 1975 sugar is avail-
able for 8¢ a pound, buy me two units. . .*

Irene owned her two units one day after the firm received the
letter and check, at 8¢ a pound. Tier 1 was in place immediately, as
Irene had expected. When you are thinking about going for a Tier
8, you know where prices are and you know it everyday. Because of
the advances in telecommunications, because of satellite dish anten-
nae and microwave technology, Irene had access to the latest price
information, though she be hundreds of miles from the nearest city,
Yellowknife, NWT. Once her letter was sent, her die was cast.

Two units of sugar under ownership at 8¢ a pound. $1500
each, $3000 out-of-pocket margin money required. The size of each
unit? 112,000 pounds. Why such an odd number? Because 112,000
pounds equals a nice, round 50 European tons, a round figure that
translates poorly to American pounds.

If the price of sugar rises 1¢ and you have one pound of sugar,
you will make a profit of 1¢. If you have 112,000 pounds of sugar in
your unit, your unit will make $1120.00 (1¢ times 112,000 pounds =
$1120.00). If you have two units, as Irene now did, you will make
$1120 on each of your units, or a total of $2,240, should you sell
when the price rises that 1¢. If you do not sell, you have an equity
growth of value. As you know by now, in the futures unit businesses
you can use this increase in equity value to automatically, without
question, purchase additional units. All that is required to purchase
these units is to instruct your firm to do so, by phone, by mail, in
person: "buy me one more unit with my increase in equity value
after the price rise." Or, if you wish, you may ask the firm to mail
you the equity increase with a cashier's check: "If my equity value
rises $4000 at any given time, please mail me a cashier's check the
same day for $4000." It will be done, immediately and without
question, upon your instructions. It is this equity financing feature

that distinguishes the futures business from all other businesses.

Besides the buy order, Irene included a stop-loss order.

> *. . . If the price ever drops to below 3¢ after I have bought my units at 8¢, sell my units at the stop loss price or thereabouts. . .*

Irene had never, in years of investing in units, entered a purchase order without having a stop-loss order in the background to protect it.

Finally, Irene gave instructions that were to be followed if the Tier 1 order filled and she had her two units of sugar at 8¢ a pound; instructions stiffly written to avoid the possibility of their being misunderstood:

> *If I buy my 2 units of sugar at 8¢ a pound, and the market does not drop to my stop-loss point beforehand, but rises, use my equity increase at 9½¢ to buy 2 more units of sugar at that price.*
>
> *If I buy my additional units of sugar at 9½¢ and the market does not drop to my stop-loss point beforehand, but rises, use my equity increase at 11¢ a pound to buy 4 additional units of sugar at that price.*
>
> *Further instructions will be forthcoming.*

These were all the instructions she gave her firm and all the instructions she needed to give them. The tier steps were clearly defined and calculated. Two units purchased at 8¢ a pound would yield a profit of $3360.00 by the time the market rose to 9½¢ (1½¢ profit times 112,000 pounds per unit, times 2 units = $3360.00), with which she would buy two additional units. Each unit cost $1500; the additional units would cost her only $3000 out of her $3360 equity increase, leaving a bit of an edge to add to her initial $2000 reserve for any short-term price decline.

All set. The order filled: two units of sugar at 8¢ a pound, purchased in October, 1973. And what happened to price? Nothing; winter approached, Irene taught her classes, and the orders stood; if sugar reached 9½¢ a pound, she would have her second tier filled automatically; if the price reached 3¢ a pound, she would be taken out of the market automatically. She was in for the long haul; her instructions were explicit. She could not alter the line; she could only watch it, and watch it we both did, for two months. In late December, the line reached 9½¢ a pound, and Irene owned two more units. Slow momentum, but she was only asking for momentum over the long haul. Her concern was to fill Tier 2. It was filled.

In January, 1974, Irene saw—and I saw—that the line was approaching 11¢ a pound. She sent off her second set of instructions to the firm.

Mr. Mathiesson:

Re: My letter of 5 October, 1973.

If I buy my 4 additional units of sugar at 11¢ a pound, and the market does not drop to my stop-loss point but rises, use my equity increase at 12½¢ to buy 8 additional units at that price.

If I buy my 8 additional units of sugar at 12½¢ a pound, and the market does not drop to my stop-loss point, but rises, use my equity increase at 14¢ to buy me 16 additional units at that price, raising my stop loss to 8¢.

Further instructions will be forthcoming.

If the momentum came, her instructions would cover a large span of it. After starting at 8¢ in October, the sugar market rose in price to 9½¢ by Christmas of 1973. On January 14, 1974, the price rose to 11¢ a pound, and on that day, Irene owned eight units of sugar; two purchased at 8¢, two more at 9½¢ a pound, and four at 11¢. Tier 3 was complete within three months of the first day of the trade, and Tiers 4 and 5, if possible were lined up waiting for the line.

Five tiers, the limits that would be familiar to Rocky and Karen, all as a result of momentum. If the line continued up and the price reached 14¢ a pound, Irene would see her total units increase from two to thirty-two, a sixteen fold increase in units without putting an additional out-of-pocket penny into the business.

"Further instructions will be forthcoming," Irene wrote her firm, but not yet. If she reached Tier 5—if there was sufficient momentum—she would pause. The price would be 14¢ a pound. She would pause. She had been in this business longer than Rocky and Karen. She knew that there was a time for action, and a time for pausing.

Tier 4 and Tier 5 filled rather quickly; the "little momentum" that she predicted in her letter to me was there, in force. By February 15th all five tiers were in place. The price of sugar had gone from 8¢ to 9¢ to 10¢ to 11¢ to 12¢ to 13¢ to 14¢: an arithmetic progression. Her units rose in a geometric progression: 2 to 4 to 8 to 16: 32 units in all. Irene had riden 6¢ worth of momentum to increase her holdings to 32 units. She now controlled three million, five hundred and eighty-four thousand pounds of sugar. Three and a half million pounds of sugar from a cash investment in 224,000 pounds. With each 1¢ price rise now, she could multiply 3,584,000 by .01¢, or $35,840.00.

No where to go but up. Yet Irene paused. She did not send further instructions, though the price kept rising. She did not send her Tier 6 orders; she entered no Tier 7 orders. Down south, I had been watching the price of sugar closely, with Irene in mind. I watched the price and assumed that Irene was already at Tier 6, that she had bought another 32 units, that her total holdings were 64 units.

But Irene did nothing. "I know sugar, Bruce," she had written me. "I know sugar from every excess pound on this compact little body." Sugar she may have known; the line, she knew better.

Recall the "bounce-back" effect. It was the basis of Rocky and Karen's home heating oil business, as well as the impetus of most of their early trades. If you remember, Rocky and Karen looked for a price that had dropped precipitously from a high price and zone to a low price or zone. Such a price would usually recover all or part of its value, and Rocky and Karen tried to ride the momentum of that "bounce-back" to value.

If home heating oil dropped from a zone 1 level to a zone 4 level, it was quite likely to rise again to the top of zone 2. Rocky and Karen have now seen the phenomenon many times; Irene had seen it countless times. She knew that once a dramatic event has occurred, the chances are good that the effect of the dramatic event will continue. But first the momentum will be tested. The price of home heating oil falls, but recovers; "bounce-back." The price of sugar soars, but weakens; "bounce-back." Testing of price, testing of momentum. In sugar many traders start selling, taking advantage of their profits after the 6¢ rise in price. So prices drop. But Irene was not looking to sell for a 6¢ profit. She had no intention of selling. She was still looking to **buy**; she was looking for a Tier 8, and the "bounce-back" would tell her whether a Tier 8 would be possible.

Irene paused. The price continued up. Several times the price touched the point where she could use her equity to purchase the 32 units that made up Tier 6; I assumed she had. But she was following a rule, a rule of her own invention.

"After reaching Tier 5, always allow 60 days for bounce-back. Proceed to higher tiers thereafter, if possible."

She knew sugar, but she knew the line better. How many times had she traded to Tier 8 "on paper" before attempting one? Enough to make a rule, enough to realize that she should expect a bounce-back, a reaction, at her Tier 5 area.

Her stop-loss had been raised to 8¢ a pound, to protect all the units she had purchased. Whether her trade would continue or not depended on whether or not that stop loss would be touched. A lot depended on other buyers of sugar, the ones like Rocky and Karen a few years later, who would be watching for the drop, who upon seeing the price fall from 14¢ a pound, would start buying again. It would be the other buyers who, by their combined decisions, would end the "bounce-back" effect.

The price of sugar fell to 11¢, nowhere near her 8¢ stop loss. The buyers jumped on the line in droves, now that the price was lower. Thousands of businessmen across the world, watching a line move across a piece of graph paper, from the top to the bottom, and then from the bottom to the top. They were buying, then. But Irene sat quietly, she was waiting to expand, to use the momentum to the utmost.

When the 60 day "bounce-back" period had passed, the decline in price had been well established, and it had ended. There was no missing it; buyers were jumping on, forcing the price higher. Irene would take the higher prices, gladly; she was in for the long haul and it would be the higher prices that would **finance** her trip. Toward the end of the two-months, she finally sent the delayed instruction to her firm:

Mr. Mathiesson:

Re: Letters of 5 October, 1973 and 5 January, 1974.

No sooner than April 15th, but any time thereafter, if the price of sugar rises to 15½¢, use my equity increase to buy me 32 additional units at that price.

If I buy my 32 additional units at 15½¢ a pound, and the market does not drop to my stop-loss point of 8¢ a pound, but rises, use my equity increase at 17¢ a pound to buy 64 additional units at that price.

If I buy my 64 additional units at 17¢ a pound, and the market does not drop to my stop-loss point, but rises, use my equity increase at 18½¢ a pound to buy me 128 additional units at that price.

At that point, raise my stop-loss to 12½¢.

Further instructions will be forthcoming.

A Tier 8 plan. We have seen Rocky and Karen successfully run a Tier 4 plan to their advantage, and a Tier 3. But Irene was looking at the stratosphere; once the bounce-back was over, she **knew** she could pull it off. Her instructions were specific. The line would do what the line would do. She could not influence it. She would continue to quietly teach school. It was her vocation: the plan was defined, and now all **we** could do was to watch the line.

*   *   *   *   *   *

Much later, I wrote Irene and asked her if these last Tiers caused her as much suffering as they caused me, because I was at the outer limits. I was a nervous wreck, and I didn't have a penny in the sugar market. I had seen the price rise; I had assumed she had already filled at least Tier 6, and then I saw the price drop to 11¢, and assumed that she had got out for a loss. She was in her programmed pause, her 60-day wait, but I had no way of knowing that. She answered no, she hadn't worried. What for? She had planned the trade for some time. Her instructions were sent. She had work at school to do. She simply watched the price. If the tiers filled, the tiers filled. If they didn't, they didn't. She tried to stay as emotionless as possible.

I happen not to believe her.

The tiers began to fill.

Tier 6 filled on April 18th, at 15½¢.

Tier 7 filled on May 2nd, at 17¢.

Tier 8 filled on May 8th, at 18½¢.

And then it was done, a Tier 8 plan, fully accomplished. And until the day I die, I will never believe she remained through it all "as emotionless as possible."

It was just a line moving from the bottom of the piece of graph paper back toward the top, but a line with so much meaning.

To Irene, to myself, and to all the others watching the price of sugar that year.

The profits were starting to add up, **quickly.**

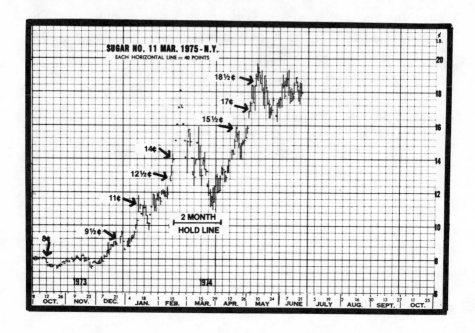

At 18½ cents, Irene already had a profit of $426,720.00. By the time her tier 8 leg filled, she had already made nearly half a million dollars from her initial $3,000.00 investment. You can calculate it this way, **with prices at 18½¢:**

2 units purchased at 8¢ now had a 10½¢ profit.
2 units purchased at 9½¢ now had a 9¢ profit.
4 units purchased at 11¢ now had a 7½¢ profit.
8 units purchased at 12½¢ now had a 6¢ profit.
16 units purchased at 14¢ now had a 4½¢ profit.
32 units purchased at 15½¢ now had a 3¢ profit.
64 units purchased at 17¢ now had a 1½¢ profit.
128 units purchased at 18½¢ were, as of now, without profit.

—334—

2 units times	10½ ¢	times $1,120 per 1¢	equals $	23,520.00
2 units times	9 ¢	times $1,120 per 1¢	equals $	20,160.00
4 units times	7½ ¢	times $1,120 per 1¢	equals $	33,600.00
8 units times	6 ¢	times $1,120 per 1¢	equals $	53,760.00
16 units times	4½ ¢	times $1,120 per 1¢	equals $	80,640.00
32 units times	3 ¢	times $1,120 per 1¢	equals $	107,520.00
64 units times	1½ ¢	times $1,120 per 1¢	equals $	107,520.00
128 units times	0 ¢	times $1,120 per 1¢	equals $	0.00

By the time the eighth tier filled, Irene had seven previous tiers showing profits of $426,720.00. She had invested $3,000, and not another penny of her cash. By the time the eighth tier filled she had earned 14,224% rate of interest on her investment. **Fourteen thousand percent**, almost a half a million dollars, and Irene had the gall to write me and say, "I just watch the line, as emotionless as possible." Nobody has **that** good a poker face.

Irene may have been cool, calm and collected —hah— but I was a total wreck. I knew that **if** she was still in the sugar business, she had made herself a half-million dollars. **If** she was still in. I wrote her, asked for a quick reply. Here is the complete text of the Mailgram she sent me in answer:

"Yes."

I was relieved, and then had a moment to think. She had written me, saying that she was in for the long haul. It was May, 1974. There were still **ten months** until March of 1975. Not once had she ever revealed her selling strategy to me, her selling level. It looked like a long ten months of suffering for **me** on the horizon. "I know sugar, Bruce." And she may well have. But what about me? I couldn't live another ten months of this, why hadn't she written me when there were only 17 days left, not the original 17 months?

Seven months down and ten months to go.

And then the long haul began.

And with it began the fun.

$$* \quad * \quad * \quad * \quad * \quad *$$

Take a ball. Roll it across a table. Your hand has given momentum to the ball; the amount of momentum determines how far the ball will roll before stopping.

That is the simplest form of momentum.

Take a ball. Roll it down a hill. Your hand begins the momentum, but an additional force, gravity, will supply additional momentum. The ball will roll faster and faster, gaining speed until a counterforce acts against it. The same flick of your wrist that rolled the ball across the table has sent the ball rolling down the hill, yet momentum has sent the ball rolling at 5, 10, 25 miles per hour: Other forces can act on momentum.

$$* \quad * \quad * \quad * \quad * \quad *$$

Hypothetical "ABC" Beet Sugar Company is the largest sugar company in the world. Shares of that corporation are traded on America's largest stock exchanges. It is a mammoth food service corporation with tens of thousands of employees worldwide and over 7,000 area managers, one for every 23.3 employees. In 1974, ABC Beet Sugar Company made $42 million dollars, which is a lot of money. To do that, ABC had to cope with organizational problems, collection problems, inventory problems, merchandising problems, marketing problems, distribution problems, overhead problems, employee problems, bureaucracy problems, legal problems, tax problems, insurance problems, government interference, environmental concerns, zoning codes, and a souring economy. They would have to make enough during the good years to wait out the bad years, which would surely return. It is quite likely that ABC Beet Sugar Company had more than $3,000 invested in their worldwide operations in 1974. In truth, $3,000 probably wouldn't have paid a single monthly phone bill of a single field office for ABC Sugar.

Irene's Sugar Company had no employees, no inventory, and no overhead. It was operated out of a four room house, with rent paid by the Canadian government, in the town of Inturak, Northwest Territories, Canada, a village of 79 people. Irene's Sugar Company was formed in October of 1973 with $5,000 of capital, $3,000 for actual use and $2,000 for reserve. What were the consequences of her decision to go Tier 8 that year? Irene purchased her last units at 18½¢ a pound on May 8th, 1974. She then had a total of 256 units: 28,672,000 pounds of sugar under her control. Each 1¢ of price rise would now return her 256 times $1,120, or $286,720.00. Each 1¢ of price rise above the 18½¢ price level would return Irene 9,557% on her initial investment. She had been looking for a "little momentum" in sugar and in those seventeen months, she **found** it.

Perhaps Boyd Hawley put it best, after missing out on so much of the momentum in his silver tier opportunity. "If the momentum is running in your favor, protect your profits with a stop and then LET THE MARKET RUN!"

May 8th and Tier 8 were not the end of the sugar price run during those seventeen months. It was the beginning. The beginning of what, even Irene never knew at the start. But as long as the momentum continued, she would ride it. And ride it she did. The price staggered, just a day or two, in the middle of November, at about 55¢ a pound, and continued up. She had had enough; I was dead. With the gyrations at 60¢, working at the stratospheric levels, concentration on the one room school room full of students was getting dif-

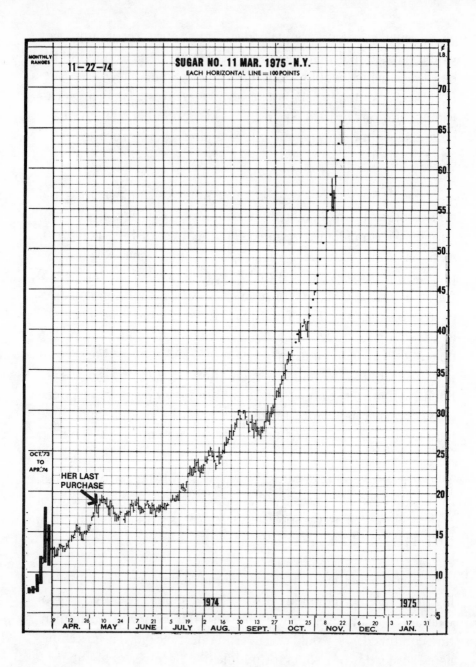

SUGAR NO. 11 MAR. 1975 - N.Y.
EACH HORIZONTAL LINE = 100 POINTS

11-22-74

MONTHLY RANGES

OCT.'73 TO APR.'74

HER LAST PURCHASE

—338—

ficult. She sent her last instructions to her firm, this time via telegram, backed up with a telephone call:

Sell all units at 56¢ by moving my stop-loss immediately up to that level.

When Mr. Mathiesson received the instructions the price was already above 60¢. Irene was "stopped-out" on the way back down. She got her 56¢ a pound, and thereby missed the top of the sugar market by 10¢. She was content. All things end. All momentum ends. She rode the momentum to new, high ground, saw the momentum lurch for a moment on the way up at the 55¢ level; it was enough. She was out, the game was over.

In 1974, Irene Sarnoff, a schoolteacher in the Northwest Territories, Canada, owner and operator of the Irene Sarnoff Sugar Company, made $11,178,720.00. Eleven million, one hundred and seventy-eight thousand, seven-hundred and twenty dollars. Her initial investment had been $3000.00. She had not invested a penny more. She earned 372,624% return on her investment. She had held her units from October of 1973 until December of 1974, or fourteen months. The last units, *half* of her total holdings, had been bought in May of 1974, and were held only seven months. She had no employees, no overhead, no accounting problems, no inventory, and no environmental problems. Her broker was her accountant: when she finally sold out on that December day a **certified check** was on its way to Inturak by 5:00 p.m. Nothing unusual about that, it was standard operating procedure. In units for future delivery, the day you sell is the day you get paid.

Irene Sarnoff was a wealthy woman, at the age of 34.

* * * * * *

Moreover, Irene was not the only person to emerge from the sugar price increase in 1973-74 with such unbelievable profits, there were many others. I tell her story because I know her story and the details of her tiers. But other individuals did as spectacularly well.

Do you need proof, I can offer it; it can be **verified** with a trip to your public library and the few minutes it will take you to examine the bound copies of the *Wall Street Journal* for 1973 and 1974.

In October of 1973, when Irene first bought two units of sugar, there were over 15,000 units being bought and sold each day. She only bought 2 of 15,000. In December of 1974, over 22,000 units were owned. Of these, Irene owned 256. Her holdings, enormous as it may seem represented about 1% of the total.

1974 SUGAR UNITS OWNED
(In Thousands of Units)

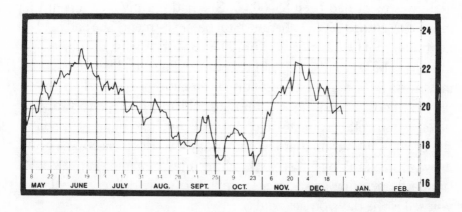

There were a great many more players in this game than Irene. Thousands and thousands more; and that was only in sugar. There were equally as many opportunities for profit in the **other** businesses available for ownership.

You require some **more** proof about the opportunities for profit through a tier investment in the momentum of the line in these fields of investment, I can offer it, too. A total compilation would take another book, but an **idea** of the potential for profit can be presented in a few more pages. Sugar advanced in 1973 and 1974 and made Irene a millionairess. What about the other markets? How did they do in 1974, or in the intervening years since 1974? Let's take a look.

We recognize the pattern now, corn prices rose steadily in 1973 and then "bounced-back." Was it the time to buy?

It sure was. Like sugar, corn made an advance, "bounced-back" and then resumed its upward momentum. Unlike sugar, the "bounce-back" period lasted longer than 60 days. However, remember that Irene would not finance her 6th, 7th, and 8th tier until prices rose to the higher levels. Not only did she wait for 60 days, she also waited for higher prices; a dual requirement. If Irene was playing the corn market of 1974, she made a fortune there also.

I am going to show you several years of history now, so read slowly.

PORK BELLIES (FROZEN) FEB. 1976 - CHI.
EACH HORIZONTAL LINE = 100 POINTS

10 –10 –75

1974   1975

TOTAL OPEN INTEREST &
VOLUME (All Contracts)

OPEN INTEREST
(1969 – 1974 AVG.)

CURRENT OPEN INTEREST

VOLUME

    The next year offered advancing prices in many units, and the
price of bacon—raw, uncured bacon, or "pork bellies"—was one
of the first to move. Do you remember the high price of bacon at
the grocery? That price rise appeared as a line, first. Units for future
delivery took off because of scarcity of supply; after the futures
units rose, the price at the local supermarket quickly and inevitably
followed. Prices dropped to zone 4, made a 1-2-3 bottom, and then
advanced. It should be familiar to you by now.

The wild ride of the
price of coffee lasted
for many months.
But if you bought
below $1.00 — and
there was ample time
to do so — at the
zone 4 level, there
was no way you
could lose. It was on-
ly a question of how
much money you
were going to make.

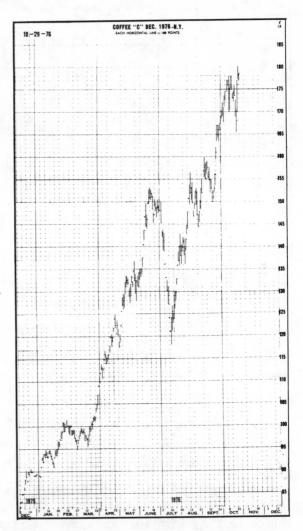

COFFEE "C" DEC. 1976 -N.Y.
EACH HORIZONTAL LINE = 100 POINTS

10-29-76

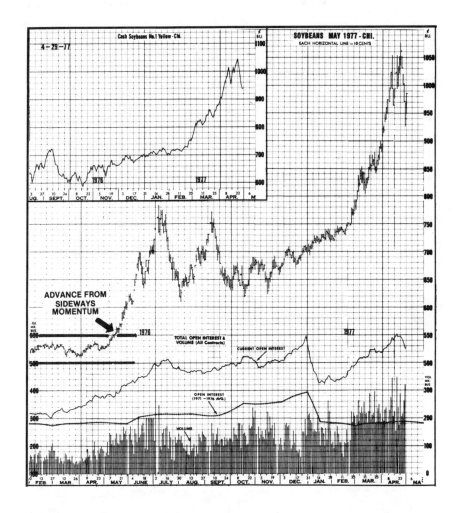

In 1977 many lines offered soaring momentum, and the farm business of soybeans led the way: each 10¢ price advance returned $500 profit **per unit**. Do you think only a few canny traders took advantage of these profits? There were **120,000 units** of soybeans owned by investors. Each 10¢ price advance supplied $60,000,000 in profits. Look at the number of 10¢ price advances shown on this graph. **It was the year 1977.**

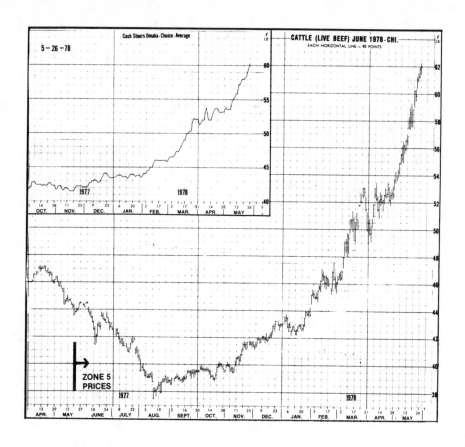

The great beef boycott of 1978: macaroni and cheese, fish, chicken became the staples in many American households. The graph above tells you why. Beef dropped to below 38¢ a pound and then rallied 24¢, a 63% advance in price in less than a year. At 38¢, beef was in an historic zone 5, a **super** buy. With the price advancing over 50%, the returns were phenomenal. **A nice, easy, advancing market** with an excellent tier opportunities built right in. A few **tens of thousands** of traders rode the line up. **The year was 1978.**

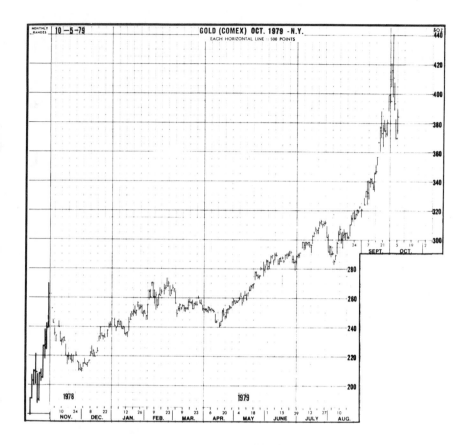

GOLD (COMEX) OCT. 1979 - N.Y.
EACH HORIZONTAL LINE : 500 POINTS

$0z 440

1979 was a year for gold, for advancing gold prices; the momentum was staggering. The black lines to the far left of the above graph tell the story you would have been charting when looking for this momentum: a 1-2-3 bottom, back in 1978. Dramatic momentum: how many investors rode it? Thousands. Nor was the gold the only advancing market in 1979; there were many others. $440 an ounce gold. Was that the end of the momentum? Yes, it was... **for 1979.** But $440 an ounce wasn't the end of the gold price rise. It was just the beginning. By the time 1980 was over, prices would run to over $950 an ounce, over **twice** the 1979 peak. How many people owned units of gold during 1980? Thousands. And what were their profits? They **exceeded** those taken by Irene with her opportunity in sugar. **The profits were staggering.**

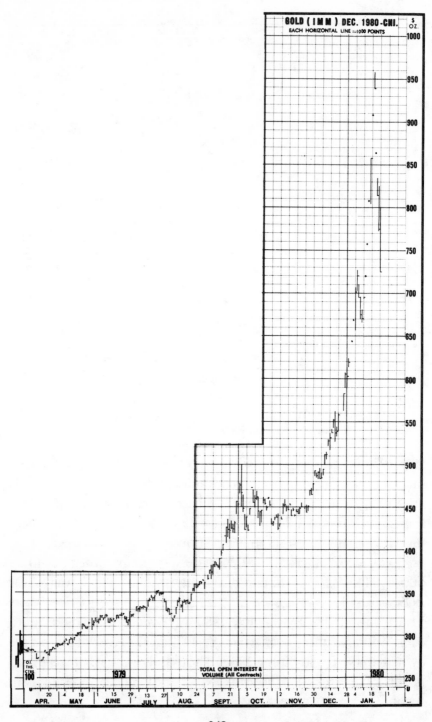

GOLD (I M M) DEC. 1980 -CHI.
EACH HORIZONTAL LINE ≈ 1000 POINTS

$ OZ.

TOTAL OPEN INTEREST &
VOLUME (All Contracts)

O.I.
THS.
CTS.
100

1979

1980

20 | 4 18 | 1 15 29 | 13 27 | 10 24 | 7 21 | 5 19 | 2 16 30 | 14 28 | 4 18 | 1
APR. | MAY | JUNE | JULY | AUG. | SEPT. | OCT. | NOV. | DEC. | JAN.

—348—

Nor was gold the only metal to rise in 1979 and 1980. Copper also advanced during those years, substantially so, rising from a **zone 5** level of 70¢ to above $1.40 a pound. Some people hoarded pennies in hopes of taking advantage of this price rise; others bought units of copper, because each 1¢ price advance returned a profit of $250.00 for each unit owned of the thousands owned. $250 per unit, for every 1¢ price rise. The price rose 75¢. Zone 5 to zone 1.

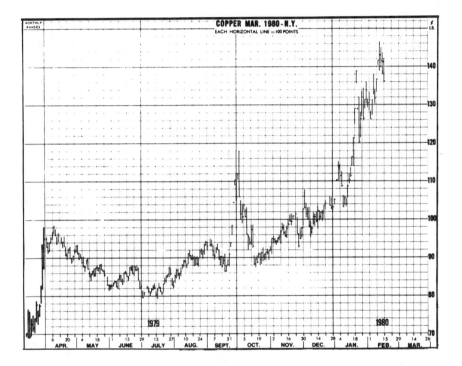

Some investors traded the line in gold; others traded the line of copper prices; still others traded other fields, other businesses with substantial momentum in their price lines, always watching for zones, buying when the time was right. **The year was 1980.**

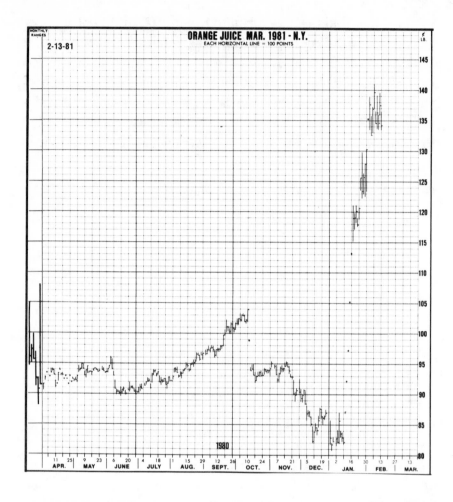

ORANGE JUICE MAR. 1981 - N.Y.
EACH HORIZONTAL LINE = 100 POINTS

¢
LB.

145

140

135

130

125

120

115

110

105

100

95

90

85

80

1980

| APR. | MAY | JUNE | JULY | AUG. | SEPT. | OCT. | NOV. | DEC. | JAN. | FEB. | MAR. |

11 25 | 9 23 | 6 20 | 4 18 | 1 15 29 | 12 26 | 10 24 | 7 21 | 5 19 | 2 16 30 | 13 27 | 13

    1981, the year of the big freeze. We watched NBC News and saw the citrus trees of Florida covered with icicles, bathers at Miami Beach wearing overcoats. In December of 1980 there were thousands of units owned in orange juice for future delivery. For each of these units, a 1¢ price rise returned $150. Between January 9 and February 6, 1981, in less than a month, the price rose 59¢: $8,850 for each and every one of the thousand of units owned. **The year was 1981.**

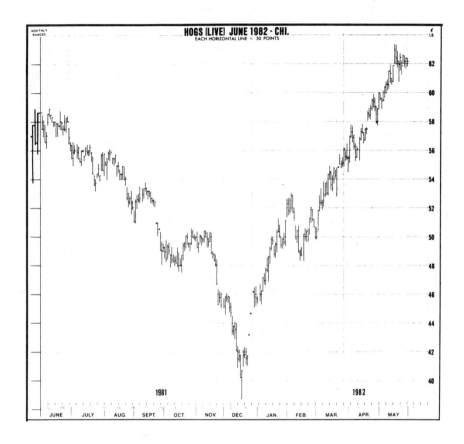

1982. Another year, and more momentum. The price for hogs and bacon was very weak as 1981 ended, drifting in zone 5, below 40¢ a pound. But as the new year entered, the strength was daily. The price of bacon at the grocery rose; the price of ham went up. We all paid more. But thousands of people, also paying the increased prices at the store, owned units of ham and bacon for future delivery. They suffered not at all. **They made fortunes. The year was 1982.**

New markets in a new world of tradition. There is ample room for new players, no limit in fact, and often a reward at the end. Two things will make your success possible:

1.   *The line moving across a piece of graph paper.*

2.   *Your own knowledgeable use of that line.*

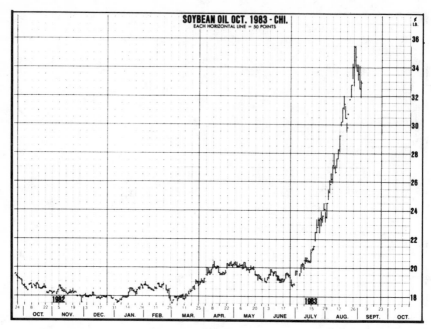

SOYBEAN OIL OCT. 1983 - CHI.
EACH HORIZONTAL LINE = 50 POINTS

¢/LB.

1983

MONTHLY RANGES

COFFEE MAY 1984 - N.Y.
EACH HORIZONTAL LINE = 100 POINTS

¢/LB.

CONTRACT COMPLETED
MAY 21, 1984
HIGH   LOW
158.50   108.50

1984

—352—

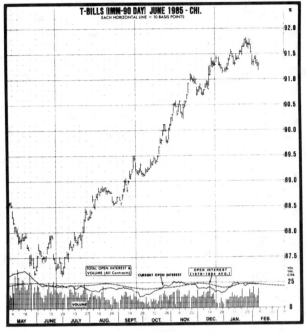

T-BILLS (IMM-90 DAY) JUNE 1985 - CHI.
EACH HORIZONTAL LINE = 10 BASIS POINTS

1985

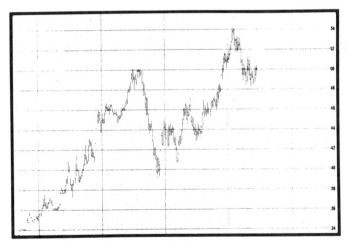

1986

The momentum of that line took four-foot-eleven Irene from 8¢ a pound to 66¢ in a little more than a year. A single unit of sugar, purchased at 8¢ and sold at 56¢—ten cents below the top and a single unit—yielded a profit of $53,760.00. That is a **lot** from a little; from just one unit.

But out of that potential of $53,000.00 per single investment could be taken $11 million. No longer was the investor taking from a single unit; the investor was taking from a lot of units, 256 units in fact, each made up of 112,000 pounds of sugar and each 1¢ price rise returning $286,720 of additional profit.

At the top who did Irene sell to? Unfortunately, for them, she sold her units to new "weak hands" entering the market for the first time with no experience, trading on paper history, or record of success. All they knew was that sugar prices were high and it was the time to buy. It was **not** the time to buy, it was the time to sell, and Irene did just that. The weak hands never knew what hit them. She had taken her single dollar and gone her way. **She knew the principle of momentum.** Start with knowledge, about where you are and where you plan to go. Seek your start-up point. As momentum moves in your direction, increase your investing both vertically and horizontally at the same time. Maximize your units a penny at a time and take a little off the top from each. Don't attempt a large tier structure at a high zone price, start at the bottom and work up. From that low price level, increase your tiers as rapidly as experience and your record of success recommends and have all your tiers in place *before* the majority of the move in price begins. One day the price move will end; if you have taken your positions at the lowest levels, that end will return you fabulous profits. By the time sugar had risen from only 8¢ to 18½¢ Irene had a profit of $450,000. By the time she sold at 56¢, she made $11 million. All based on a single principle: **The same principle that has made everyone wealthy from the beginning of time: Maximizing momentum.**

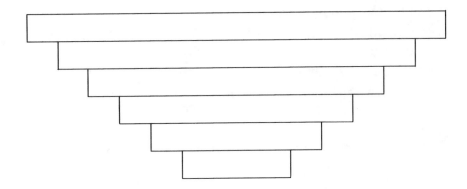

What about Irene's ride in sugar itself; was that sugar move the ride of a lifetime? It was certainly a ride which would be remembered forever. But six years later in 1980, **the sugar market ran again**. It had retreated to its original starting area and then moved back up, from the bottom of the page to the top.

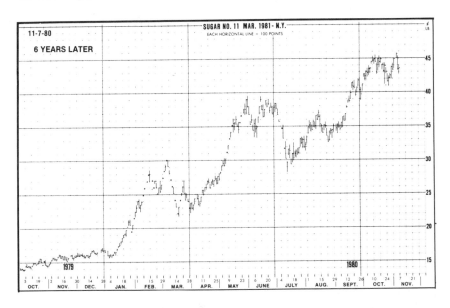

By November of 1980, almost **an identical six years** since Irene sold her 1974 sugar units, the price had risen from a base of 15¢ to a peak of 45¢. It wasn't the same killer of 1974, but **still** one single unit purchased at 15¢ and sold at 45¢ yields a profit of $33,600.

Several units purchased on the momentum of the line could have easily returned a million dollars. And was that the end? It was the end in sugar for a while; but it was really just the beginning of another big move. By 1982, sugar had again retreated to the 8¢ level and those who bought "for the long haul," were bound to make several million more the **next** time the price headed up.

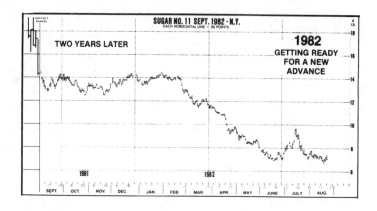

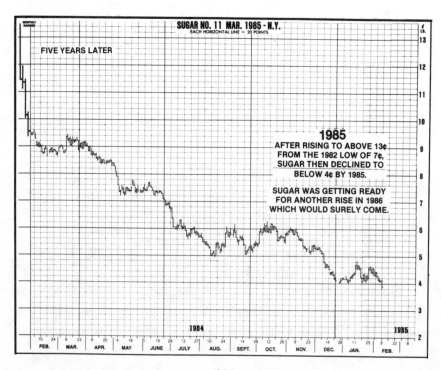

If you learn nothing more from this book than the huge profits available in sugar every few years, it will be worth its price. Sugar rises for a while, overproduction occurs, the price drops, production stops, and then prices rise again. Each ride up returns millions, true millions, to buyers of units for future delivery. **Simply be patient**, wait for sugar to be below 10¢ a pound, and expect another rise. It **will** come.

What of Irene? Does she live on the Riviera now?

No. She lives in the village of Inturak, teaching children. She loves the work. She is going to retire soon: the cold and the severity of the life digs deeper each year. She is older now. Hers will be a sumptuous retirement; she has the satisfaction both of financial success, in the investments she loves, and personal happiness, in the Northwest Territories. She has anonymously donated a great deal of money to the Indians with whom she lives and teaches.

She travels more now, spending a part of each winter in Florida, so I suppose that is where it all began. She said, in her letter from St. Petersburg, that she often went south and normally took a few of her "kids" from the far north with her. She also said, that starting 1977 there had been a string of cold winters in Florida, but she never minded at all. She had devised a great way to cope with the Florida cold and when she told me, I knew it was the same Irene, the sugar queen of 1974. She said she would buy orange juice now, each year, anticipating her travels south. If the weather was warm, and nothing would happen to the price of her orange juice units, they would have a great vacation. But if the weather was cold, she was prepared.

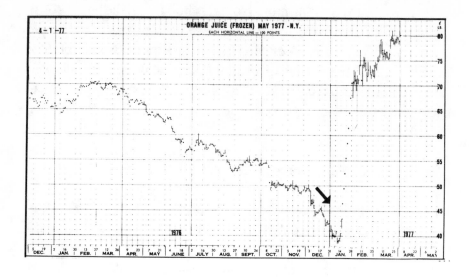

ORANGE JUICE (FROZEN) MAY 1977 - N.Y.
EACH HORIZONTAL LINE = 100 POINTS

In **1977**, the weather got real cold, the crops froze, and Irene made $6000 per unit of orange juice for future delivery. I don't know how many units she had, but by that time I am sure she started with more than one.

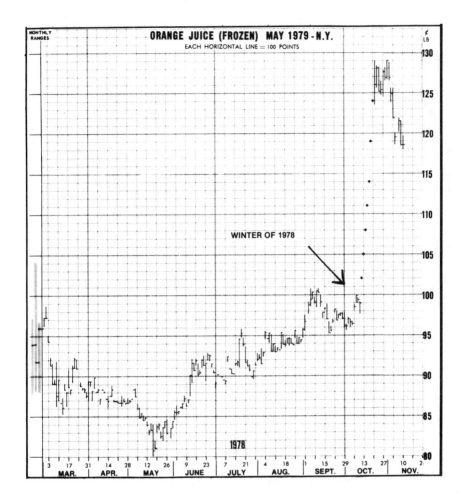

ORANGE JUICE (FROZEN) MAY 1979 - N.Y.

EACH HORIZONTAL LINE = 100 POINTS

WINTER OF 1978

1978

In 1978, the cold weather came before her vacation. That didn't matter. Now she could enjoy the best of both worlds; she could take her "little from a lot" and also enjoy the sun when she arrived in January. Orange juice was being good to Irene, it paid her another $6000 per unit that year. She had a lot of units.

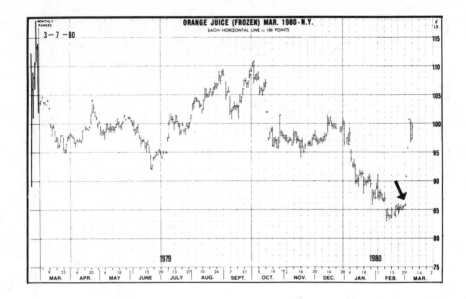

In 1980, she again was able to spent January in Florida with relative warmth. By the time she returned home, within a few weeks, the price advanced $2,250 per unit. Two units of ownership would have paid her two weeks in Florida in the grandest style.

The thing she liked most about Orange Juice units, Irene wrote, is that she seemed to be able to find substantial price action with cold weather every year. With sugar, she would buy on the down cycles and ride up on the uptrend, but there might be a two or three year period between the momentum. With orange juice, not only did it add an interesting twist to her Florida vacations, but it also enabled her to pay for them.

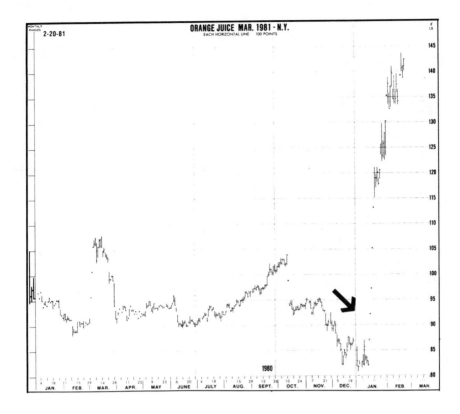

ORANGE JUICE MAR. 1981 - N.Y.
EACH HORIZONTAL LINE 100 POINTS

¢
LB

145

140

135

130

125

120

115

110

105

100

95

90

85

80

1980

JAN. | FEB. | MAR. | APR. | MAY | JUNE | JULY | AUG. | SEPT. | OCT. | NOV. | DEC. | JAN. | FEB. | MAR.

And 1981 was no different. Along came January, along came the trip to Florida, and along came the cold weather. In 1981, Irene made $8000 per single unit, her best year ever. She was rapidly becoming additionally wealthy simply by her annual trips to Florida.

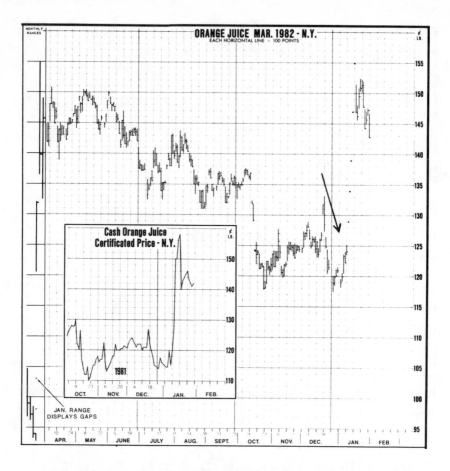

ORANGE JUICE MAR. 1982 - N.Y.
EACH HORIZONTAL LINE = 100 POINTS

Cash Orange Juice
Certificated Price - N.Y.

1981

She didn't do quite as well **in 1982**, the price ran only $4500 per unit for her that year. But she was more than satisfied. The weather was cold, the vacation not much, but they were able to enjoy it just the same, **financed** by a freeze in the citrus groves and the $4500 per unit profit of Irene.

I haven't corresponded with Irene since 1982, so I don't know everything about her since then. But, in a way, we do correspond. The graph is our means of communication. All I have to do is take out my graph of orange juice prices about January or February

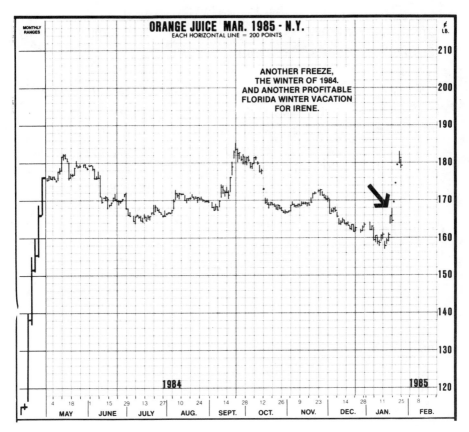

ORANGE JUICE MAR. 1985 - N.Y.
EACH HORIZONTAL LINE = 200 POINTS

MONTHLY RANGES

¢ LB.

ANOTHER FREEZE,
THE WINTER OF 1984.
AND ANOTHER PROFITABLE
FLORIDA WINTER VACATION
FOR IRENE.

210
200
190
180
170
160
150
140
130
120

1984   1985

4 18 | 1 15 29 | 13 27 | 10 24 | 14 28 | 12 26 | 9 23 | 14 28 | 11 25 | 8

MAY   JUNE   JULY   AUG.   SEPT.   OCT.   NOV.   DEC.   JAN.   FEB.

each year to receive a message from Irene. If the graph is steady, she is telling me the vacation was great and the weather terrific. If the price soars; it is Irene's way of letting me know that cold weather didn't ruin her vacation, she made another several thousand on each of the units she owned. It was our unique way of communicating.

I picked up a little news from Rocky and Karen Becket, also. They are still in Modesto, California, and are still charting prices, discussing tiers, watching tiers, watching home heating oil, as well as all the other business opportunities, and raising two toddlers. Karen said they successfully negotiated their first five tier trade and were very happy. There were doing well and their future seemed assured.

The only problem that Boyd Hawley seems to have is listening to the "voice from the sky." He is never sure if it is telling him to buy or to sell. But he, too, is happy.

You have seen enough now to understand, and if you follow prices on paper for a while you will appreciate, the observation even more: **There is not a single year that passes without numerous opportunities**, being measured in the tens, hundreds, and thousands of percent, being offered to skillful investors in the **new tradition of units for future delivery.** Not a single year. We reviewed some examples from 1974 but there will be just as many examples forward to 1994 and there were equally as many examples from 1964 to 1974. Each year the opportunities are numerous. Advisors seeking to handle your money in one form or another stress caution, and caution is good advice.

But caution will only hold onto capital already made; if you haven't yet made yours, you have to try a different approach. Or, if you have made yours already, but have an extra $5000 or $10,000 to work with, you may enjoy seeing if you can turn that into something a bit larger.

There is a route to wealth accumulation, and you now know it.

It begins with a starting point; you have to start looking.

It continues until you find your stopping point, be it Avon products, or sugar, McDonald's or copper, Shaklee or silver.

Once you find your stopping point, then the fun begins.

If your stopping point is one of the businesses discussed in this book, your work can begin **tomorrow.** Take a newspaper. Buy some graph paper at a local stationery store. Record a price of any of the items we have covered, the *Wall Street Journal* will have them all, your local newspaper most all. Then wait one day and record another price for that same item. Draw a line connecting the two and see what you have: Momentum.

You are starting to watch momentum.

The movement of price over time; and the opportunities for profit therein.

It is as easy as that to begin; get some graph paper, find and record the price of any item you have some familiarity with: heating oil, bacon, sugar, plywood, interest rates or cotton. And start watching the momentum.

Wait for prices to drop from a high price zone to a low price zone, and then buy "on paper" one single unit. With time you will realize you are walking on the path of real wealth accumulation.

The old tradition **won't** work anymore.

We **must** be pioneers seeking the new, and in the process, we will be blazing a new tradition for the generations to come.

There is a future ahead.

A dynamic growing future.

Momentum is movement over time.

Learn to ride the line, to ride that momentum and you can accumulate substantial wealth within your lifetime.

The line is the route to wealth accumulation.

It is the route to the future.

Take a ball, give it a shove. . . and see where the momentum carries you.

Remember how this book began. . .

Take a ball. Roll it across a table. Your hand has given momentum to the ball, the amount of momentum determines how far the ball will roll before stopping. This is the simplest form of momentum.

Take a ball. Roll it down a hill. Your hand begins the momentum, but an additional force, gravity, will supply additional momentum. The ball will roll faster and faster, gaining speed until a counterforce acts against it. The same flick of your wrist that rolled the ball a few feet across a table has started the ball down the hill, yet momentum has sent the ball rolling at 5, 10, 25 miles per hour: other forces can act on momentum.

*   *   *   *   *   *

Chapter 14

Take a ball. Roll it across a table. Your hand has given momentum to the ball, the amount of momentum determines how far the ball will roll before stopping. This is the simplest form of momentum.

Take a ball. Roll it down a hill. Your hand begins the momentum, but an additional force, gravity, will supply additional momentum. The ball will roll faster and faster, gaining speed until a counterforce acts against it. The same flick of your wrist that rolled the ball a few feet across a table has started the ball down the hill, yet momentum has sent the ball rolling at 5, 10, 25 miles per hour: other forces can act on momentum.

Chapter 15

Remember the success story of Rocky and Karen and the rules they followed on their path to success. With time, you will add your **own rules** to the following list, but these will get you started.

Rule #1. Commit no more money than you can afford to risk in this new venture. $5,000 is a very good limiting sum. If you cannot make money with $5,000 of invested capital, most likely you will not make money with $50,000 invested. Always try to keep your capital risk small and manageable.

Rule #2. Before you risk any money by trading, trade "on paper" for several weeks or months. If you can't make money "on paper," you will not make it by risking real dollars.

Rule #3. When you do risk real money, always start at the tier 1 level. First succeed "on paper." Then succeed at the tier 1 level with real money. Once you can do this over and over again, consistently, **then** consider working upward to tier 2, or 3 or even 4. But before you advance to any level higher than your current level, you must be able to prove to yourself, day in and day out, month in and month out, even year in and year out, that you are a success at the level which you are now leaving.

Rule #4. **If in doubt, stay out!** There are unlimited opportunities in this field and you never need to worry about having missed a chance that will not come again. **All** chances come again in this business, perhaps not in the same marketplace, but certainly in an equally appealing one. If you have any doubt, stand aside. It is always easier to quit and then reenter, than to be driven out by large financial losses and lose the chance to play the game again.

Rule #5. **Why do Alaskan fishermen earn $100,000 and more during a good season?** You already know the answer. It is because the risks are great and the chances of success are far from certain. One ship out of every hundred or thousand in the Alaskan waters sinks and the entire crew is lost. With this type of ratio, you **have** to pay men and women large salaries to get them to venture on the high seas. Why do people like Irene and Rocky and Karen earn such large amounts in the game you have been reading about in the pages of this book? Because the risks of loss for those who fail in this game can be as great as those faced by the Alaskan fishermen. Remember, this is a real game, with real money, with tough competitors, with lives and livelihoods at stake. Be very careful with your money. Risk only small amounts and then only very cautiously. Do not trust anyone except yourself. Always consider acting three or four times before you finally do act. Play the game "on paper" before you play "for real." Learn "on paper" when failure will be cheap, not expensive. The rewards in this venture are great but the risks are very great also. If you have any doubt, stay out. If you suffer losses, stand aside and rethink your commitment. Reenter only after gaining more experience "on paper."

Rule #6. Start with no more than one trade per month. This will give you experience, diversity, examples of successes and examples of failure. You can design your own monthly trading program, or you can use professional help of the type outlined for you in chapter 18. Either way, one trade per month at the tier 1 level is generally the **best way** to start when you actually decide to commit money to this new field.

Rule #7. The road to success has many caution signs. Go slow. Be careful. Keep close tabs on your money. Trust yourself first and foremost. If you start to lose consistently, call it quits for a while. Read as much as you can, as often as you can. Add to your working rules with each new experience. It is possible to be successful in this game, it is possible to make a great deal of money, it is possible to accumulate real wealth. **You can do it.** It is being done. Just be **extra careful** while you are in the **learning phase.** And in this field the learning phase will last your entire lifetime.

Chapter 16

The more you read, the more you will learn. With time, you will find that you will enjoy reading most of the major books written in this field. **Where to start?** I have written several other books covering the various opportunities that I have discussed in this book as well as trading techniques and money-management formulas. I think you will find my other books as interesting as you have found this one. For a complete list of **all** the books I have written in this field (including one for the publishers of the *Wall Street Journal, Dow Jones*), you can write me at the address below. Read one or two or three of my books and then go to a library or bookstore and read a few others by different authors. **This is a great way to start.** For a **free list** of my books write:

Bruce Gould
Post Office Box 16
Seattle, WA 98111

Chapter 17

Once you decide to begin, you will **need a broker** to handle your orders **and a brokerage firm** to execute your buying and selling decisions. If you already have such a person and such a firm, stay where you are. If your experience has been successful, stick with it. But if you are brand new, or if you are looking for a change, you can write me. I know many firms, from the largest to the smallest, and many individual brokers. **I will always be happy to recommend both a firm and a broker to you.**

Write me and I will quickly tell you how to begin.

Chapter 18

A special program for the readers of this book who would like to become involved in this field of investment, but who don't have the experience to proceed has been designed. I call it the **"Monthly Trading Program"** and here is how it works.

Each month I personally examine all the trading opportunities that exist in the various fields of investment discussed in this book and recommend **one opportunity** to you which I feel offers exceptional profit potential. As a subscriber to this program, you are notified as to:

1. **Which opportunity** I believe offers an exceptional profit potential at that time.
2. **How you can participate** in the recommended trading opportunity.
3. **The entry day and entry price** that I personally recommend to you.
4. **The exit points** that I also personally recommend to you.
5. **The amount of risk** that I will accept in my own trading account with respect to this recommended position and how you should judge whether you wish to assume an equal, greater or lesser risk.

Once you receive all this information from me,

(A) You can follow the recommended trade **"on paper" only** to see how this investment turns out.
(B) You can **invest real money** in the recommended trade on the **tier 1** level with the brokerage firm and broker of your own choice and trade the position exactly as I recommend it and will personally trade it myself.
(C) **Or, you can invest** in the recommended position on a tier 1 level but take a position directly opposite to that which I recommend. With time you can discover whether you can make more money by betting "with" me or "against" me. This should be an educational and rewarding experience for you.

Each month **after** my recommendation is given to my subscribers, I will then **invest my own money** in the recommended **"Monthly Trade"** exactly as I have recommended it to you. I will buy or sell exactly as I have outlined the trade to you and I will place **real money** behind each of my recommendations.

If the recommended trade calls for us to "buy October sugar on January 31st, at the market price on the open," then on January 31st, "at the market price on the open" I will personally buy the October sugar contract in my own investment account. If the November recommended trade is to "sell March wheat on the 10th," then on November 10th, in my own personal investment account, I will "sell March wheat." **Whatever I recommend to you,** I will do myself, in my own account, with my own money.

In addition, once I close out my position for any recommended monthly trade (meaning I have both bought and sold the unit for future delivery that I recommended to you), **I will send you a copy of my personal brokerage statement for this transaction.** This statement will show when I bought, when I sold, and what my personal profit or loss was for this monthly recommended trade.

I will buy when I recommend that you buy and I will sell when I recommend that you sell. I will use real money and I will trade on the tier 1 level. You can duplicate my investment with your own money, you can follow "on paper without investing real money," or you can bet against me and take a position directly opposite to that which I recommend. With this **"Monthly Trading Program"** you can watch me at work in such markets as cattle, copper, corn, heating oil, interest rates, gasoline, gold, hogs, lumber, orange juice, bacon, silver, soybeans, stock indices, sugar, wheat and a variety of other markets and then **use my trades for your own account** once you gain sufficient confidence and experience.

This program was developed specifically for you, the reader of this book. It is my way of helping you get started in this new investment field at the tier 1 level and thereby gain judgment and experience at the same time you are watching me invest my own money in these profitable market opportunities. I think you will enjoy and benefit from this program and if you are interested in learning more about it you can write the following address for full details:

The Monthly Trading Program
Post Office Box 16
Seattle, WA 98111

Chapter 19

Take a ball. Roll it across a table. Your hand has given momentum to the ball, the amount of momentum determines how far the ball will roll before stopping. This is the simplest form of momentum.

Take a ball. Roll it down a hill. Your hand begins the momentum, but an additional force, gravity, will supply additional momentum. The ball will roll faster and faster, gaining speed until a counterforce acts against it. The same flick of your wrist that rolled the ball a few feet across a table has started the ball down the hill, yet momentum has sent the ball rolling at 5, 10, 25 miles per hour: other forces can act on momentum.

Take a ball. Roll it across a table. Your hand begins the momentum. . . **and where it will take you, only you can now decide.**

THE END

About the author. . .

Bruce G. Gould is a professional commodities trader and consultant to the commodities industry. He has worked as a buyer for one of the largest institutional purchasers of grains and has visited all of the major commodity exchanges. He holds a Doctorate of Jurisprudence degree from the University of Washington Law School and is a recognized authority on the legal aspects of commodity futures contracts. Mr. Gould's efforts to educate the public on commodities was described by one authority as "embarrassing to find that Mr. Gould has been able to make a complex subject so much simpler than we have been able to do." Besides his current book, *Dow Jones-Irwin Guide to Commodities Trading, Revised Edition,* Dr. Gould is the author of *Commodity Trading Manual, How to Make Money in Commodities, Bruce Gould on Commodities* volumes 1 through 9, the *Commodity Advisors Manual,* and *The Greatest Money Book Ever Written.* He currently analyzes market opportunities for the *Bruce Gould Monthly Trading Program.*

All price charts used in this book are the product of

CRB FUTURES CHART SERVICE
75 Montgomery Street, Jersey City, NJ 07302
(201-451-7500)

I highly recommend their charts to you and suggest that you write them for a subscription to their services. If you mention my name they should give you very good service.

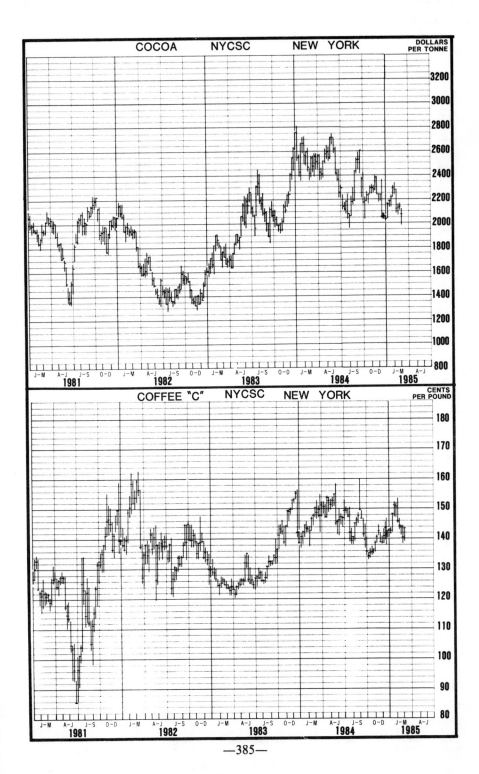

COCOA   NYCSC   NEW YORK   DOLLARS PER TONNE

3200
3000
2800
2600
2400
2200
2000
1800
1600
1400
1200
1000
800

J-M A-J J-S O-D J-M A-J J-S O-D J-M A-J J-S O-D J-M A-J J-S O-D J-M A-J
1981   1982   1983   1984   1985

COFFEE "C" NYCSC   NEW YORK   CENTS PER POUND

180
170
160
150
140
130
120
110
100
90
80

J-M A-J J-S O-D J-M A-J J-S O-D J-M A-J J-S O-D J-M A-J J-S O-D J-M A-J
1981   1982   1983   1984   1985

—385—

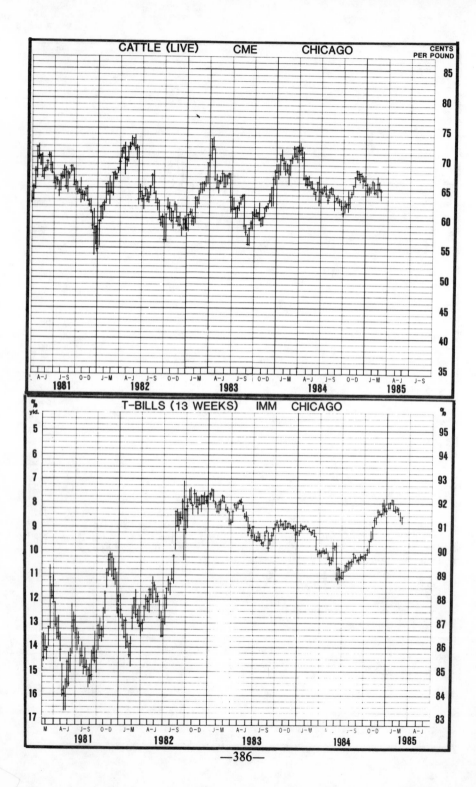

CATTLE (LIVE)   CME   CHICAGO   CENTS PER POUND

T-BILLS (13 WEEKS)   IMM   CHICAGO

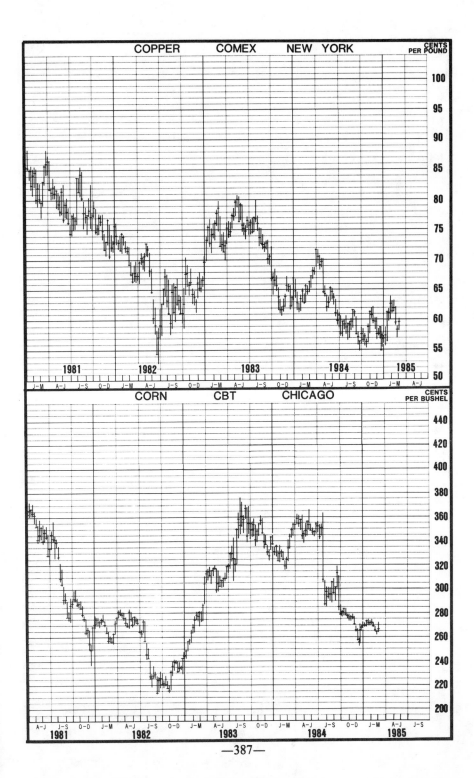

COPPER   COMEX   NEW   YORK   CENTS PER POUND

1981   1982   1983   1984   1985

J-M   A-J   J-S   O-D   J-M   A-J   J-S   O-D   J-M   A-J   J-S   O-D   J-M   A-J   J-S   O-D   J-M   A-J

CORN   CBT   CHICAGO   CENTS PER BUSHEL

1981   1982   1983   1984   1985

A-J   J-S   O-D   J-M   A-J   J-S   O-D   J-M   A-J   J-S   O-D   J-M   A-J   J-S   O-D   J-M   A-J   J-S

—387—

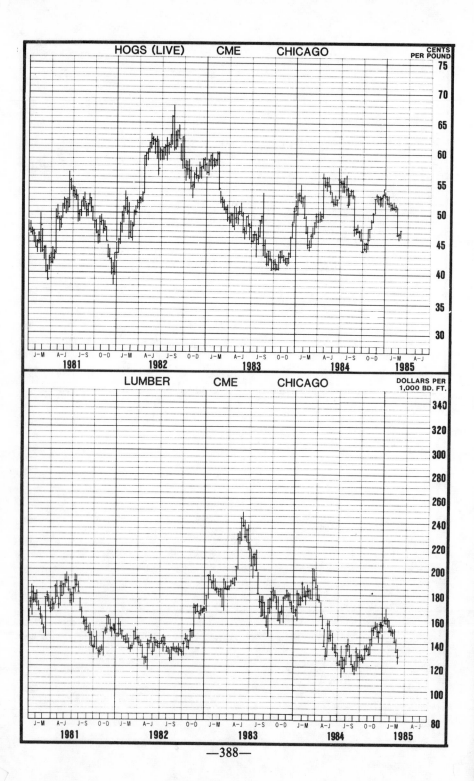

HOGS (LIVE)   CME   CHICAGO   CENTS PER POUND

75
70
65
60
55
50
45
40
35
30

J-M A-J J-S O-D J-M A-J J-S O-D J-M A-J J-S O-D J-M A-J J-S O-D J-M A-J
1981   **1982**   **1983**   **1984**   **1985**

LUMBER   CME   CHICAGO   DOLLARS PER 1,000 BD. FT.

340
320
300
280
260
240
220
200
180
160
140
120
100
80

J-M A-J J-S O-D J-M A-J J-S O-D J-M A-J J-S O-D J-M A-J J-S O-D J-M A-J
1981   **1982**   **1983**   **1984**   **1985**

—388—

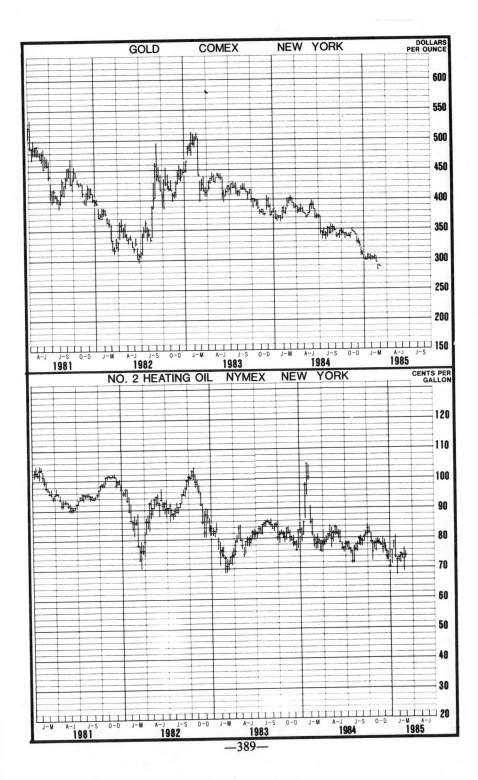

GOLD   COMEX   NEW YORK   DOLLARS
                                         PER OUNCE

NO. 2 HEATING OIL NYMEX NEW YORK   CENTS PER
                                          GALLON

—389—

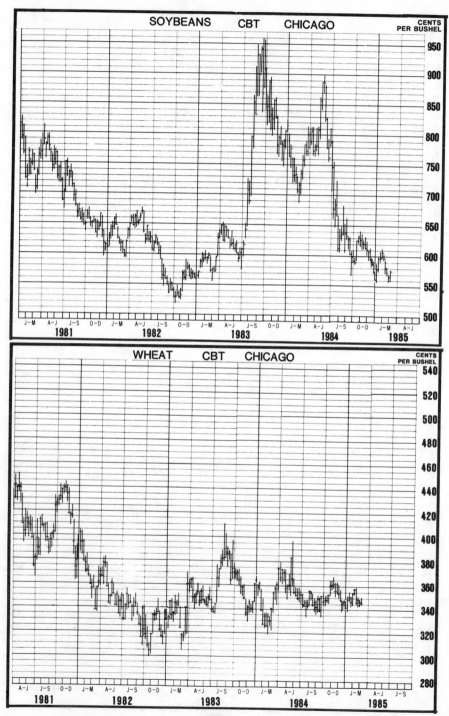

SOYBEANS   CBT   CHICAGO   CENTS PER BUSHEL

WHEAT   CBT   CHICAGO   CENTS PER BUSHEL

—390—

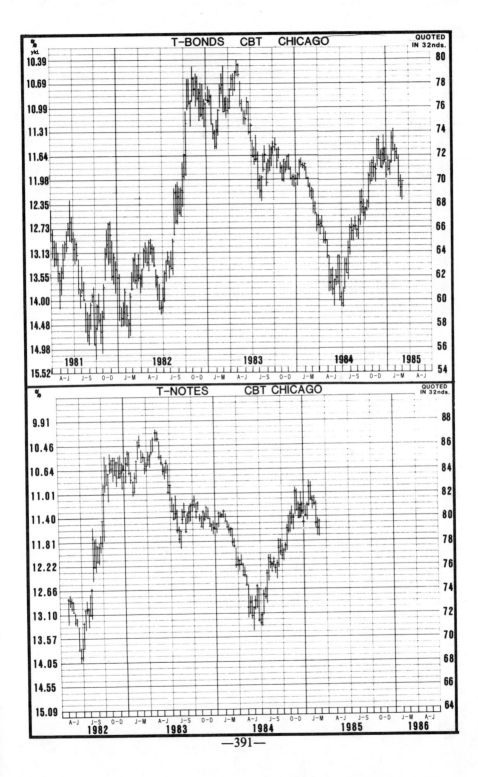